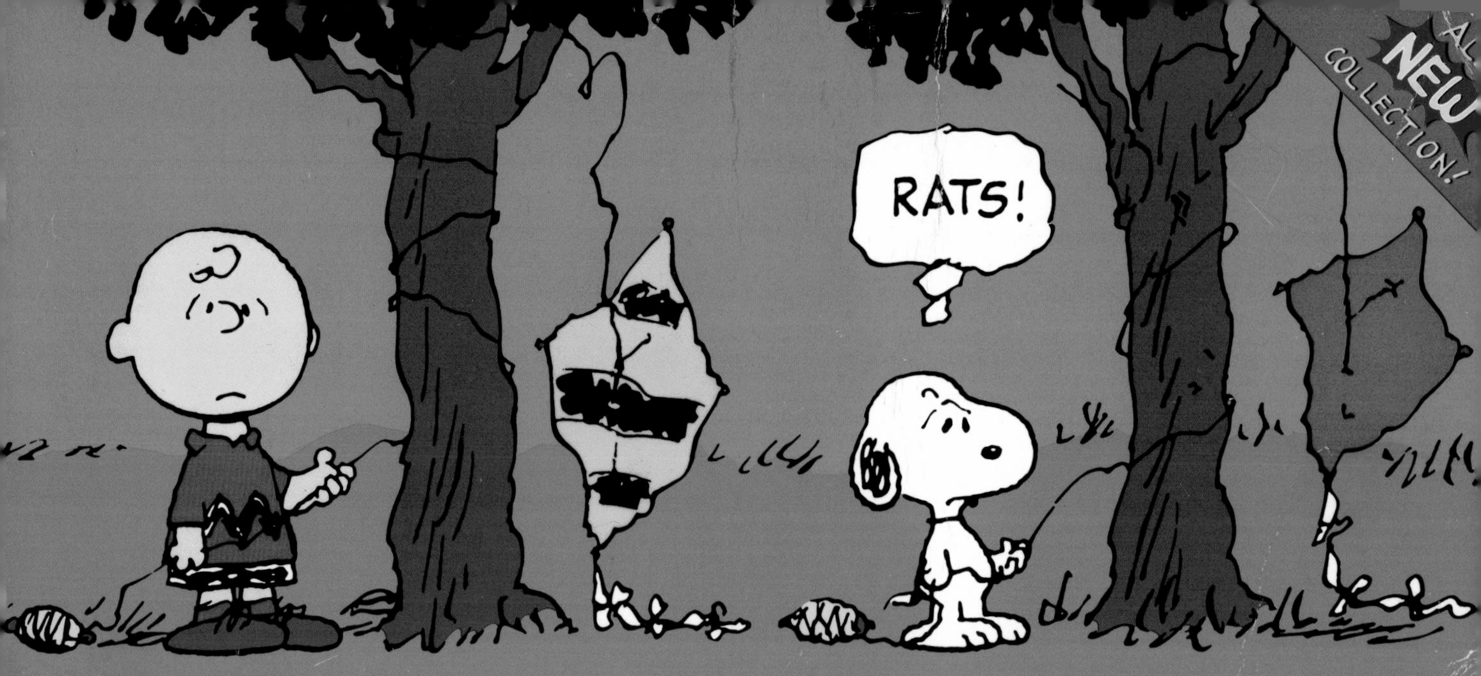
RATS!
NEW
COLLECTION!

The World Is Filled With Mondays

PEANUTS™ TREASURY

Charles M. Schulz

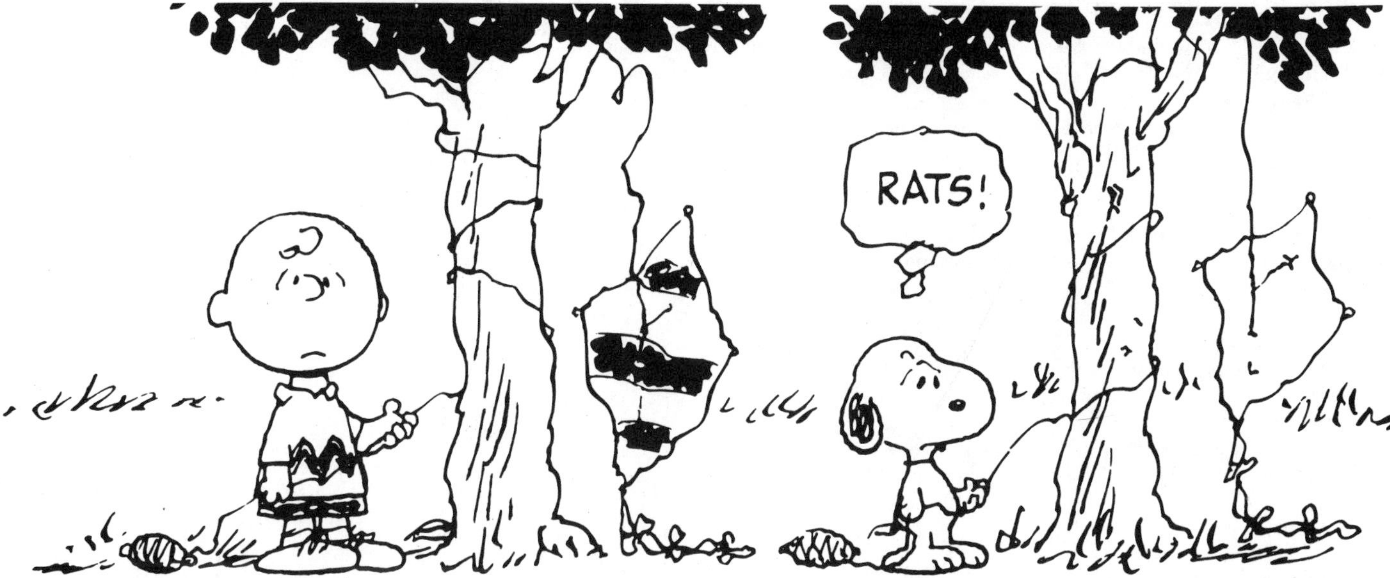
RATS!

The World Is Filled With Mondays

PEANUTS TREASURY

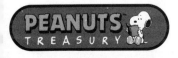

Charles M. Schulz

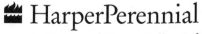

HarperPerennial
A Division of HarperCollinsPublishers

Based on the PEANUTS® comic strip by Charles M. Schulz.
http://www.snoopy.com

HarperCollins books may be purchased for educational, business, or sales promotional use.
For information please write to:
Special Markets Department, HarperCollins Publishers, Inc.,
10 East 53rd Street, New York, NY 10022

http://www.harpercollins.com

Designed by Christina Bliss, Staten Island

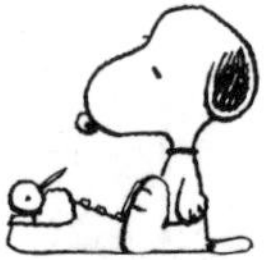

ISBN 0-06-107564-7

Printed in U.S.A.

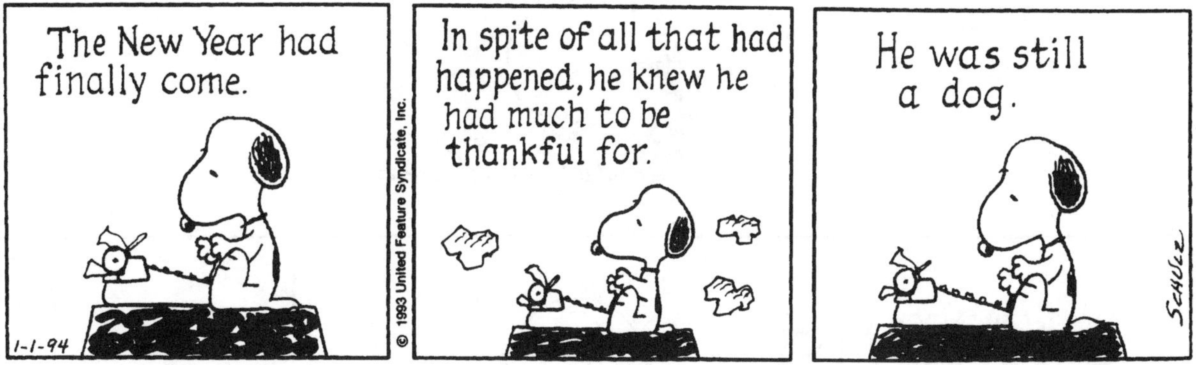
The New Year had finally come.
1-1-94
© 1993 United Feature Syndicate, Inc.
In spite of all that had happened, he knew he had much to be thankful for.
He was still a dog.
SCHULZ

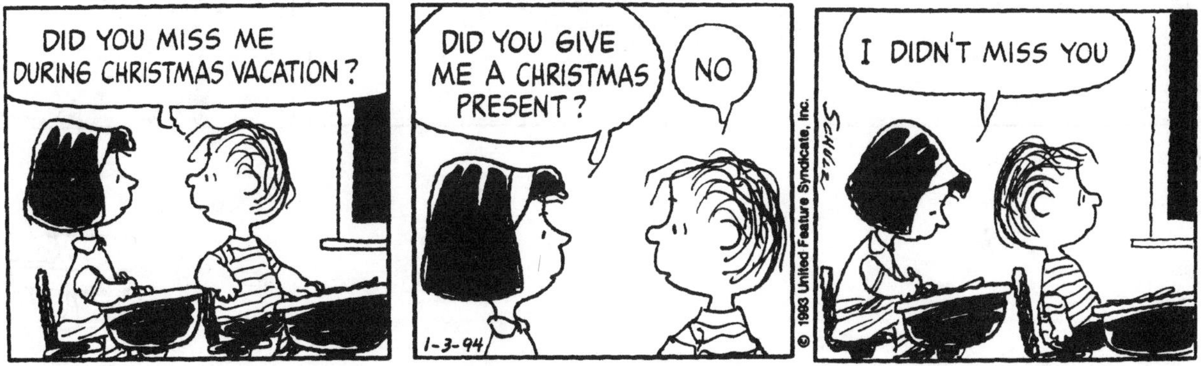
DID YOU MISS ME DURING CHRISTMAS VACATION?
DID YOU GIVE ME A CHRISTMAS PRESENT?
NO
1-3-94
© 1993 United Feature Syndicate, Inc.
SCHULZ
I DIDN'T MISS YOU

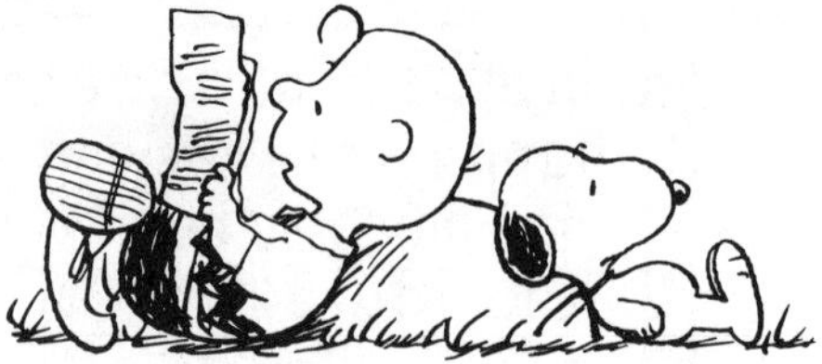

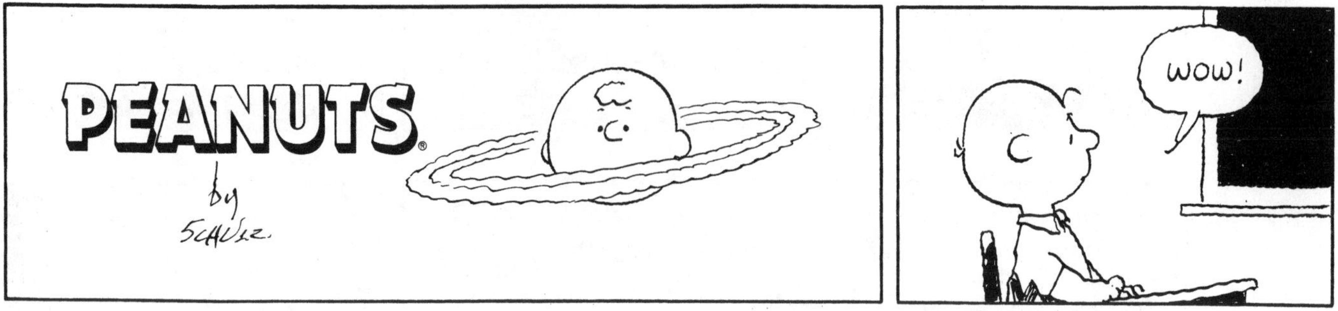
PEANUTS®
by SCHULZ
WOW!

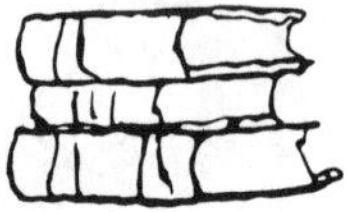

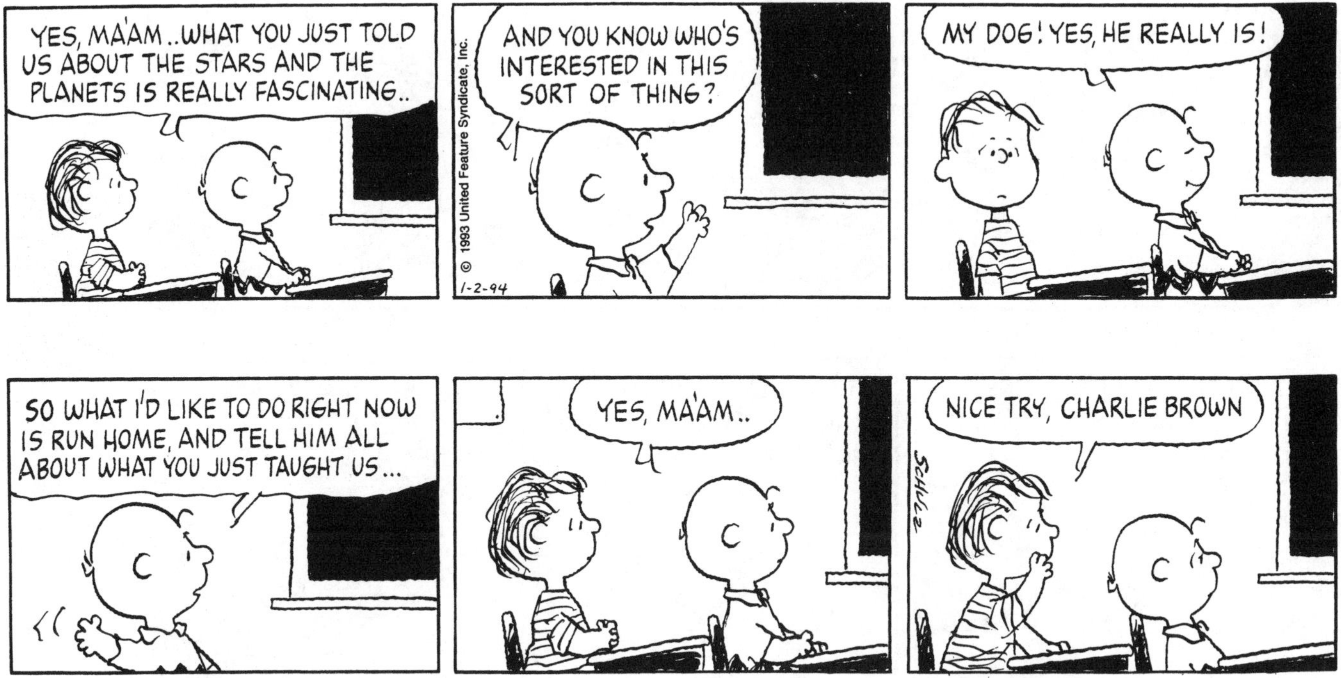
YES, MA'AM ..WHAT YOU JUST TOLD US ABOUT THE STARS AND THE PLANETS IS REALLY FASCINATING..
AND YOU KNOW WHO'S INTERESTED IN THIS SORT OF THING?
© 1993 United Feature Syndicate, Inc.
1-2-94
MY DOG! YES, HE REALLY IS!
SO WHAT I'D LIKE TO DO RIGHT NOW IS RUN HOME, AND TELL HIM ALL ABOUT WHAT YOU JUST TAUGHT US...
YES, MA'AM..
NICE TRY, CHARLIE BROWN
SCHULZ

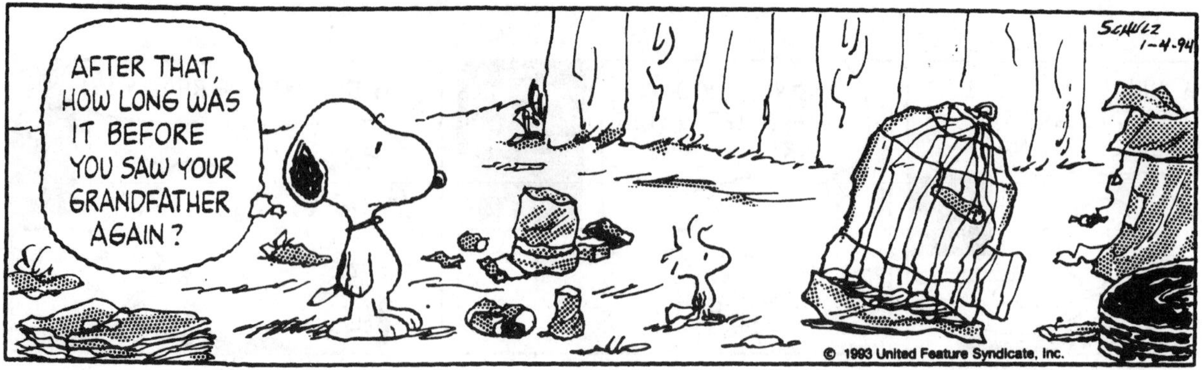
AFTER THAT, HOW LONG WAS IT BEFORE YOU SAW YOUR GRANDFATHER AGAIN ?
SCHULZ 1-4-94
© 1993 United Feature Syndicate, Inc.

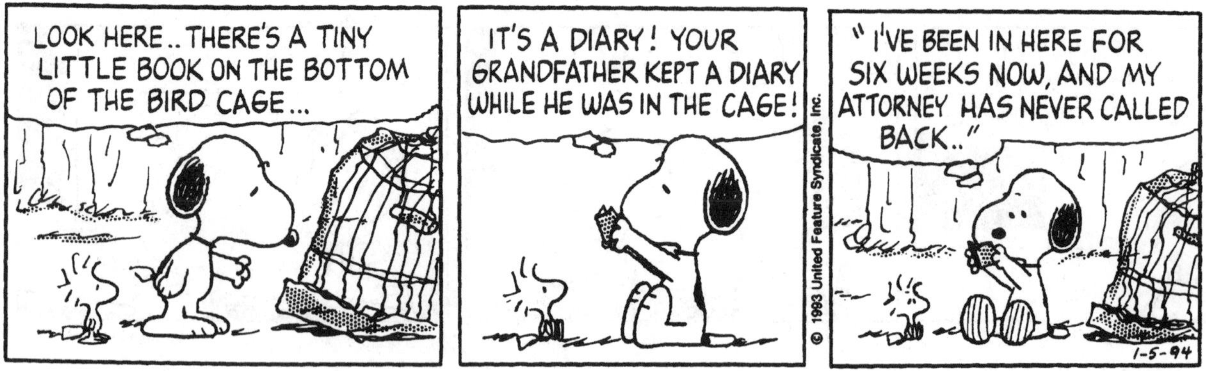
LOOK HERE.. THERE'S A TINY LITTLE BOOK ON THE BOTTOM OF THE BIRD CAGE...
IT'S A DIARY! YOUR GRANDFATHER KEPT A DIARY WHILE HE WAS IN THE CAGE!
© 1993 United Feature Syndicate, Inc.
"I'VE BEEN IN HERE FOR SIX WEEKS NOW, AND MY ATTORNEY HAS NEVER CALLED BACK.."
1-5-94

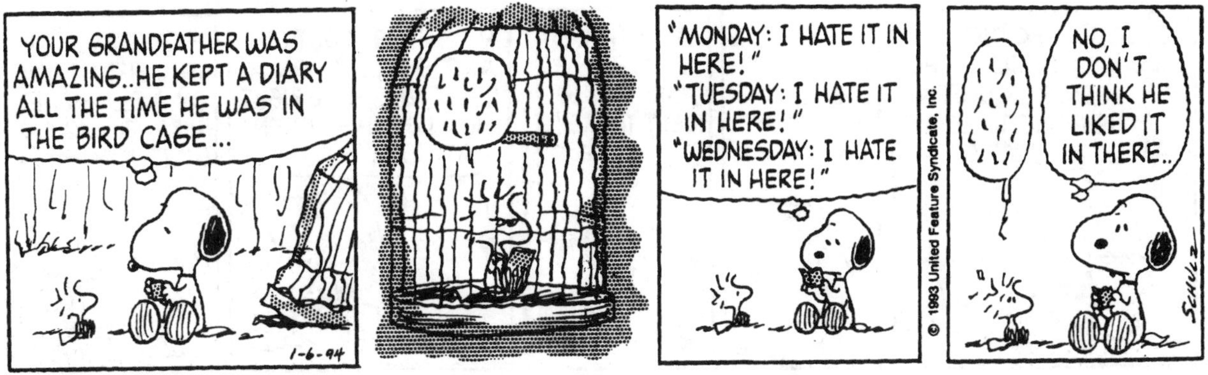
YOUR GRANDFATHER WAS AMAZING..HE KEPT A DIARY ALL THE TIME HE WAS IN THE BIRD CAGE...
1-6-94
"MONDAY: I HATE IT IN HERE!"
"TUESDAY: I HATE IT IN HERE!"
"WEDNESDAY: I HATE IT IN HERE!"
© 1993 United Feature Syndicate, Inc.
NO, I DON'T THINK HE LIKED IT IN THERE..
SCHULZ

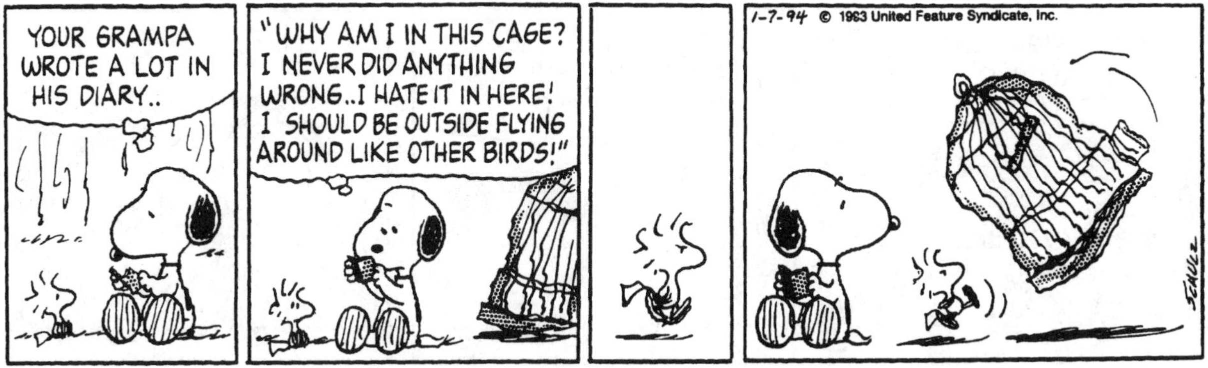
YOUR GRAMPA WROTE A LOT IN HIS DIARY..
"WHY AM I IN THIS CAGE? I NEVER DID ANYTHING WRONG..I HATE IT IN HERE! I SHOULD BE OUTSIDE FLYING AROUND LIKE OTHER BIRDS!"
1-7-94 © 1993 United Feature Syndicate, Inc.
SCHULZ

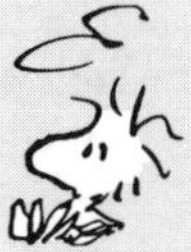

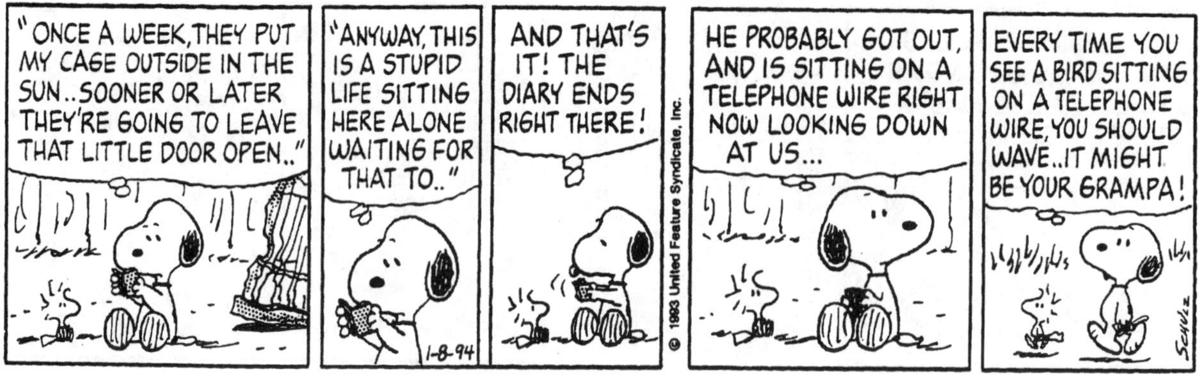
"ONCE A WEEK, THEY PUT MY CAGE OUTSIDE IN THE SUN.. SOONER OR LATER THEY'RE GOING TO LEAVE THAT LITTLE DOOR OPEN.."
"ANYWAY, THIS IS A STUPID LIFE SITTING HERE ALONE WAITING FOR THAT TO.."
1-8-94
AND THAT'S IT! THE DIARY ENDS RIGHT THERE!
© 1993 United Feature Syndicate, Inc.
HE PROBABLY GOT OUT, AND IS SITTING ON A TELEPHONE WIRE RIGHT NOW LOOKING DOWN AT US...
EVERY TIME YOU SEE A BIRD SITTING ON A TELEPHONE WIRE, YOU SHOULD WAVE.. IT MIGHT BE YOUR GRAMPA!
SCHULZ

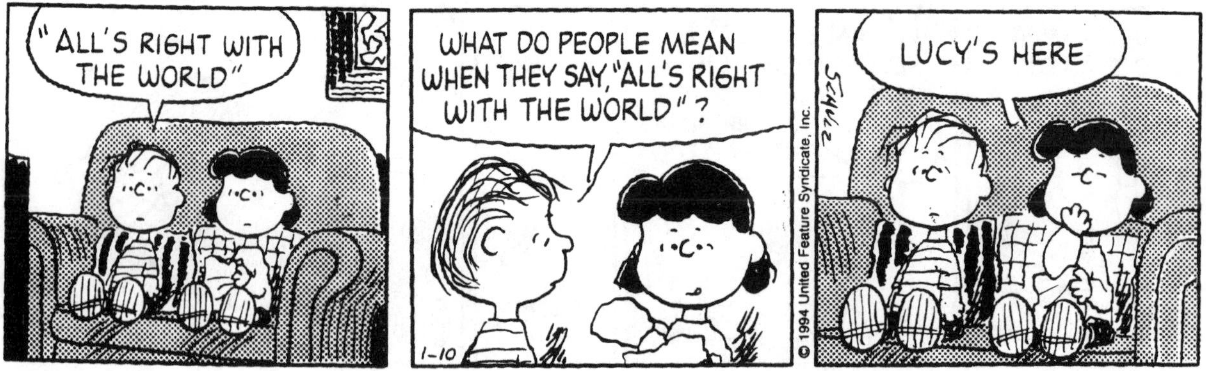
"ALL'S RIGHT WITH THE WORLD"
WHAT DO PEOPLE MEAN WHEN THEY SAY, "ALL'S RIGHT WITH THE WORLD"?
1-10
© 1994 United Feature Syndicate, Inc.
SCHULZ
LUCY'S HERE

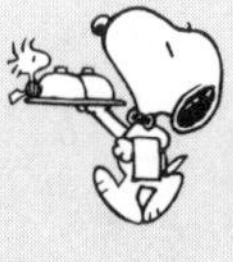

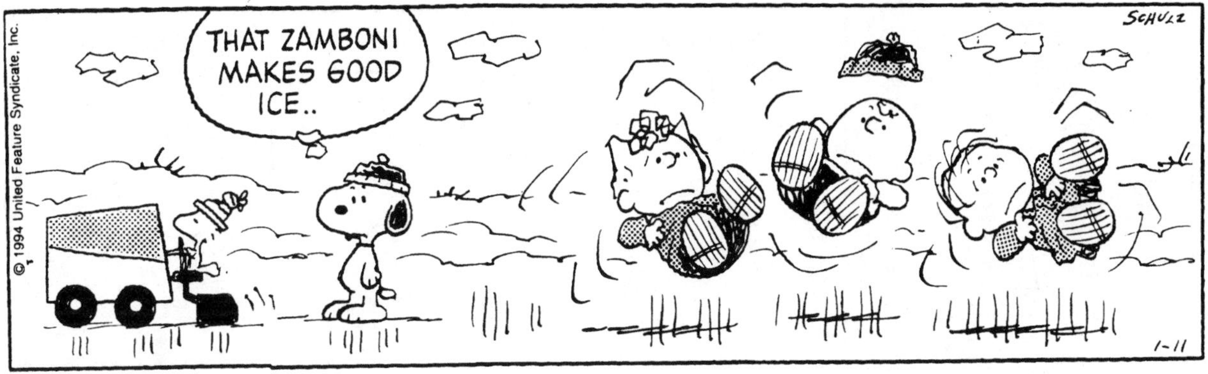

© 1994 United Feature Syndicate, Inc.
SCHULZ
THAT ZAMBONI MAKES GOOD ICE..
1-11

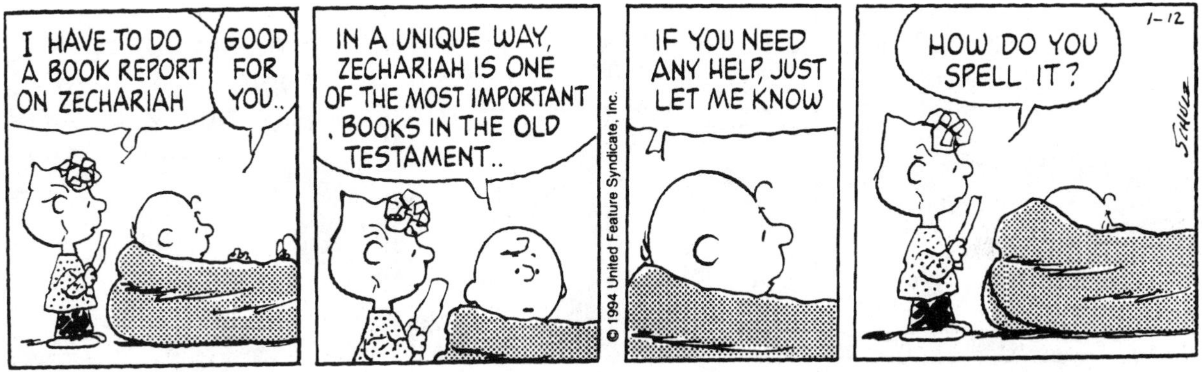

I HAVE TO DO A BOOK REPORT ON ZECHARIAH
GOOD FOR YOU..
IN A UNIQUE WAY, ZECHARIAH IS ONE OF THE MOST IMPORTANT BOOKS IN THE OLD TESTAMENT..
© 1994 United Feature Syndicate, Inc.
IF YOU NEED ANY HELP, JUST LET ME KNOW
1-12
HOW DO YOU SPELL IT?
SCHULZ

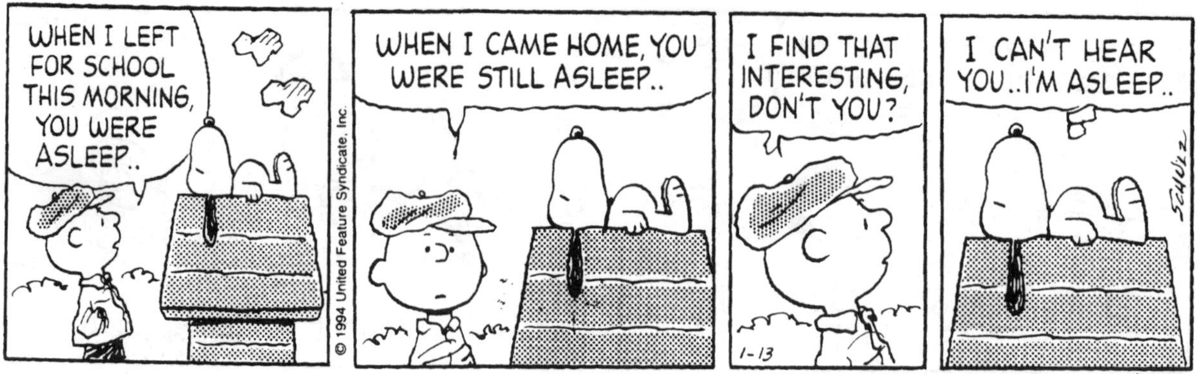
WHEN I LEFT FOR SCHOOL THIS MORNING, YOU WERE ASLEEP..
© 1994 United Feature Syndicate, Inc.
WHEN I CAME HOME, YOU WERE STILL ASLEEP..
I FIND THAT INTERESTING, DON'T YOU?
1-13
I CAN'T HEAR YOU..I'M ASLEEP..
SCHULZ

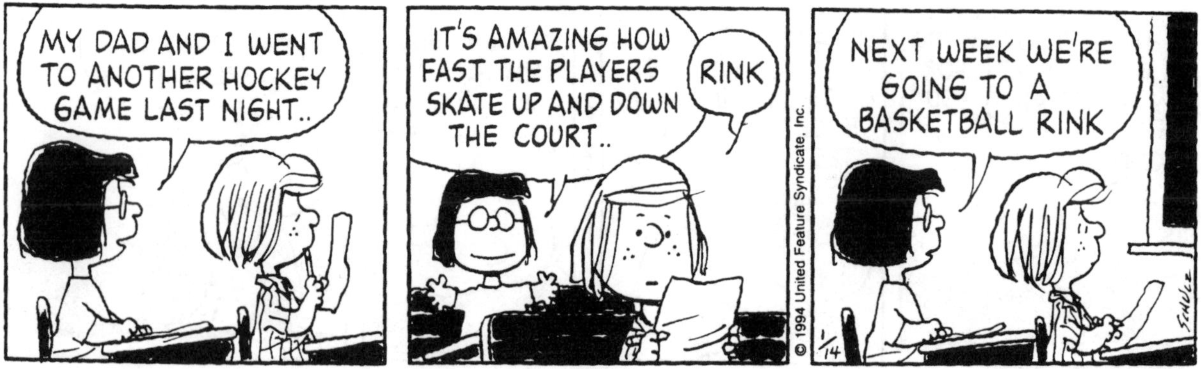
MY DAD AND I WENT TO ANOTHER HOCKEY GAME LAST NIGHT..
IT'S AMAZING HOW FAST THE PLAYERS SKATE UP AND DOWN THE COURT..
RINK
© 1994 United Feature Syndicate, Inc.
1/14
NEXT WEEK WE'RE GOING TO A BASKETBALL RINK
SCHULZ

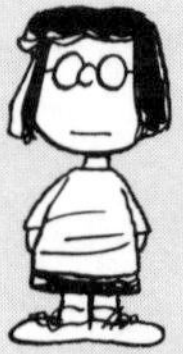

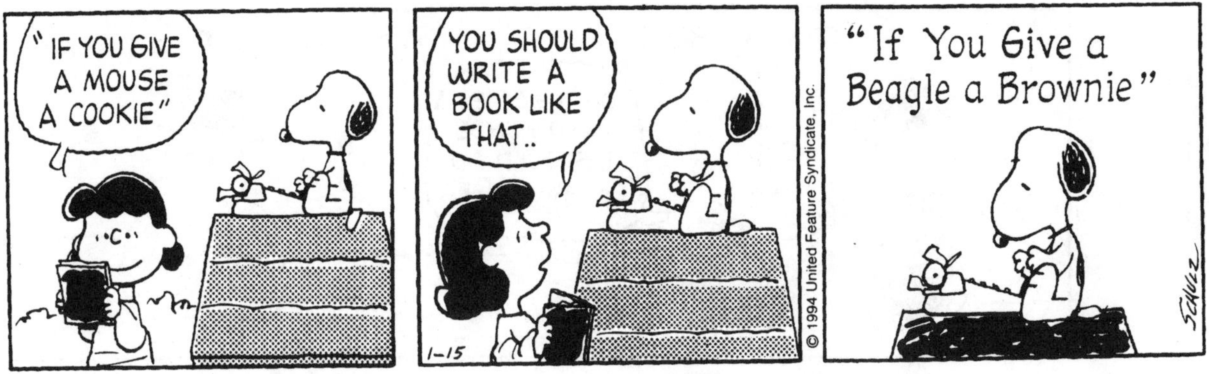
"IF YOU GIVE A MOUSE A COOKIE"
YOU SHOULD WRITE A BOOK LIKE THAT..
1-15
© 1994 United Feature Syndicate, Inc.
"If You Give a Beagle a Brownie"
SCHULZ

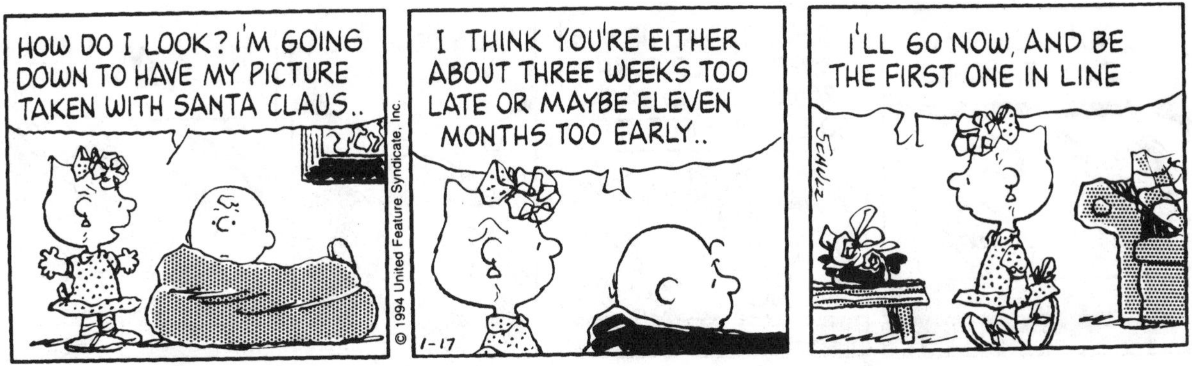
HOW DO I LOOK? I'M GOING DOWN TO HAVE MY PICTURE TAKEN WITH SANTA CLAUS..
© 1994 United Feature Syndicate, Inc.
I THINK YOU'RE EITHER ABOUT THREE WEEKS TOO LATE OR MAYBE ELEVEN MONTHS TOO EARLY..
1-17
I'LL GO NOW, AND BE THE FIRST ONE IN LINE
SCHULZ

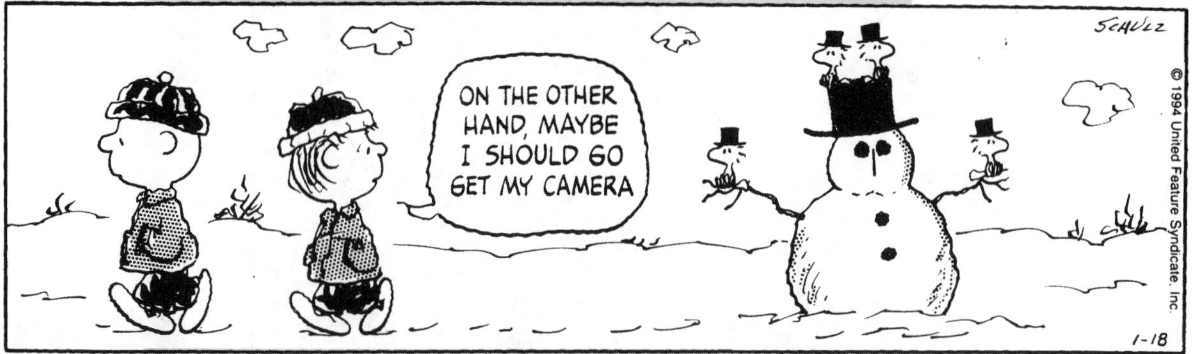
ON THE OTHER HAND, MAYBE I SHOULD GO GET MY CAMERA
© 1994 United Feature Syndicate, Inc.
1-18

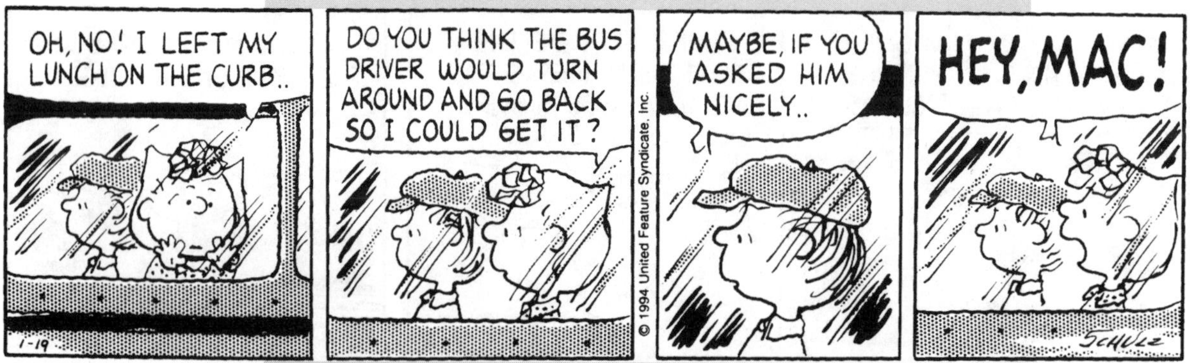
OH, NO! I LEFT MY LUNCH ON THE CURB..
1-19
DO YOU THINK THE BUS DRIVER WOULD TURN AROUND AND GO BACK SO I COULD GET IT?
© 1994 United Feature Syndicate, Inc.
MAYBE, IF YOU ASKED HIM NICELY..
HEY, MAC!

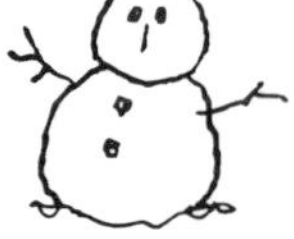

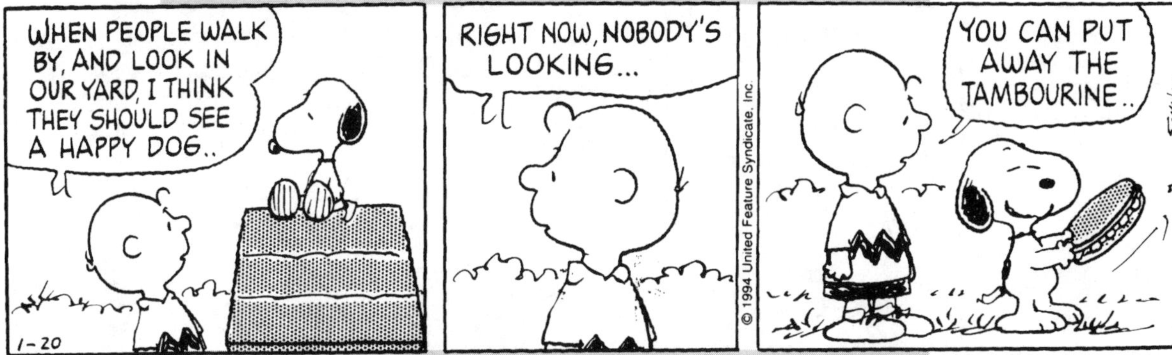
WHEN PEOPLE WALK BY, AND LOOK IN OUR YARD, I THINK THEY SHOULD SEE A HAPPY DOG..
1-20
RIGHT NOW, NOBODY'S LOOKING...
© 1994 United Feature Syndicate, Inc.
YOU CAN PUT AWAY THE TAMBOURINE..
SCHULZ

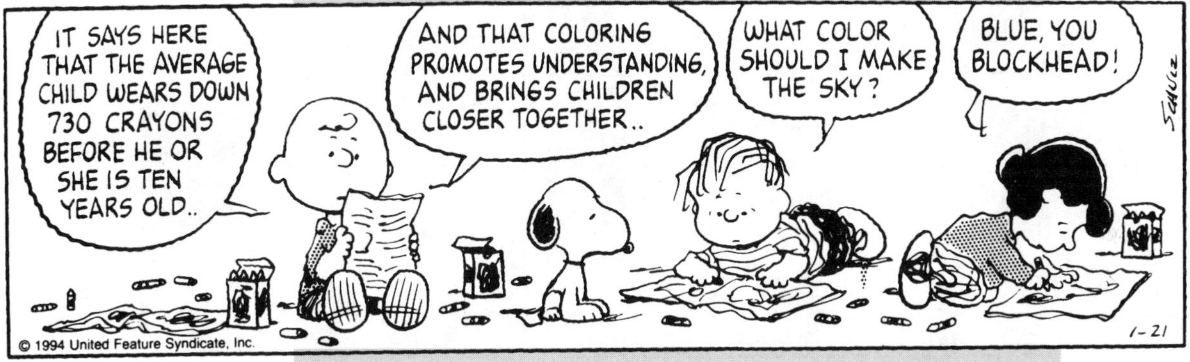
IT SAYS HERE THAT THE AVERAGE CHILD WEARS DOWN 730 CRAYONS BEFORE HE OR SHE IS TEN YEARS OLD..
AND THAT COLORING PROMOTES UNDERSTANDING, AND BRINGS CHILDREN CLOSER TOGETHER..
WHAT COLOR SHOULD I MAKE THE SKY?
BLUE, YOU BLOCKHEAD!
SCHULZ
1-21
© 1994 United Feature Syndicate, Inc.

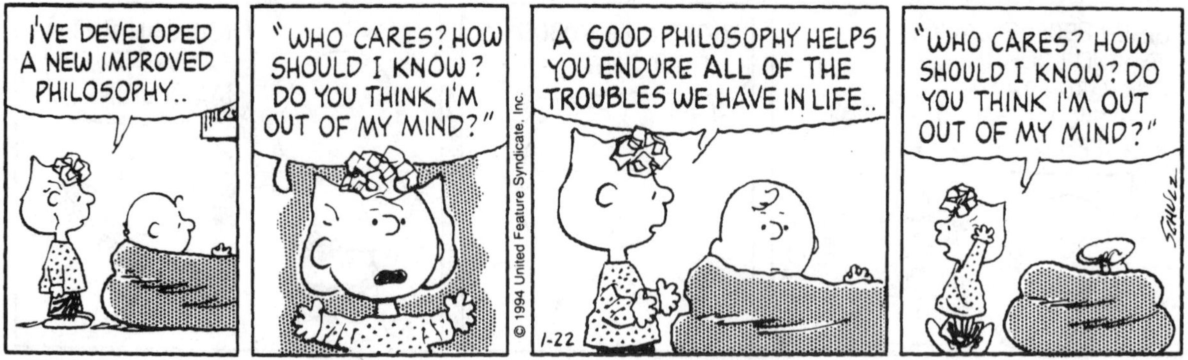
I'VE DEVELOPED A NEW IMPROVED PHILOSOPHY..
"WHO CARES? HOW SHOULD I KNOW? DO YOU THINK I'M OUT OF MY MIND?"
© 1994 United Feature Syndicate, Inc.
1-22
A GOOD PHILOSOPHY HELPS YOU ENDURE ALL OF THE TROUBLES WE HAVE IN LIFE..
"WHO CARES? HOW SHOULD I KNOW? DO YOU THINK I'M OUT OUT OF MY MIND?"
SCHULZ

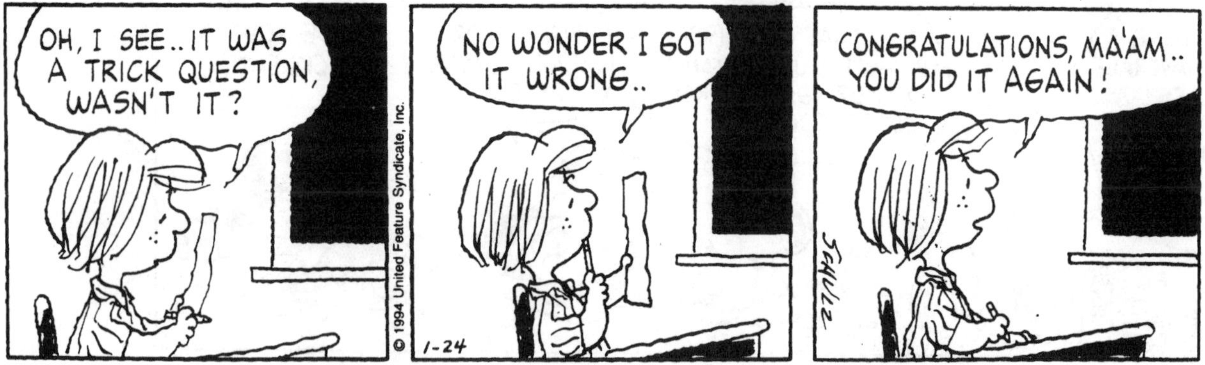
OH, I SEE.. IT WAS A TRICK QUESTION, WASN'T IT?
© 1994 United Feature Syndicate, Inc.
1-24
NO WONDER I GOT IT WRONG..
SCHULZ
CONGRATULATIONS, MA'AM.. YOU DID IT AGAIN!

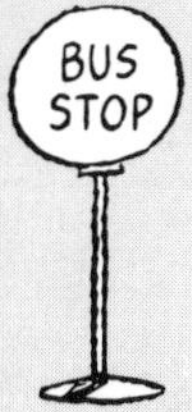
BUS STOP

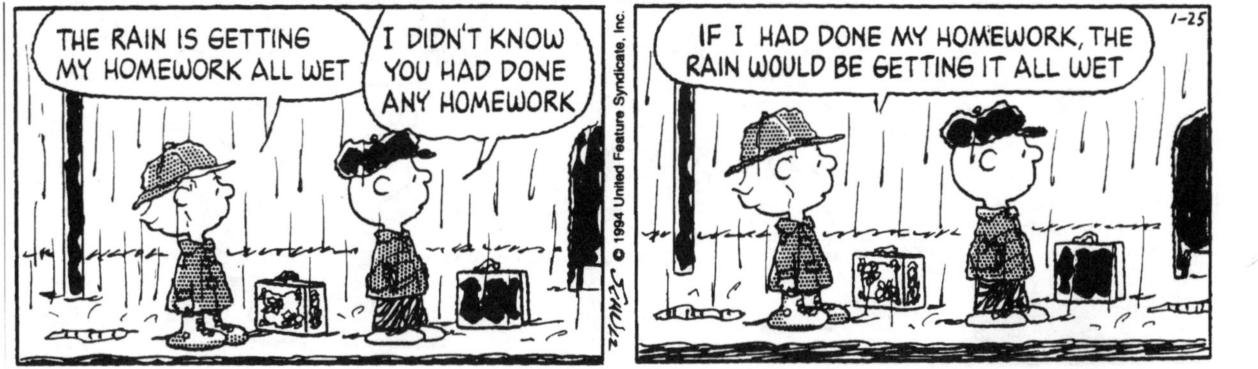
THE RAIN IS GETTING MY HOMEWORK ALL WET
I DIDN'T KNOW YOU HAD DONE ANY HOMEWORK
© 1994 United Feature Syndicate, Inc.
1-25
IF I HAD DONE MY HOMEWORK, THE RAIN WOULD BE GETTING IT ALL WET

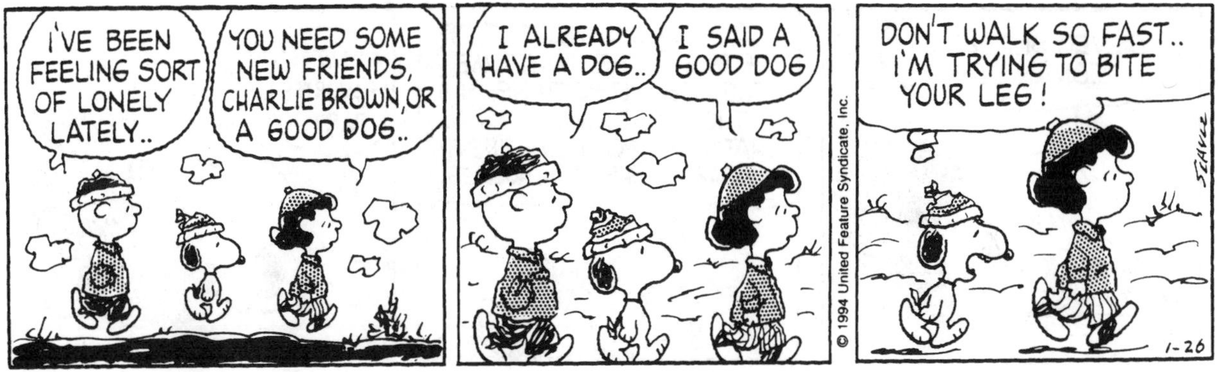
I'VE BEEN FEELING SORT OF LONELY LATELY..
YOU NEED SOME NEW FRIENDS, CHARLIE BROWN, OR A GOOD DOG..
I ALREADY HAVE A DOG..
I SAID A GOOD DOG
© 1994 United Feature Syndicate, Inc.
DON'T WALK SO FAST.. I'M TRYING TO BITE YOUR LEG!
1-26

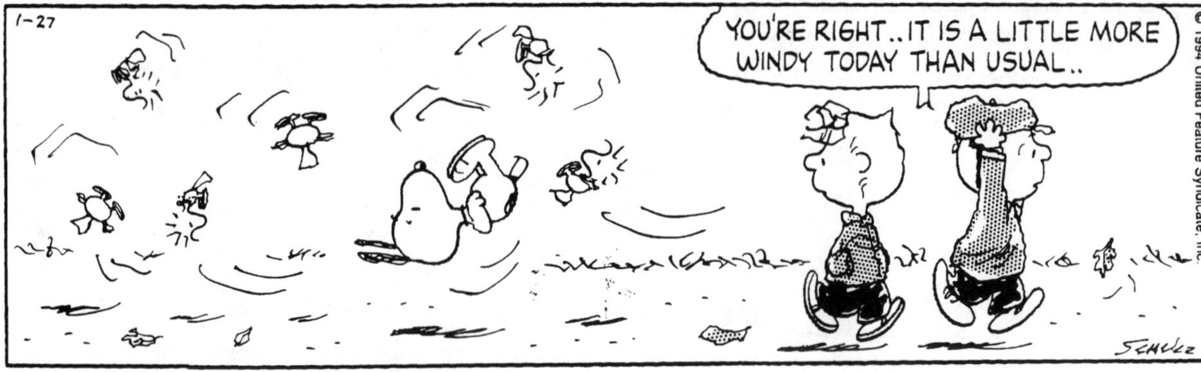
1-27
YOU'RE RIGHT..IT IS A LITTLE MORE WINDY TODAY THAN USUAL..
© 1994 United Feature Syndicate, Inc.
SCHULZ

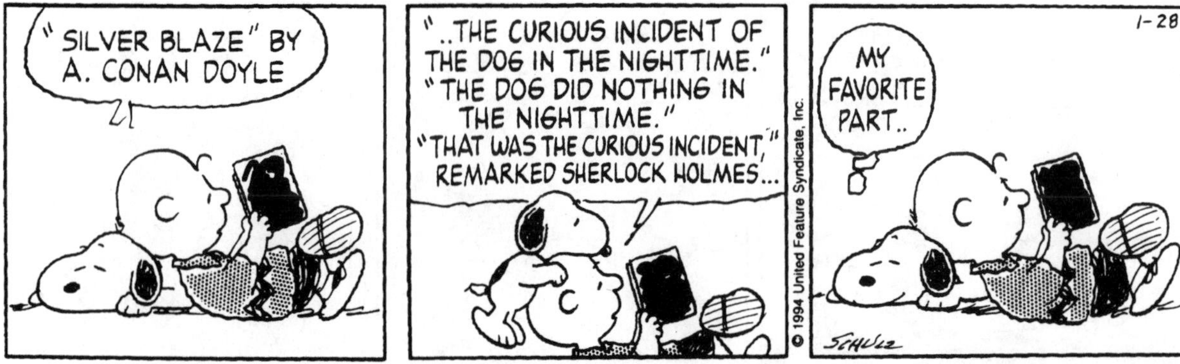
"SILVER BLAZE" BY A. CONAN DOYLE
"..THE CURIOUS INCIDENT OF THE DOG IN THE NIGHTTIME." "THE DOG DID NOTHING IN THE NIGHTTIME." "THAT WAS THE CURIOUS INCIDENT," REMARKED SHERLOCK HOLMES...
© 1994 United Feature Syndicate, Inc.
1-28
MY FAVORITE PART..
SCHULZ

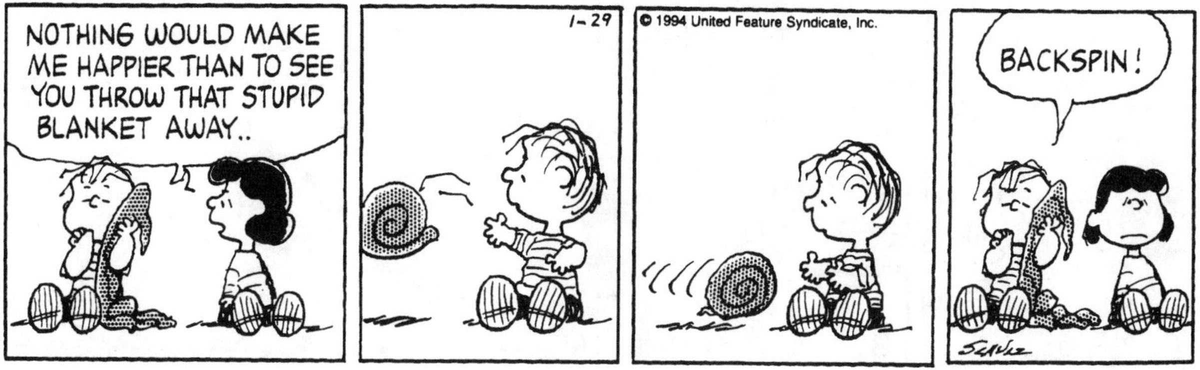
NOTHING WOULD MAKE ME HAPPIER THAN TO SEE YOU THROW THAT STUPID BLANKET AWAY..
1-29
© 1994 United Feature Syndicate, Inc.
BACKSPIN!
SCHULZ

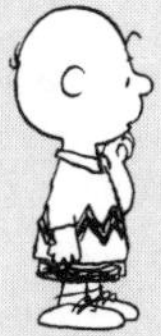

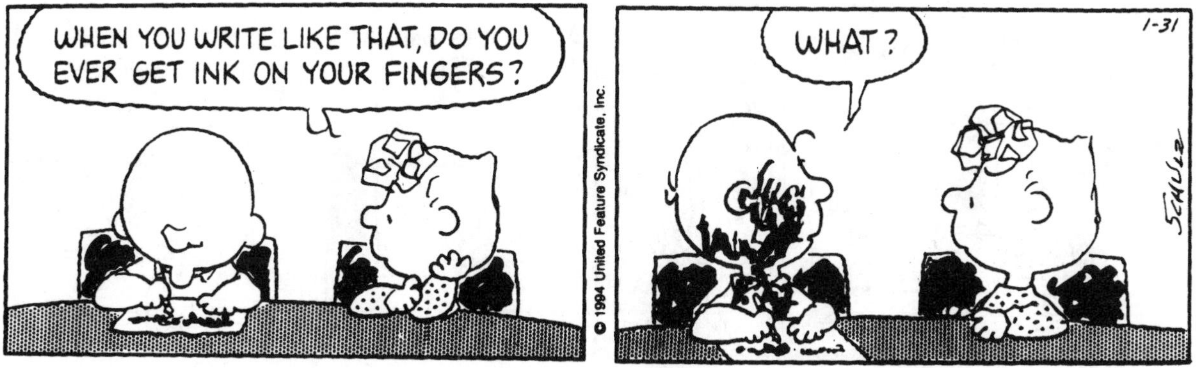
WHEN YOU WRITE LIKE THAT, DO YOU EVER GET INK ON YOUR FINGERS?
© 1994 United Feature Syndicate, Inc.
WHAT?
1-31
SCHULZ

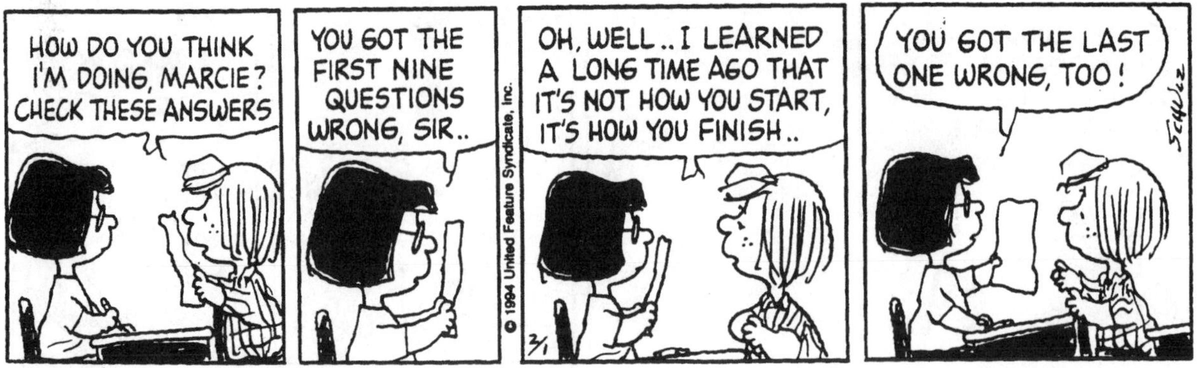
HOW DO YOU THINK I'M DOING, MARCIE? CHECK THESE ANSWERS
YOU GOT THE FIRST NINE QUESTIONS WRONG, SIR..
© 1994 United Feature Syndicate, Inc.
OH, WELL.. I LEARNED A LONG TIME AGO THAT IT'S NOT HOW YOU START, IT'S HOW YOU FINISH..
2/1
YOU GOT THE LAST ONE WRONG, TOO!
SCHULZ

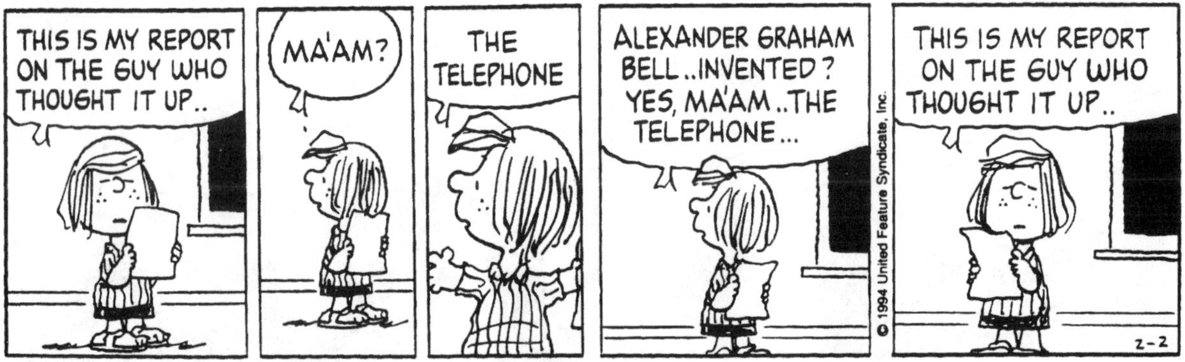
THIS IS MY REPORT ON THE GUY WHO THOUGHT IT UP..
MA'AM?
THE TELEPHONE
ALEXANDER GRAHAM BELL..INVENTED? YES, MA'AM..THE TELEPHONE...
© 1994 United Feature Syndicate, Inc.
THIS IS MY REPORT ON THE GUY WHO THOUGHT IT UP..
2-2

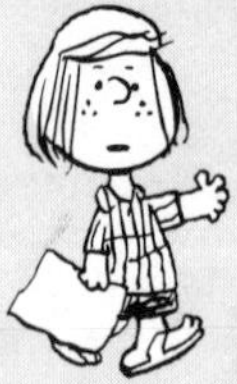

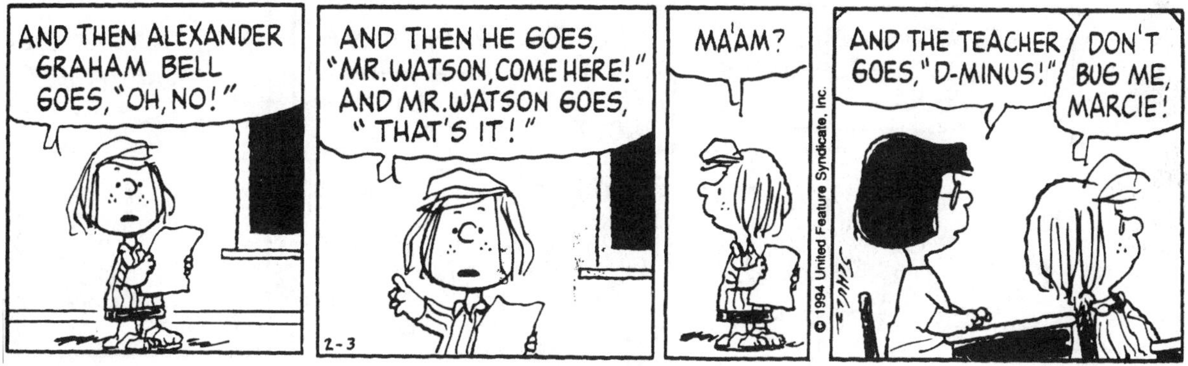
AND THEN ALEXANDER GRAHAM BELL GOES, "OH, NO!"
AND THEN HE GOES, "MR. WATSON, COME HERE!" AND MR. WATSON GOES, "THAT'S IT!"
2-3
MA'AM?
© 1994 United Feature Syndicate, Inc.
SCHULZ
AND THE TEACHER GOES, "D-MINUS!"
DON'T BUG ME, MARCIE!

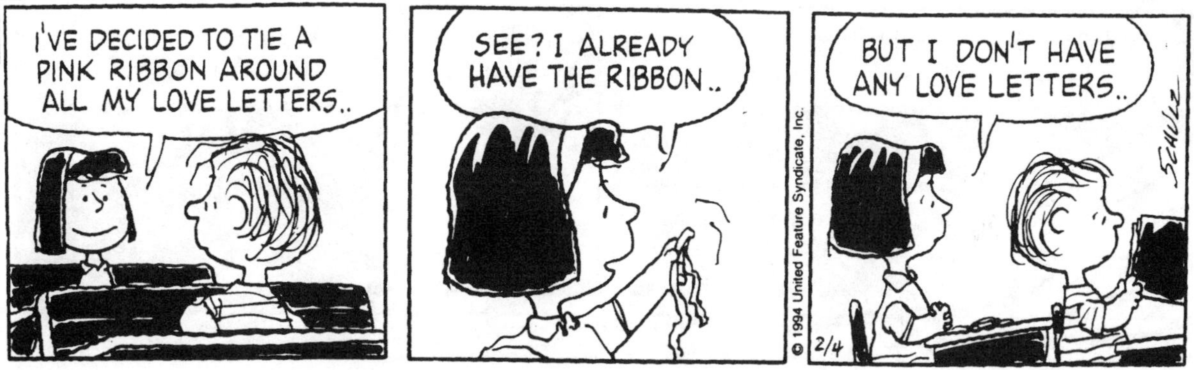
I'VE DECIDED TO TIE A PINK RIBBON AROUND ALL MY LOVE LETTERS..
SEE? I ALREADY HAVE THE RIBBON..
© 1994 United Feature Syndicate, Inc.
2/4
BUT I DON'T HAVE ANY LOVE LETTERS..
SCHULZ

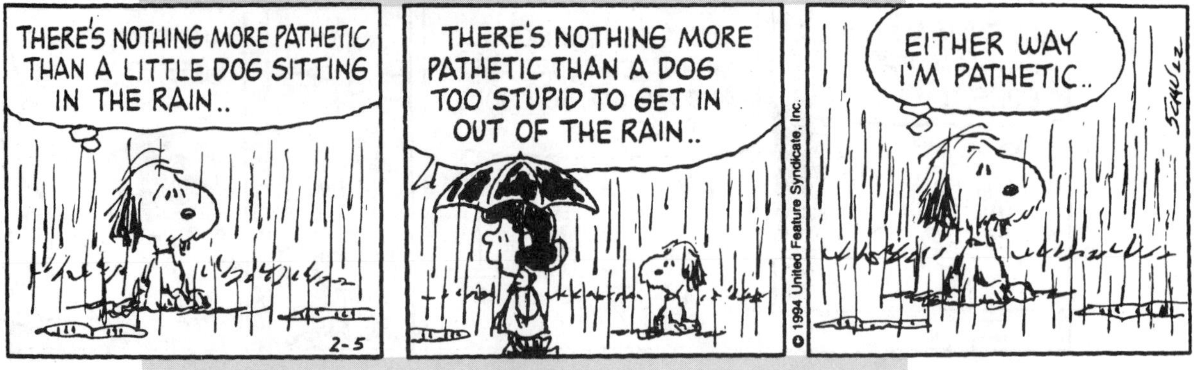
THERE'S NOTHING MORE PATHETIC THAN A LITTLE DOG SITTING IN THE RAIN..
2-5
THERE'S NOTHING MORE PATHETIC THAN A DOG TOO STUPID TO GET IN OUT OF THE RAIN..
© 1994 United Feature Syndicate, Inc.
EITHER WAY I'M PATHETIC..
SCHULZ

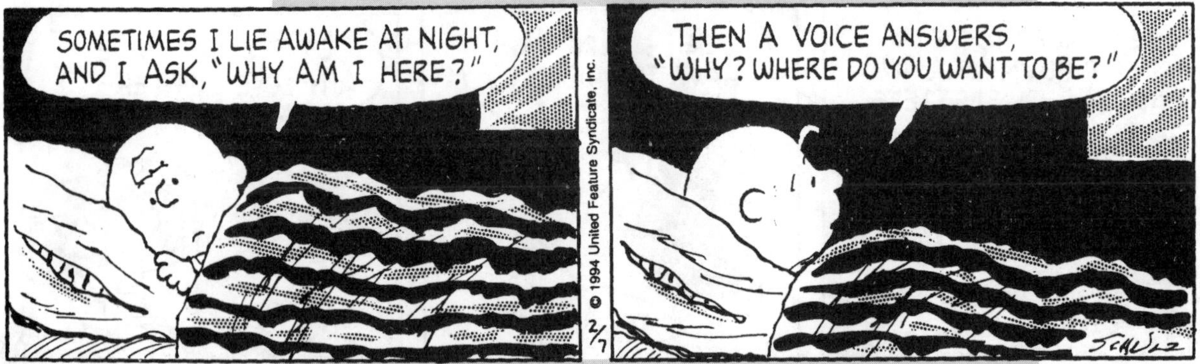
SOMETIMES I LIE AWAKE AT NIGHT, AND I ASK, "WHY AM I HERE?"
© 1994 United Feature Syndicate, Inc.
2/7
THEN A VOICE ANSWERS, "WHY? WHERE DO YOU WANT TO BE?"
SCHULZ

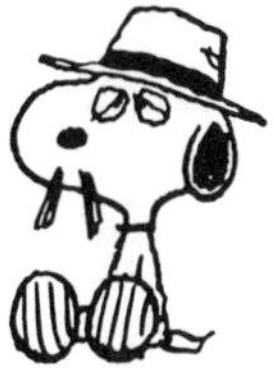

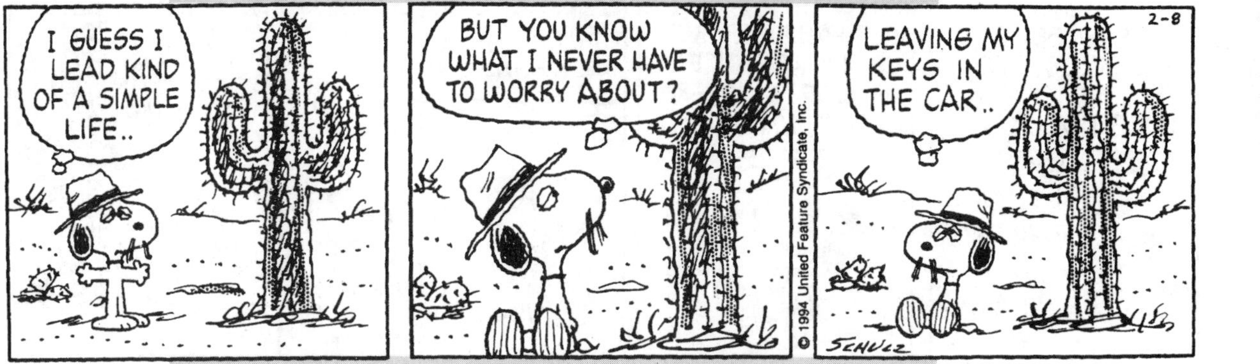

I GUESS I LEAD KIND OF A SIMPLE LIFE..
BUT YOU KNOW WHAT I NEVER HAVE TO WORRY ABOUT?
© 1994 United Feature Syndicate, Inc.
2-8
LEAVING MY KEYS IN THE CAR..
SCHULZ

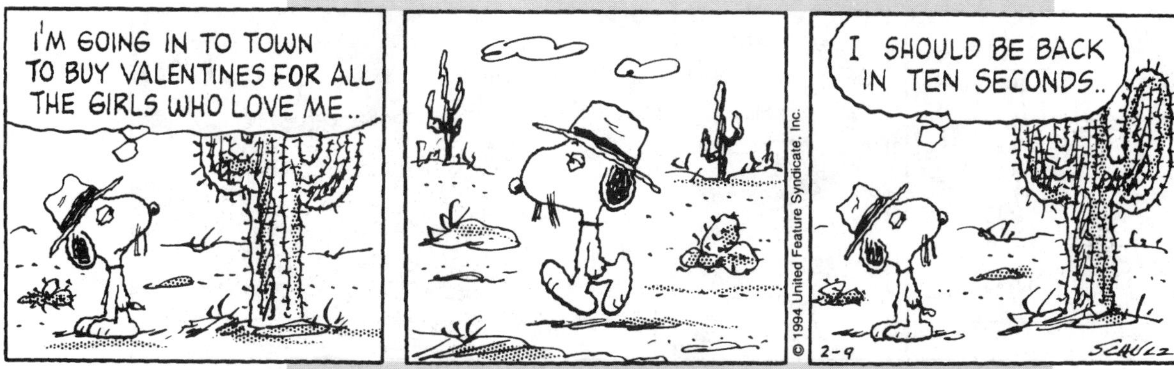

I'M GOING IN TO TOWN TO BUY VALENTINES FOR ALL THE GIRLS WHO LOVE ME..
© 1994 United Feature Syndicate, Inc.
2-9
I SHOULD BE BACK IN TEN SECONDS..
SCHULZ

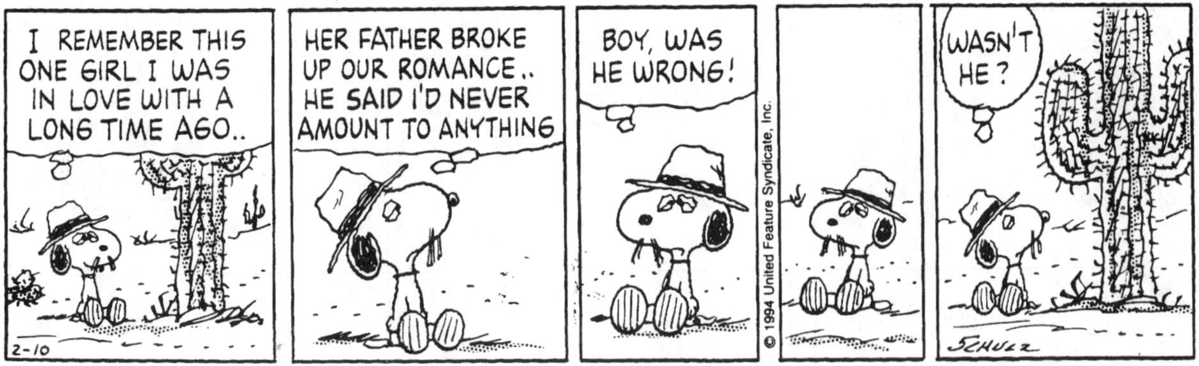
I REMEMBER THIS ONE GIRL I WAS IN LOVE WITH A LONG TIME AGO..
2-10
HER FATHER BROKE UP OUR ROMANCE.. HE SAID I'D NEVER AMOUNT TO ANYTHING
BOY, WAS HE WRONG!
© 1994 United Feature Syndicate, Inc.
WASN'T HE?
SCHULZ

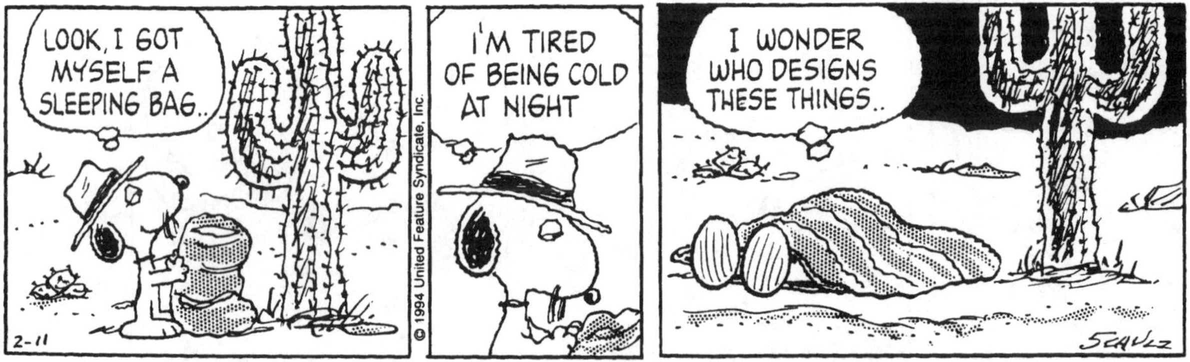
LOOK, I GOT MYSELF A SLEEPING BAG..
2-11
© 1994 United Feature Syndicate, Inc.
I'M TIRED OF BEING COLD AT NIGHT
I WONDER WHO DESIGNS THESE THINGS..
SCHULZ

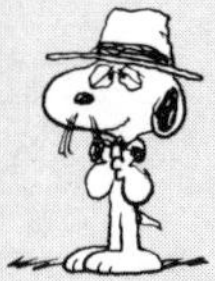

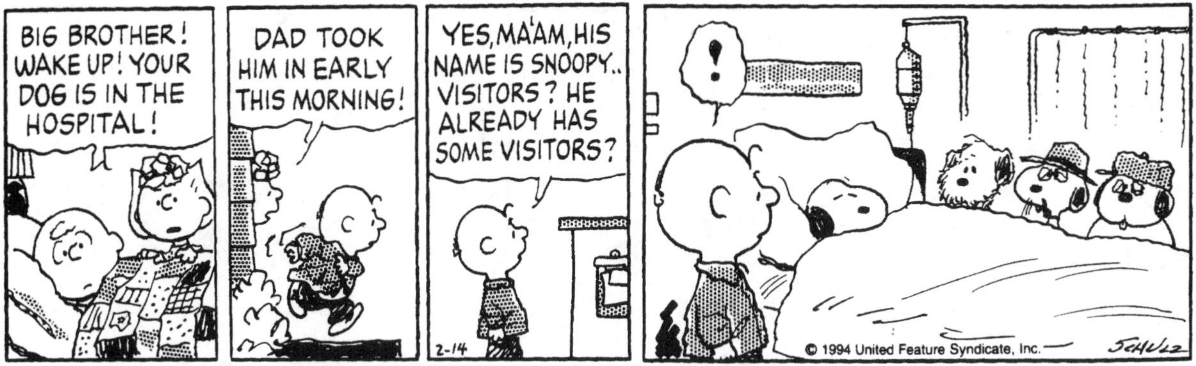
BIG BROTHER! WAKE UP! YOUR DOG IS IN THE HOSPITAL!
DAD TOOK HIM IN EARLY THIS MORNING!
YES, MA'AM, HIS NAME IS SNOOPY.. VISITORS? HE ALREADY HAS SOME VISITORS?
2-14
!
© 1994 United Feature Syndicate, Inc.
SCHULZ

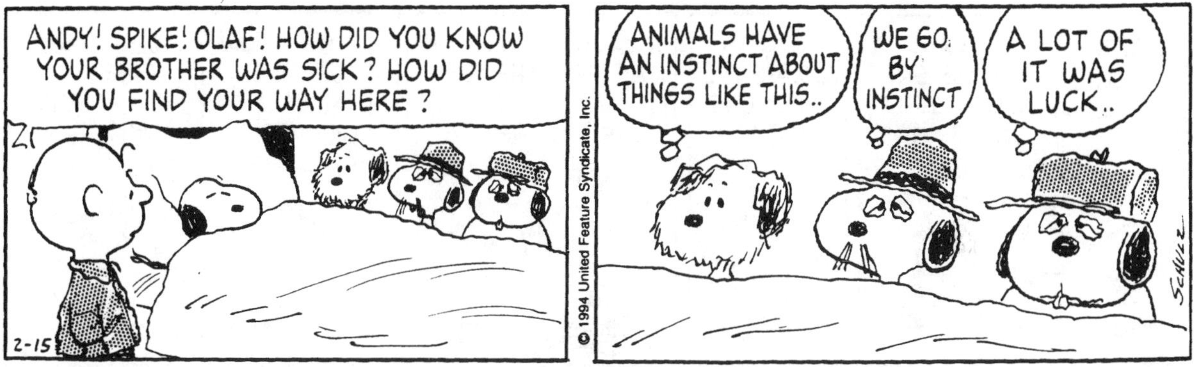
ANDY! SPIKE! OLAF! HOW DID YOU KNOW YOUR BROTHER WAS SICK? HOW DID YOU FIND YOUR WAY HERE?
Z
2-15
© 1994 United Feature Syndicate, Inc.
ANIMALS HAVE AN INSTINCT ABOUT THINGS LIKE THIS..
WE GO BY INSTINCT
A LOT OF IT WAS LUCK..
SCHULZ

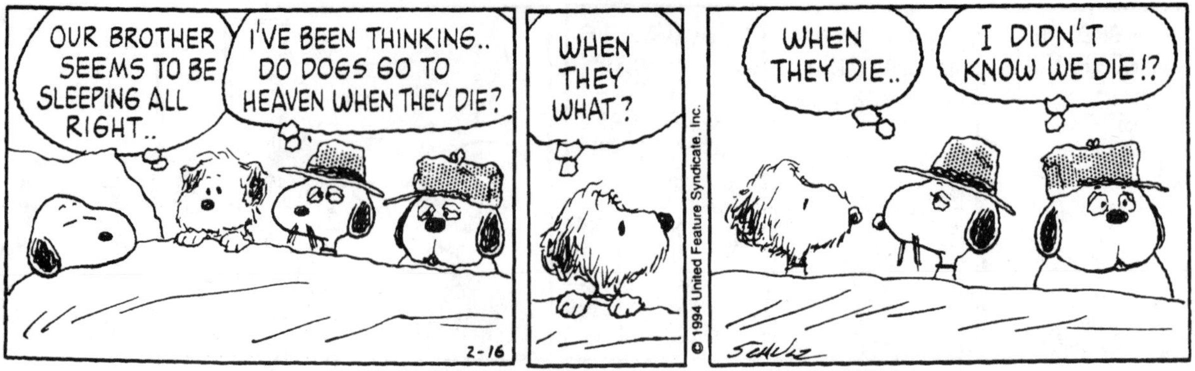
OUR BROTHER SEEMS TO BE SLEEPING ALL RIGHT..
I'VE BEEN THINKING.. DO DOGS GO TO HEAVEN WHEN THEY DIE?
2-16
WHEN THEY WHAT?
© 1994 United Feature Syndicate, Inc.
WHEN THEY DIE..
I DIDN'T KNOW WE DIE!?
SCHULZ

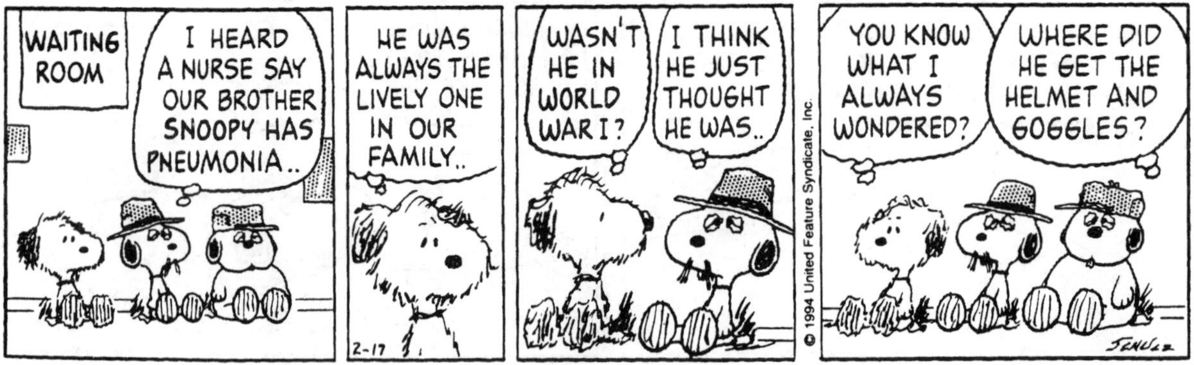
WAITING ROOM
I HEARD A NURSE SAY OUR BROTHER SNOOPY HAS PNEUMONIA..
HE WAS ALWAYS THE LIVELY ONE IN OUR FAMILY..
2-17
WASN'T HE IN WORLD WAR I?
I THINK HE JUST THOUGHT HE WAS..
© 1994 United Feature Syndicate, Inc.
YOU KNOW WHAT I ALWAYS WONDERED?
WHERE DID HE GET THE HELMET AND GOGGLES?
SCHULZ

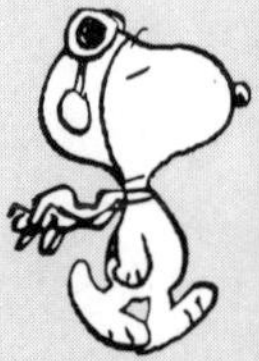

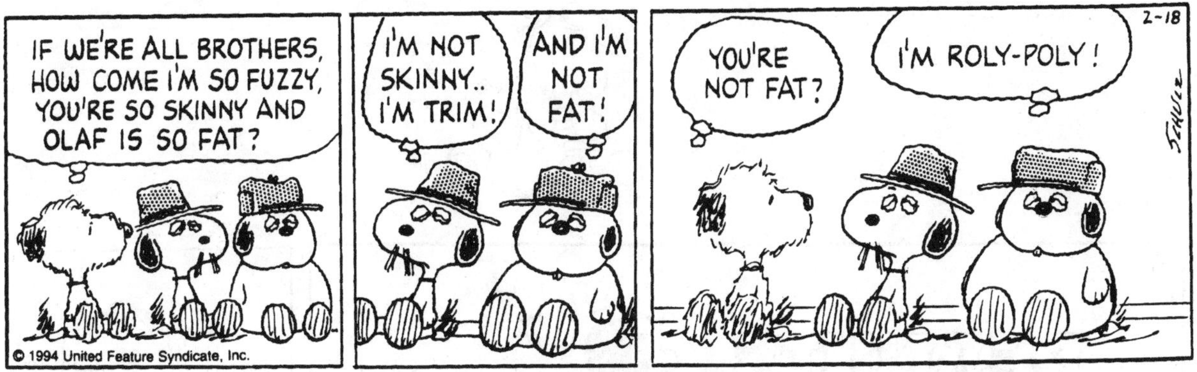
IF WE'RE ALL BROTHERS, HOW COME I'M SO FUZZY, YOU'RE SO SKINNY AND OLAF IS SO FAT?
© 1994 United Feature Syndicate, Inc.
I'M NOT SKINNY.. I'M TRIM!
AND I'M NOT FAT!
2-18
YOU'RE NOT FAT?
I'M ROLY-POLY!
SCHULZ

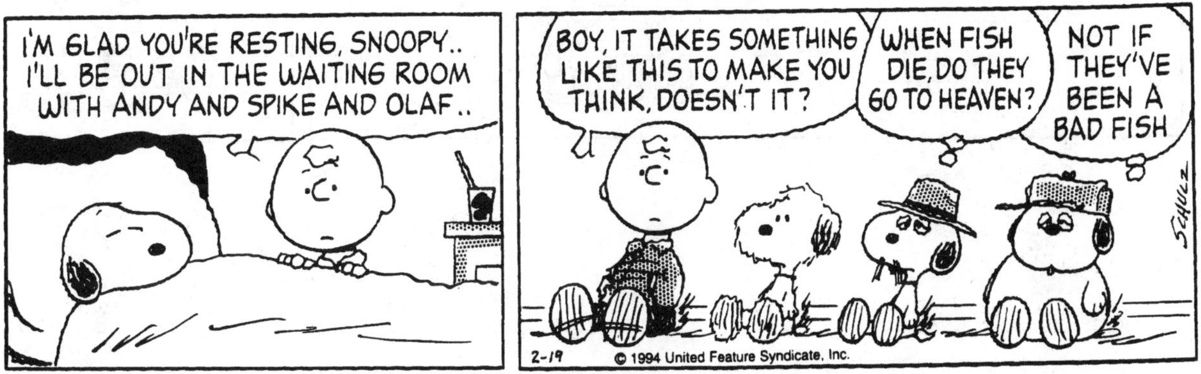
I'M GLAD YOU'RE RESTING, SNOOPY.. I'LL BE OUT IN THE WAITING ROOM WITH ANDY AND SPIKE AND OLAF..
BOY, IT TAKES SOMETHING LIKE THIS TO MAKE YOU THINK, DOESN'T IT?
WHEN FISH DIE, DO THEY GO TO HEAVEN?
NOT IF THEY'VE BEEN A BAD FISH
SCHULZ
2-19
© 1994 United Feature Syndicate, Inc.

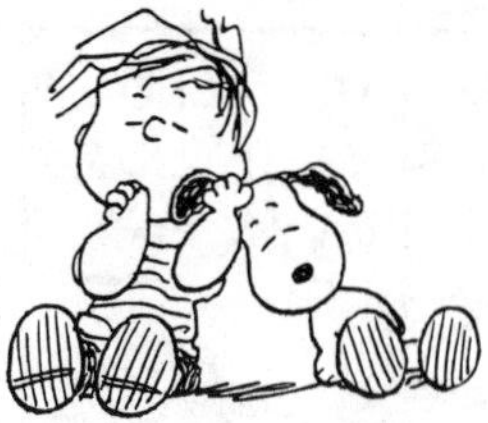

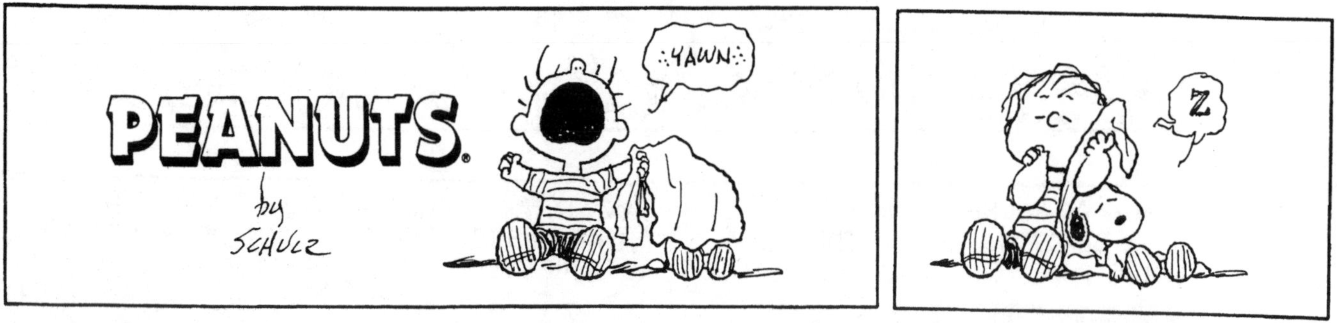
PEANUTS
by SCHULZ
YAWN
Z

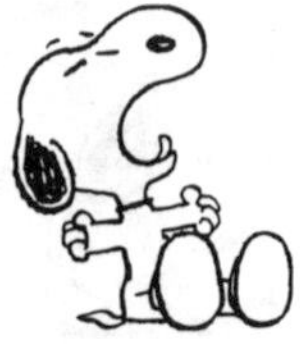

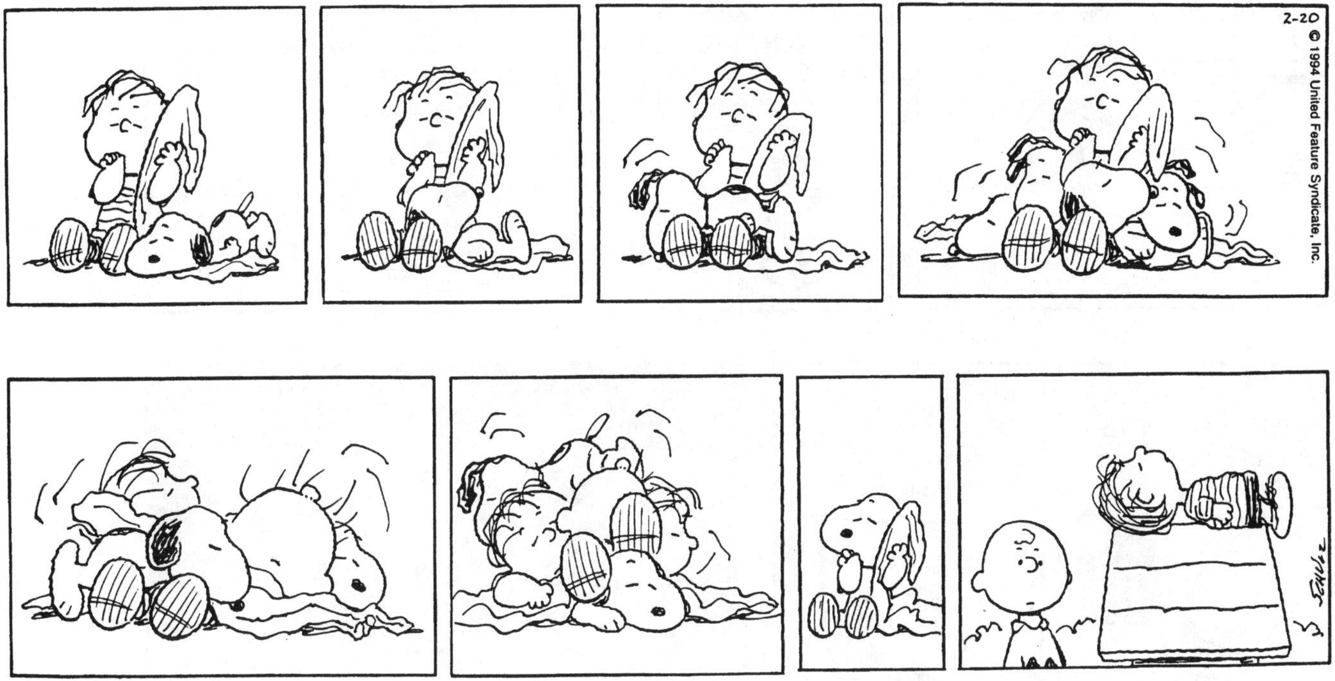
2-20 © 1994 United Feature Syndicate, Inc.
SCHULZ

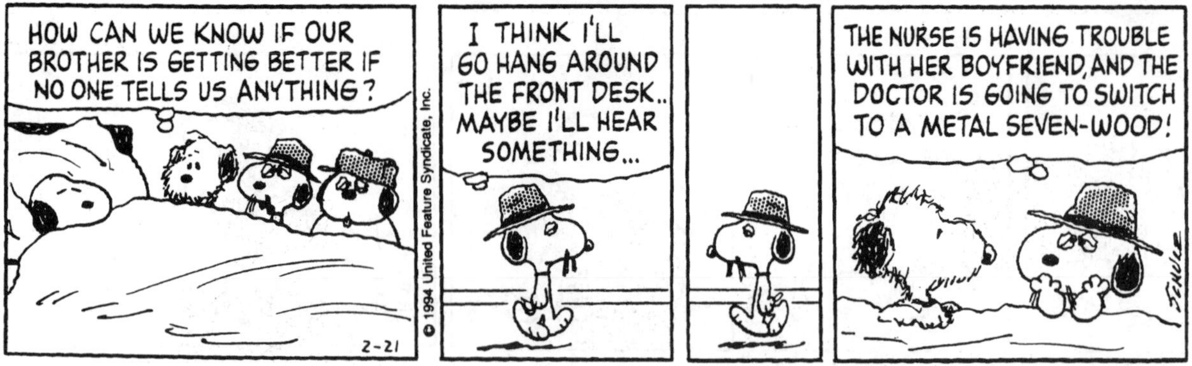
HOW CAN WE KNOW IF OUR BROTHER IS GETTING BETTER IF NO ONE TELLS US ANYTHING?
2-21
© 1994 United Feature Syndicate, Inc.
I THINK I'LL GO HANG AROUND THE FRONT DESK.. MAYBE I'LL HEAR SOMETHING...
THE NURSE IS HAVING TROUBLE WITH HER BOYFRIEND, AND THE DOCTOR IS GOING TO SWITCH TO A METAL SEVEN-WOOD!

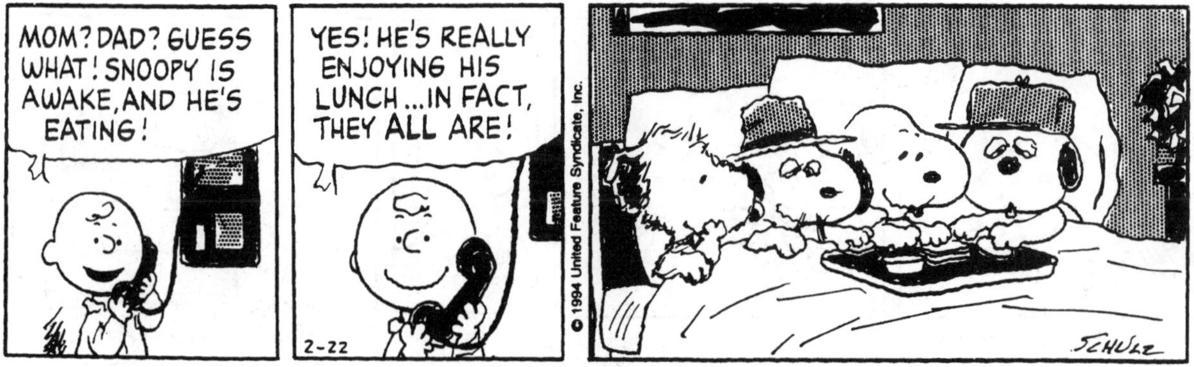
MOM? DAD? GUESS WHAT! SNOOPY IS AWAKE, AND HE'S EATING!
YES! HE'S REALLY ENJOYING HIS LUNCH ...IN FACT, THEY ALL ARE!
2-22
© 1994 United Feature Syndicate, Inc.

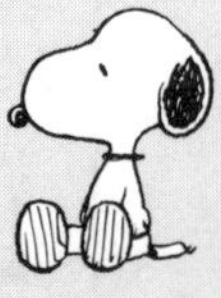

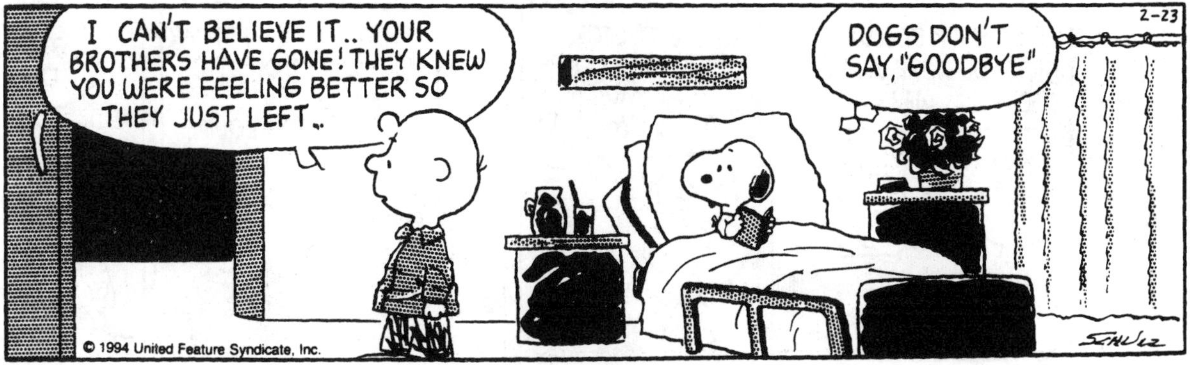
I CAN'T BELIEVE IT.. YOUR BROTHERS HAVE GONE! THEY KNEW YOU WERE FEELING BETTER SO THEY JUST LEFT..
2-23
DOGS DON'T SAY, "GOODBYE"
© 1994 United Feature Syndicate, Inc.

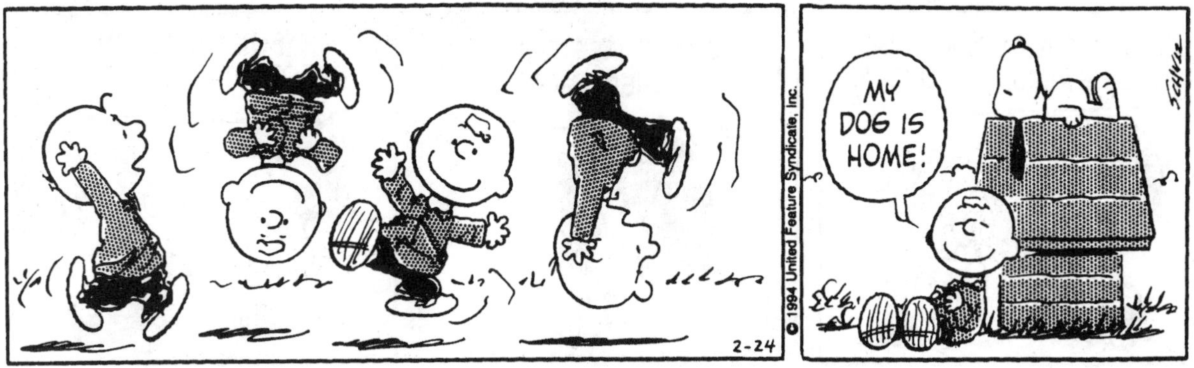
2-24
© 1994 United Feature Syndicate, Inc.
MY DOG IS HOME!

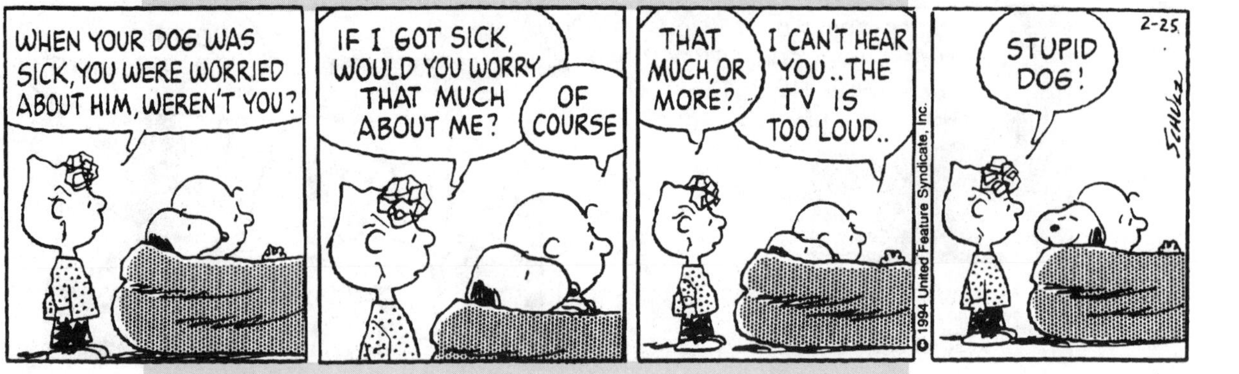
WHEN YOUR DOG WAS SICK, YOU WERE WORRIED ABOUT HIM, WEREN'T YOU?
IF I GOT SICK, WOULD YOU WORRY THAT MUCH ABOUT ME?
OF COURSE
THAT MUCH, OR MORE?
I CAN'T HEAR YOU..THE TV IS TOO LOUD..
© 1994 United Feature Syndicate, Inc.
2-25
STUPID DOG!
SCHULZ

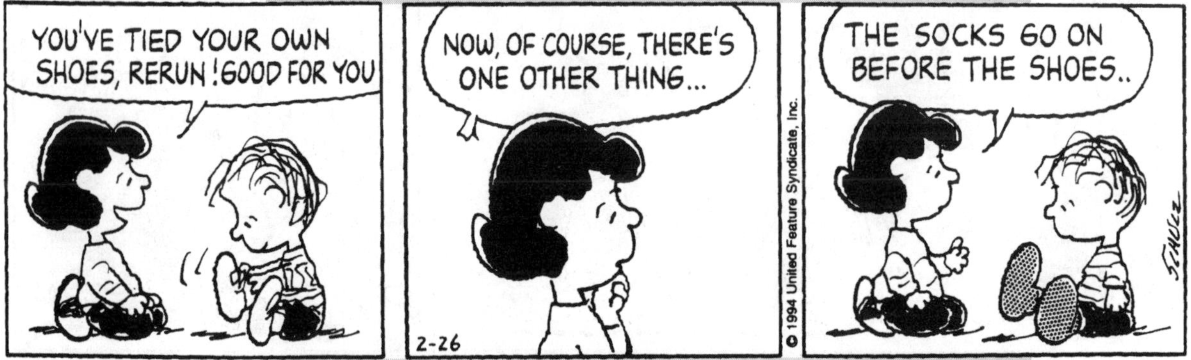
YOU'VE TIED YOUR OWN SHOES, RERUN! GOOD FOR YOU
NOW, OF COURSE, THERE'S ONE OTHER THING...
2-26
© 1994 United Feature Syndicate, Inc.
THE SOCKS GO ON BEFORE THE SHOES..
SCHULZ

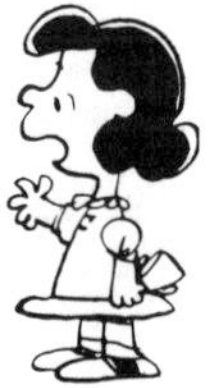

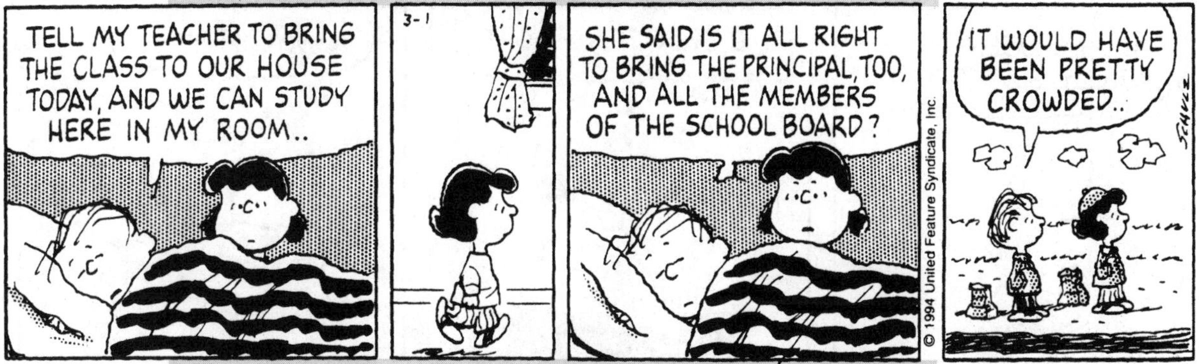
3-1
TELL MY TEACHER TO BRING THE CLASS TO OUR HOUSE TODAY, AND WE CAN STUDY HERE IN MY ROOM..
SHE SAID IS IT ALL RIGHT TO BRING THE PRINCIPAL, TOO, AND ALL THE MEMBERS OF THE SCHOOL BOARD?
© 1994 United Feature Syndicate, Inc.
IT WOULD HAVE BEEN PRETTY CROWDED..
SCHULZ

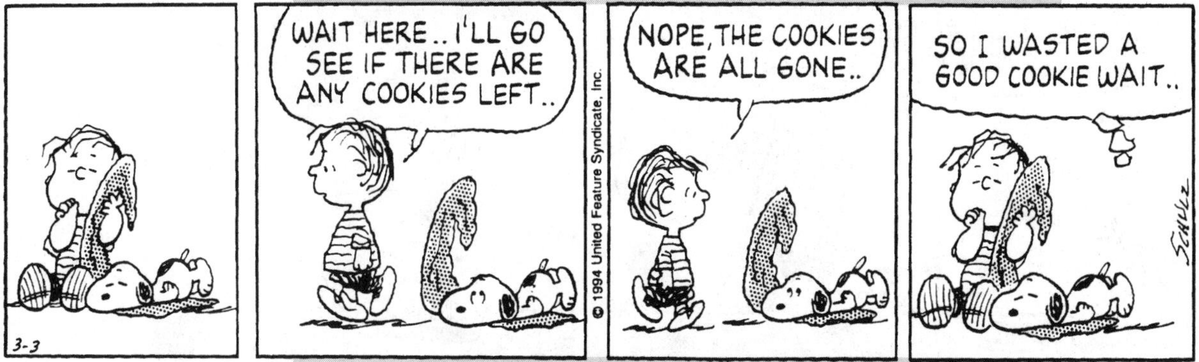
3-3
WAIT HERE.. I'LL GO SEE IF THERE ARE ANY COOKIES LEFT..
© 1994 United Feature Syndicate, Inc.
NOPE, THE COOKIES ARE ALL GONE..
SO I WASTED A GOOD COOKIE WAIT..
SCHULZ

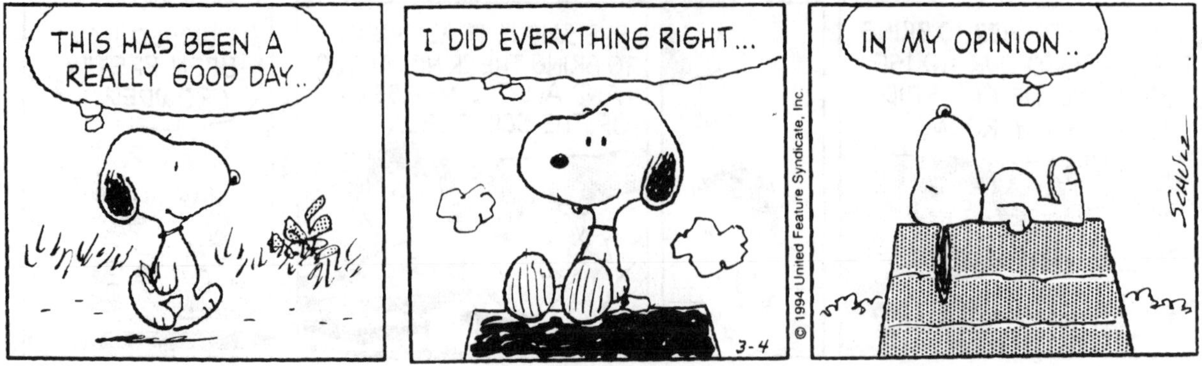
THIS HAS BEEN A REALLY GOOD DAY..
I DID EVERYTHING RIGHT...
3-4
© 1994 United Feature Syndicate, Inc.
IN MY OPINION..
SCHULZ

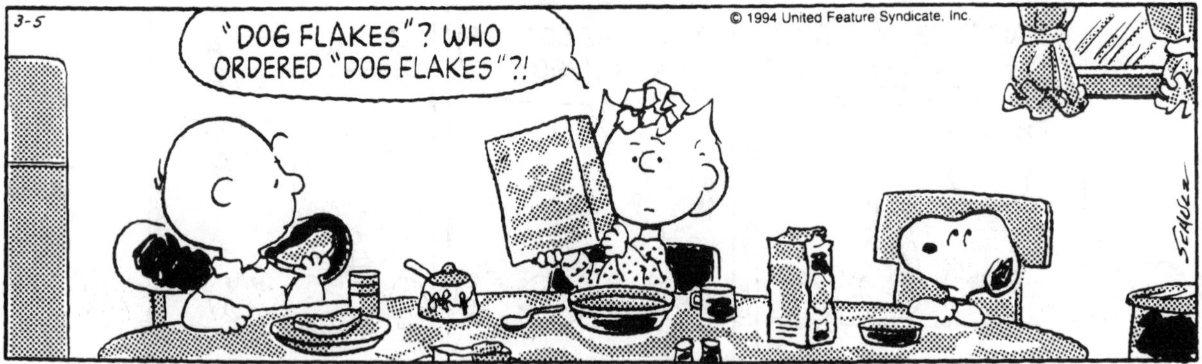
3-5
"DOG FLAKES"? WHO ORDERED "DOG FLAKES"?!
© 1994 United Feature Syndicate, Inc.
SCHULZ

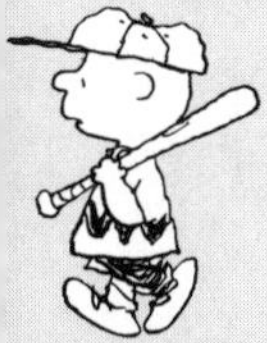

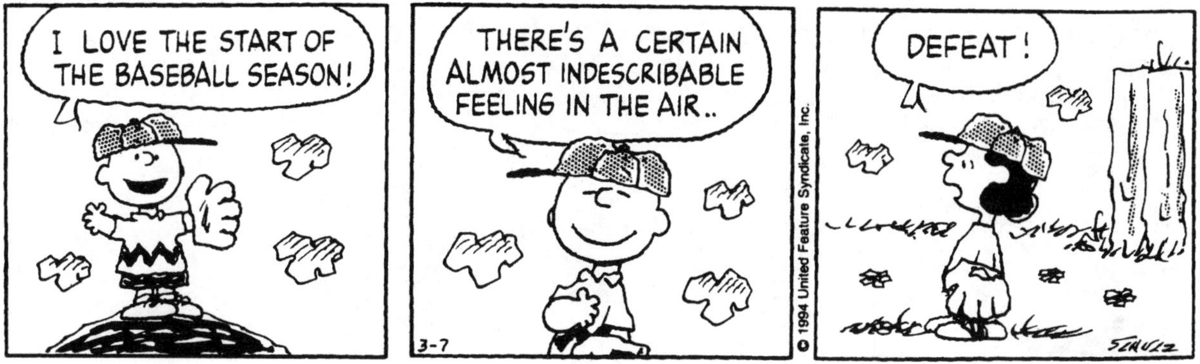

I LOVE THE START OF THE BASEBALL SEASON!
THERE'S A CERTAIN ALMOST INDESCRIBABLE FEELING IN THE AIR..
3-7
© 1994 United Feature Syndicate, Inc.
DEFEAT!

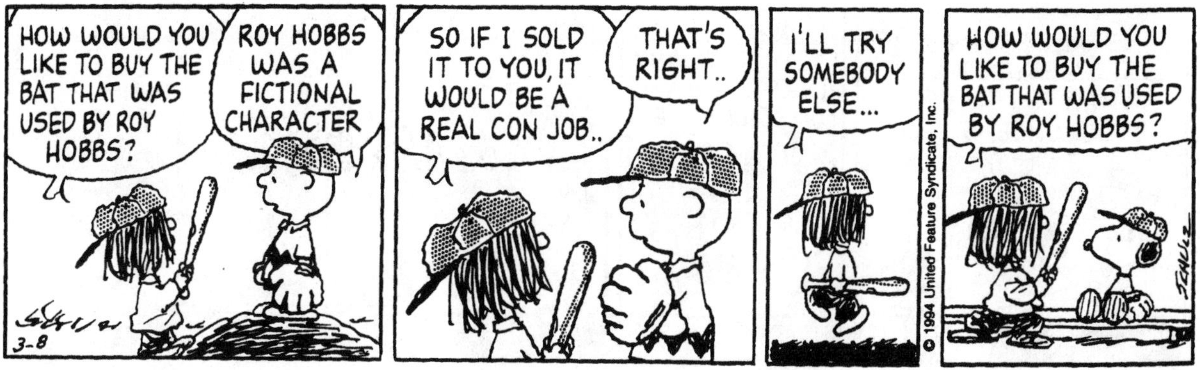

HOW WOULD YOU LIKE TO BUY THE BAT THAT WAS USED BY ROY HOBBS?
ROY HOBBS WAS A FICTIONAL CHARACTER
3-8
SO IF I SOLD IT TO YOU, IT WOULD BE A REAL CON JOB..
THAT'S RIGHT..
I'LL TRY SOMEBODY ELSE...
© 1994 United Feature Syndicate, Inc.
HOW WOULD YOU LIKE TO BUY THE BAT THAT WAS USED BY ROY HOBBS?

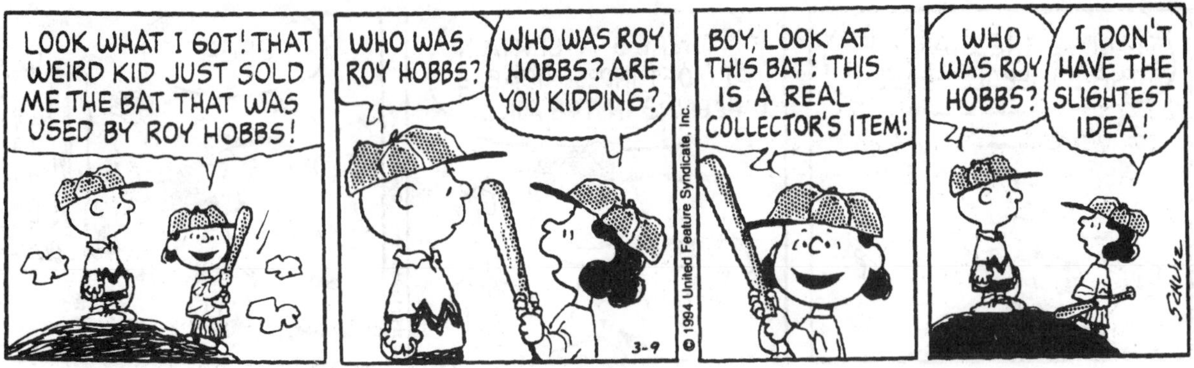
LOOK WHAT I GOT! THAT WEIRD KID JUST SOLD ME THE BAT THAT WAS USED BY ROY HOBBS!
WHO WAS ROY HOBBS?
WHO WAS ROY HOBBS? ARE YOU KIDDING?
3-9
© 1994 United Feature Syndicate, Inc.
BOY, LOOK AT THIS BAT! THIS IS A REAL COLLECTOR'S ITEM!
WHO WAS ROY HOBBS?
I DON'T HAVE THE SLIGHTEST IDEA!
SCHULZ

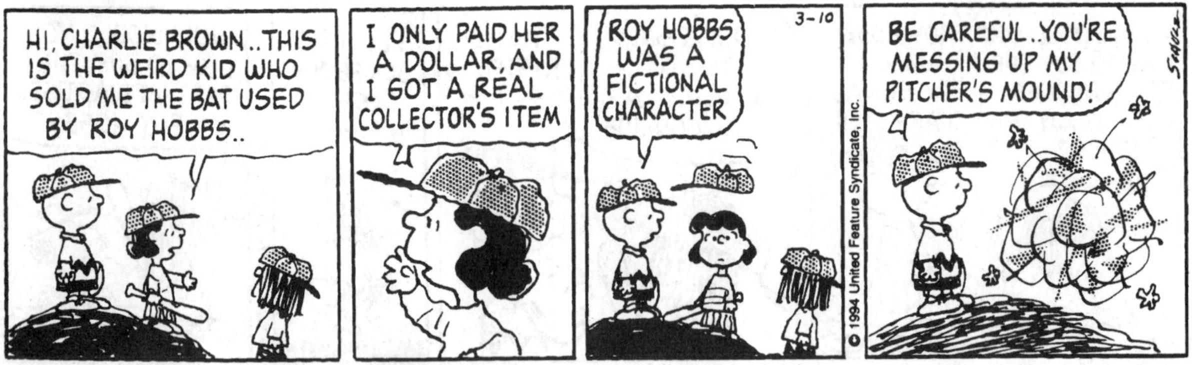
HI, CHARLIE BROWN..THIS IS THE WEIRD KID WHO SOLD ME THE BAT USED BY ROY HOBBS..
I ONLY PAID HER A DOLLAR, AND I GOT A REAL COLLECTOR'S ITEM
ROY HOBBS WAS A FICTIONAL CHARACTER
3-10
© 1994 United Feature Syndicate, Inc.
BE CAREFUL..YOU'RE MESSING UP MY PITCHER'S MOUND!
SCHULZ

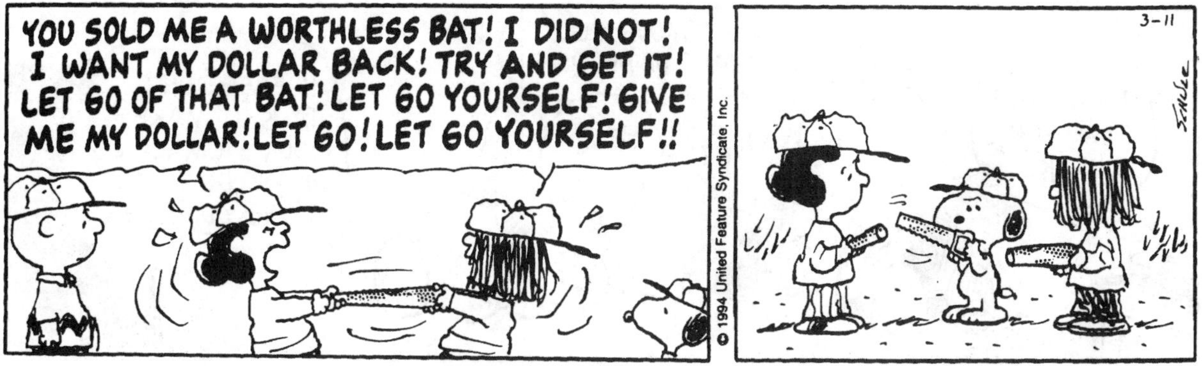
YOU SOLD ME A WORTHLESS BAT! I DID NOT! I WANT MY DOLLAR BACK! TRY AND GET IT! LET GO OF THAT BAT! LET GO YOURSELF! GIVE ME MY DOLLAR! LET GO! LET GO YOURSELF!!
© 1994 United Feature Syndicate, Inc.
3-11

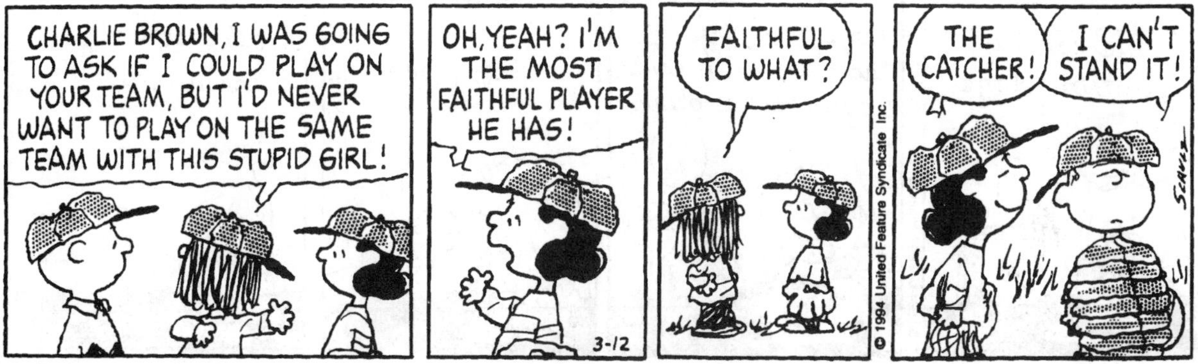
CHARLIE BROWN, I WAS GOING TO ASK IF I COULD PLAY ON YOUR TEAM, BUT I'D NEVER WANT TO PLAY ON THE SAME TEAM WITH THIS STUPID GIRL!
OH, YEAH? I'M THE MOST FAITHFUL PLAYER HE HAS!
3-12
FAITHFUL TO WHAT?
© 1994 United Feature Syndicate, Inc.
THE CATCHER!
I CAN'T STAND IT!

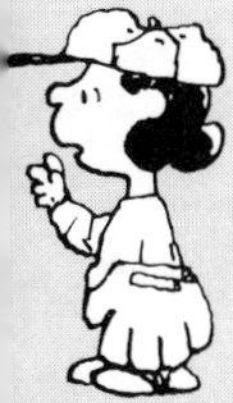

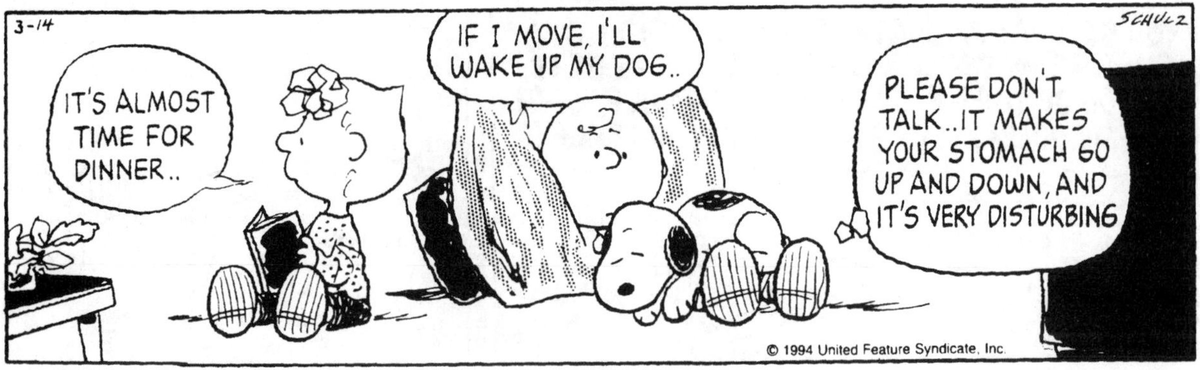
3-14
SCHULZ
IT'S ALMOST TIME FOR DINNER..
IF I MOVE, I'LL WAKE UP MY DOG..
PLEASE DON'T TALK..IT MAKES YOUR STOMACH GO UP AND DOWN, AND IT'S VERY DISTURBING
© 1994 United Feature Syndicate, Inc.

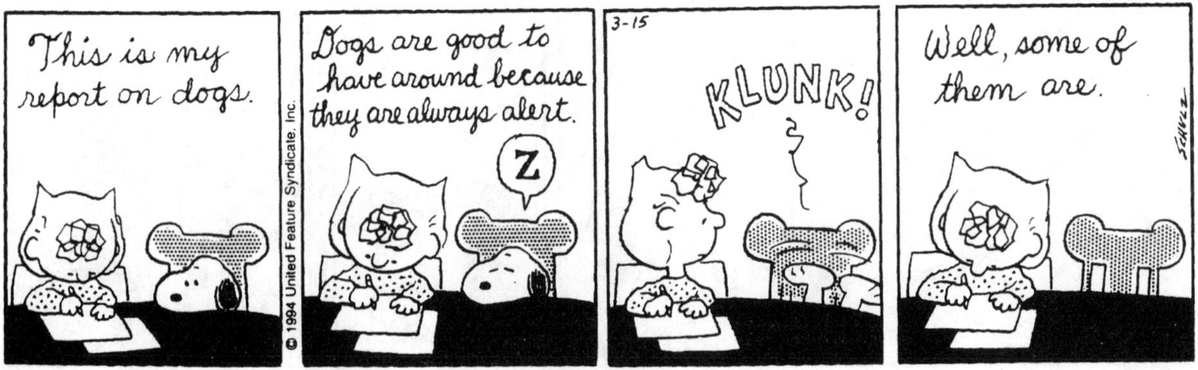
This is my report on dogs.
© 1994 United Feature Syndicate, Inc.
Dogs are good to have around because they are always alert.
Z
3-15
KLUNK!
Well, some of them are.
SCHULZ

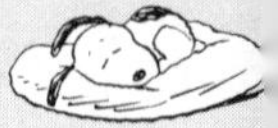

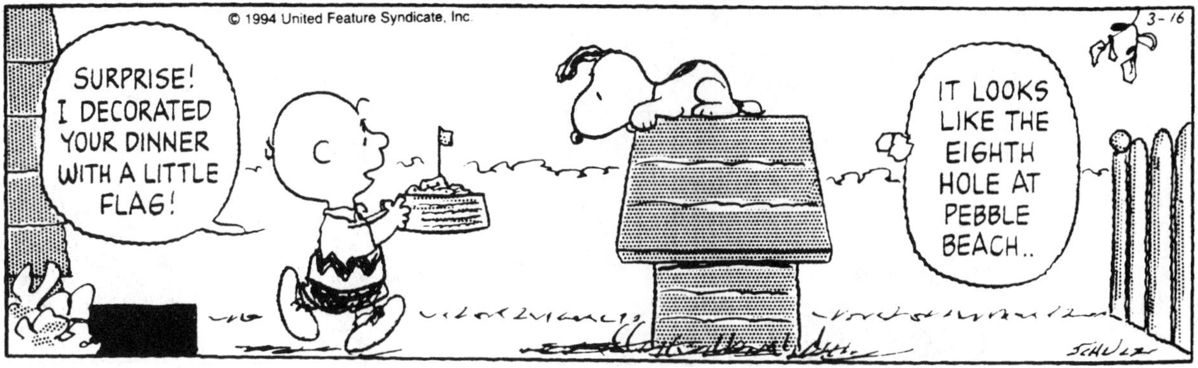
© 1994 United Feature Syndicate, Inc.
3-16
SURPRISE! I DECORATED YOUR DINNER WITH A LITTLE FLAG!
IT LOOKS LIKE THE EIGHTH HOLE AT PEBBLE BEACH..
SCHULZ

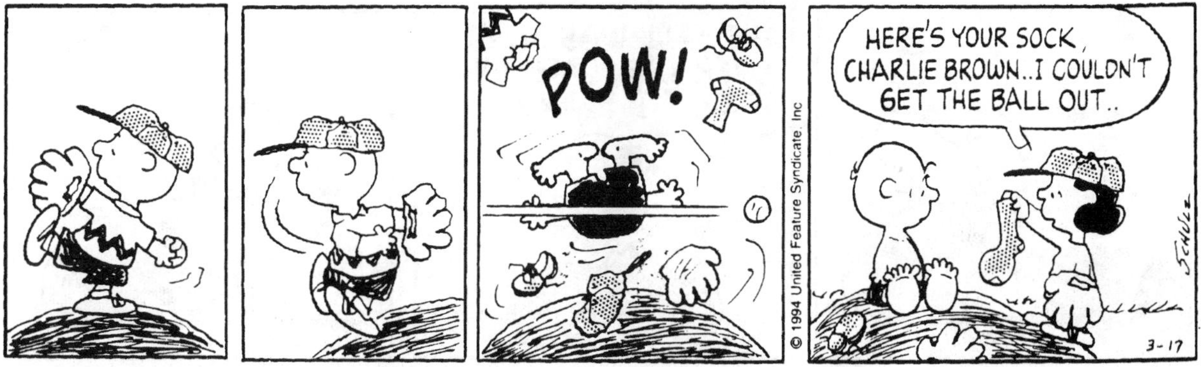
POW!
© 1994 United Feature Syndicate, Inc
HERE'S YOUR SOCK, CHARLIE BROWN..I COULDN'T GET THE BALL OUT..
SCHULZ
3-17

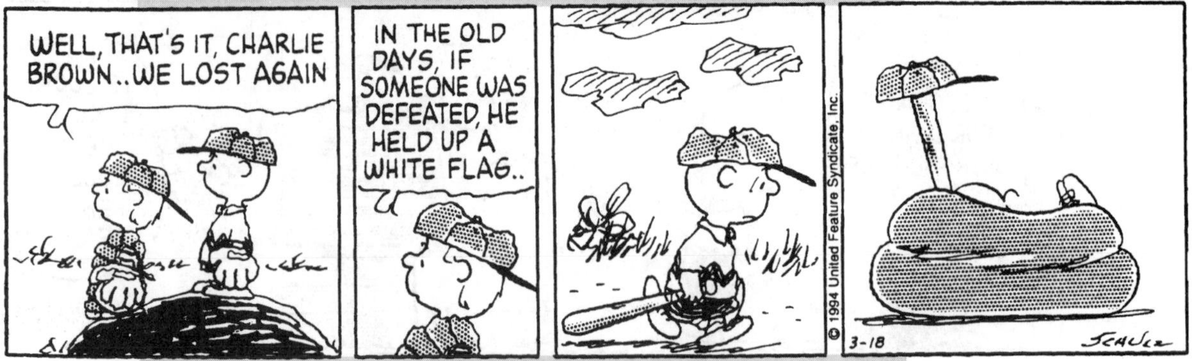
WELL, THAT'S IT, CHARLIE BROWN..WE LOST AGAIN
IN THE OLD DAYS, IF SOMEONE WAS DEFEATED, HE HELD UP A WHITE FLAG..
© 1994 United Feature Syndicate, Inc.
3-18
SCHULZ

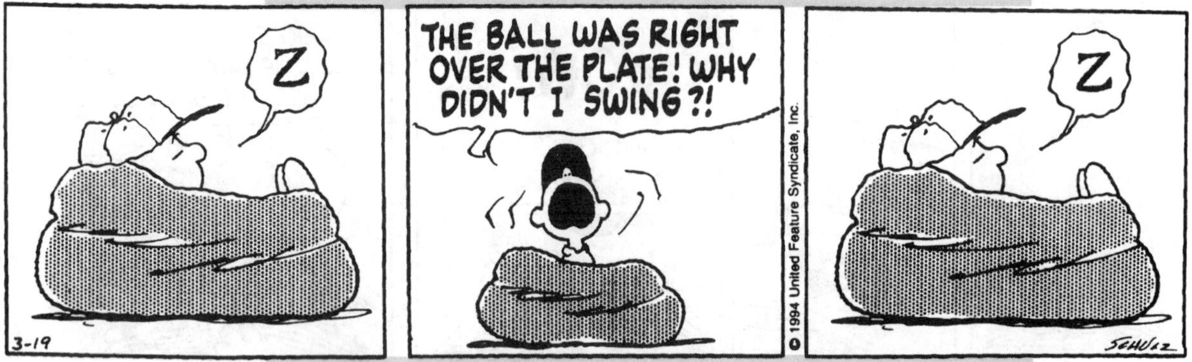
Z
3-19
THE BALL WAS RIGHT OVER THE PLATE! WHY DIDN'T I SWING?!
© 1994 United Feature Syndicate, Inc.
Z
SCHULZ

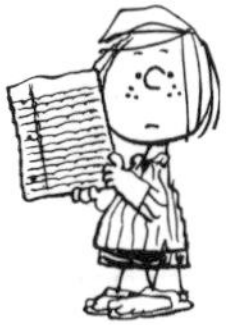

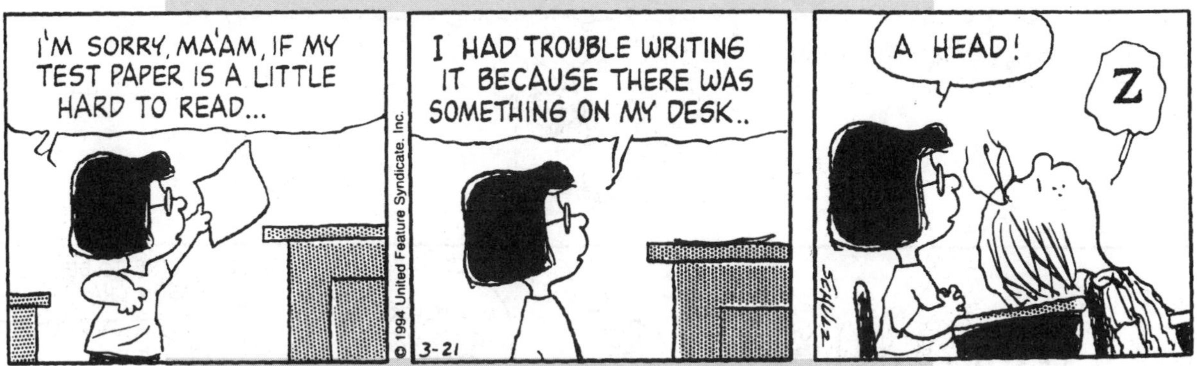
I'M SORRY, MA'AM, IF MY TEST PAPER IS A LITTLE HARD TO READ...
I HAD TROUBLE WRITING IT BECAUSE THERE WAS SOMETHING ON MY DESK..
A HEAD!
Z
© 1994 United Feature Syndicate, Inc.
3-21

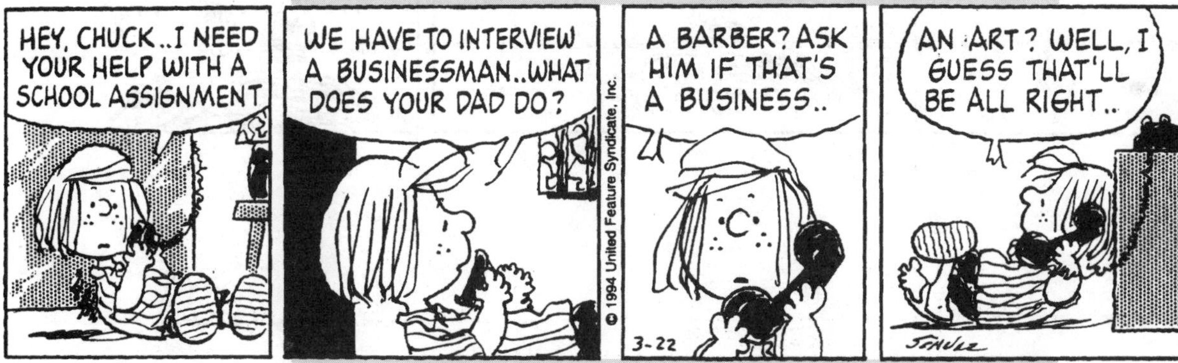
HEY, CHUCK..I NEED YOUR HELP WITH A SCHOOL ASSIGNMENT
WE HAVE TO INTERVIEW A BUSINESSMAN..WHAT DOES YOUR DAD DO?
A BARBER? ASK HIM IF THAT'S A BUSINESS..
AN ART? WELL, I GUESS THAT'LL BE ALL RIGHT..
© 1994 United Feature Syndicate, Inc.
3-22

PEANUTS.

by SCHULZ

MY PITCHER'S MOUND LOOKS GREAT..

IT'S GOING TO BE A GOOD SEASON, CHARLIE BROWN!

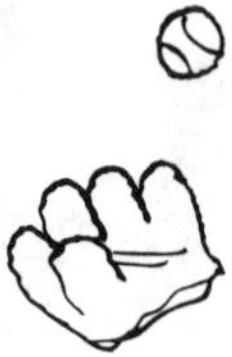

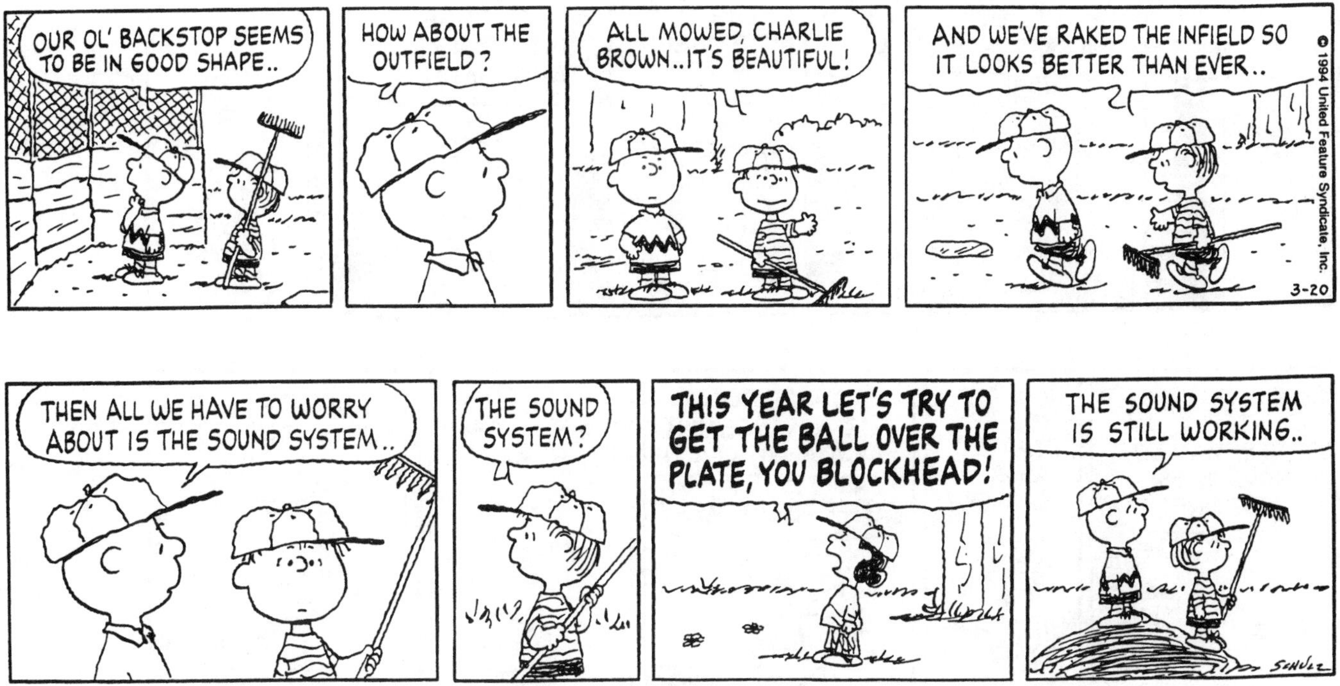
OUR OL' BACKSTOP SEEMS TO BE IN GOOD SHAPE..
HOW ABOUT THE OUTFIELD?
ALL MOWED, CHARLIE BROWN..IT'S BEAUTIFUL!
AND WE'VE RAKED THE INFIELD SO IT LOOKS BETTER THAN EVER..
© 1994 United Feature Syndicate, Inc.
3-20
THEN ALL WE HAVE TO WORRY ABOUT IS THE SOUND SYSTEM..
THE SOUND SYSTEM?
THIS YEAR LET'S TRY TO GET THE BALL OVER THE PLATE, YOU BLOCKHEAD!
THE SOUND SYSTEM IS STILL WORKING..
SCHULZ

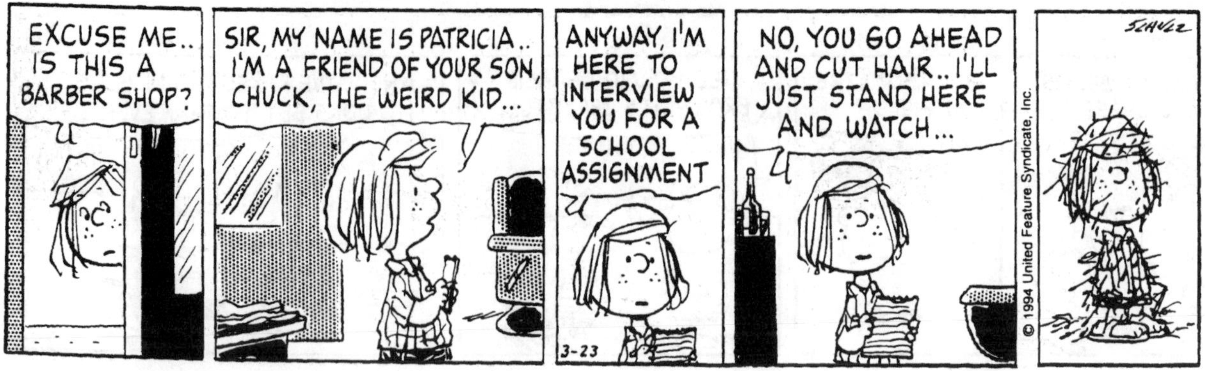
EXCUSE ME.. IS THIS A BARBER SHOP?
SIR, MY NAME IS PATRICIA.. I'M A FRIEND OF YOUR SON, CHUCK, THE WEIRD KID...
ANYWAY, I'M HERE TO INTERVIEW YOU FOR A SCHOOL ASSIGNMENT
3-23
NO, YOU GO AHEAD AND CUT HAIR.. I'LL JUST STAND HERE AND WATCH...
© 1994 United Feature Syndicate, Inc.
SCHULZ

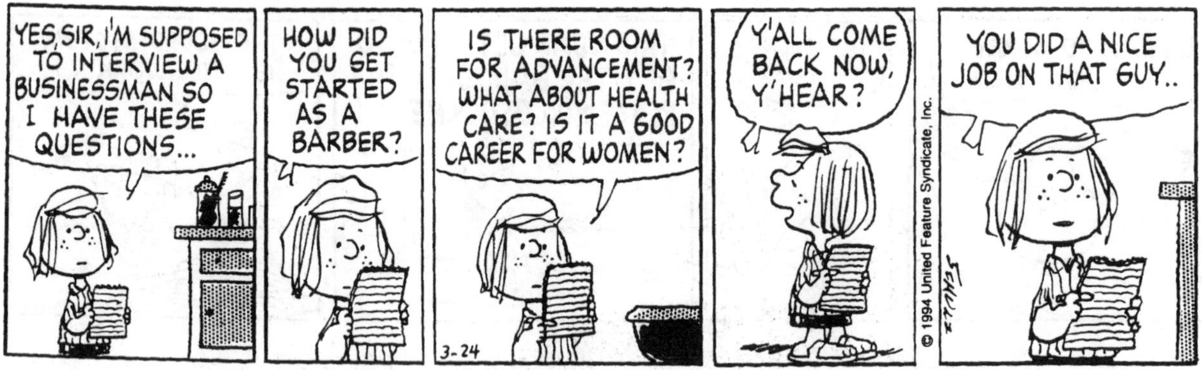
YES, SIR, I'M SUPPOSED TO INTERVIEW A BUSINESSMAN SO I HAVE THESE QUESTIONS...
HOW DID YOU GET STARTED AS A BARBER?
IS THERE ROOM FOR ADVANCEMENT? WHAT ABOUT HEALTH CARE? IS IT A GOOD CAREER FOR WOMEN?
3-24
Y'ALL COME BACK NOW, Y'HEAR?
© 1994 United Feature Syndicate, Inc.
SCHULZ
YOU DID A NICE JOB ON THAT GUY..

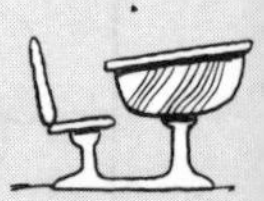

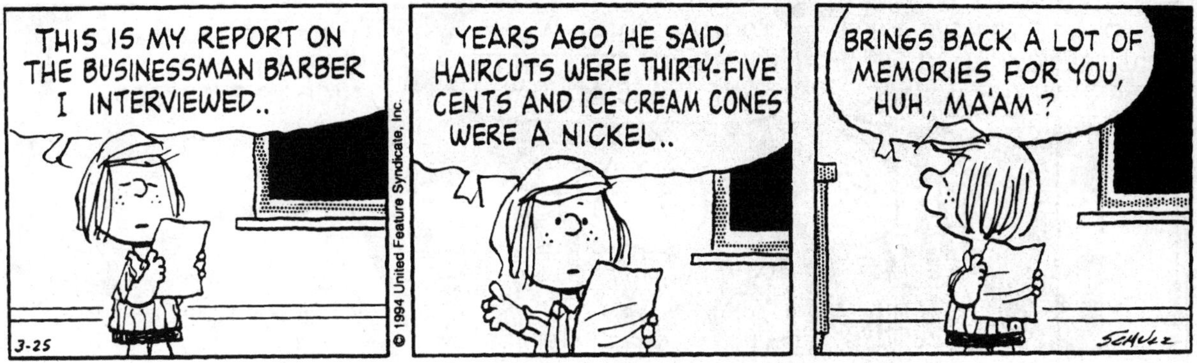
THIS IS MY REPORT ON THE BUSINESSMAN BARBER I INTERVIEWED..
YEARS AGO, HE SAID, HAIRCUTS WERE THIRTY-FIVE CENTS AND ICE CREAM CONES WERE A NICKEL..
BRINGS BACK A LOT OF MEMORIES FOR YOU, HUH, MA'AM ?
3-25
SCHULZ
© 1994 United Feature Syndicate, Inc.

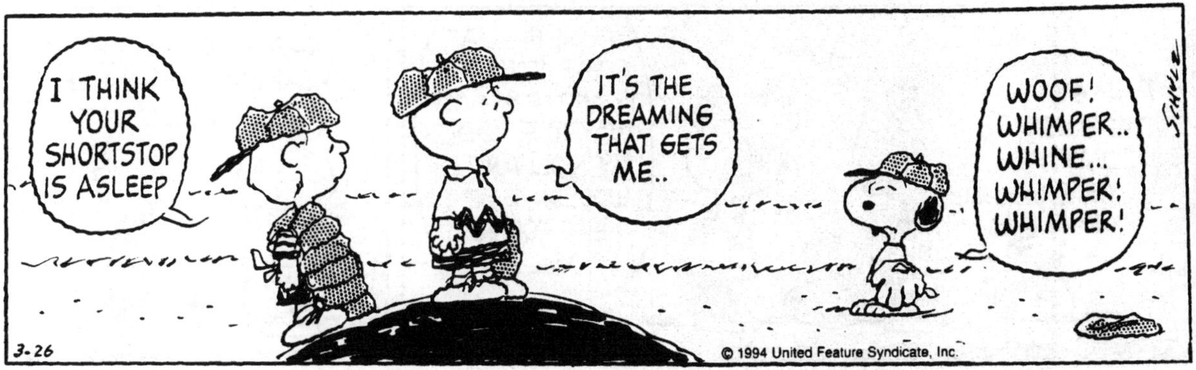
I THINK YOUR SHORTSTOP IS ASLEEP
IT'S THE DREAMING THAT GETS ME..
WOOF! WHIMPER.. WHINE... WHIMPER! WHIMPER!
SCHULZ
3-26
© 1994 United Feature Syndicate, Inc.

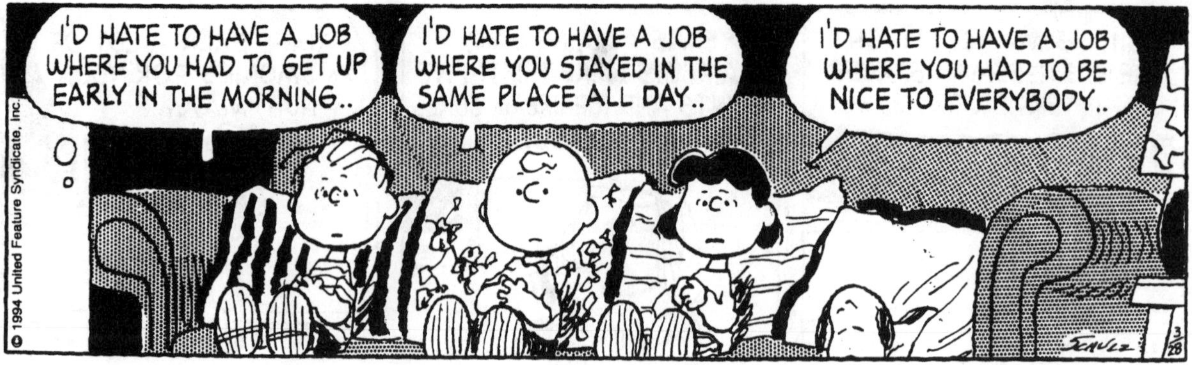
I'D HATE TO HAVE A JOB WHERE YOU HAD TO GET UP EARLY IN THE MORNING..
I'D HATE TO HAVE A JOB WHERE YOU STAYED IN THE SAME PLACE ALL DAY..
I'D HATE TO HAVE A JOB WHERE YOU HAD TO BE NICE TO EVERYBODY..
© 1994 United Feature Syndicate, Inc.

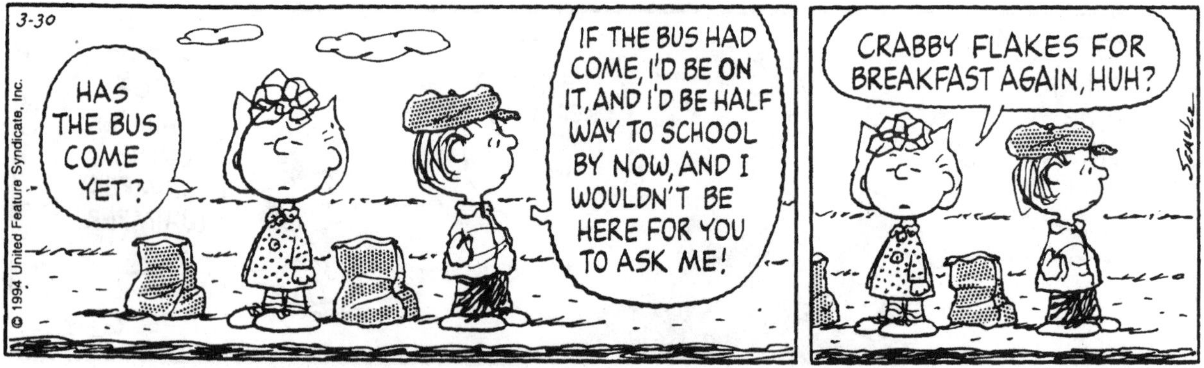
3-30
HAS THE BUS COME YET?
IF THE BUS HAD COME, I'D BE ON IT, AND I'D BE HALF WAY TO SCHOOL BY NOW, AND I WOULDN'T BE HERE FOR YOU TO ASK ME!
CRABBY FLAKES FOR BREAKFAST AGAIN, HUH?
© 1994 United Feature Syndicate, Inc.

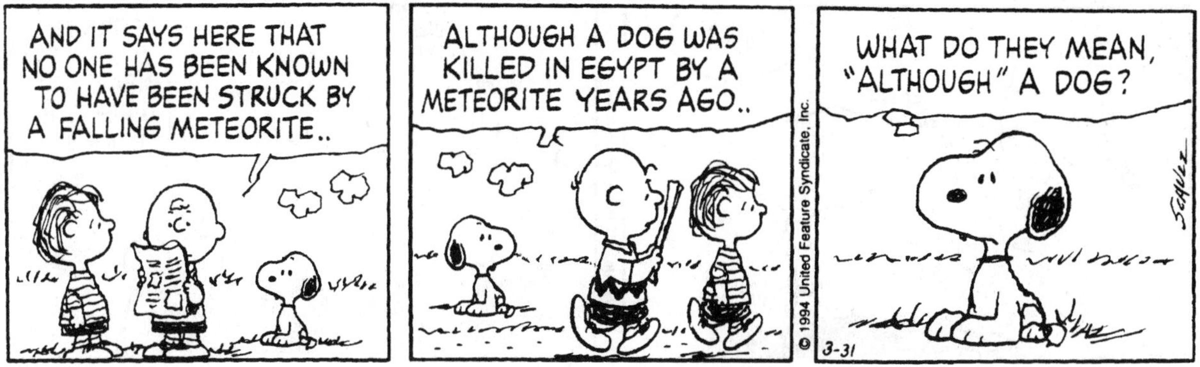
AND IT SAYS HERE THAT NO ONE HAS BEEN KNOWN TO HAVE BEEN STRUCK BY A FALLING METEORITE..
ALTHOUGH A DOG WAS KILLED IN EGYPT BY A METEORITE YEARS AGO..
WHAT DO THEY MEAN, "ALTHOUGH" A DOG?
© 1994 United Feature Syndicate, Inc.
3-31
SCHULZ

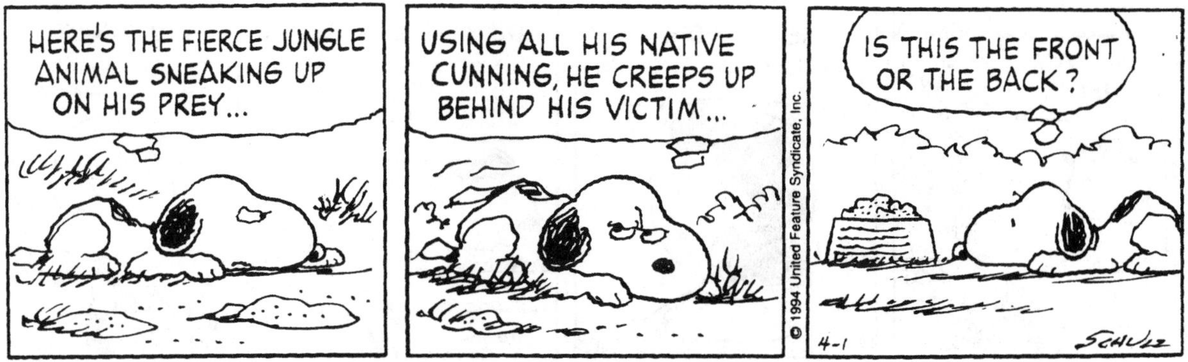
HERE'S THE FIERCE JUNGLE ANIMAL SNEAKING UP ON HIS PREY...
USING ALL HIS NATIVE CUNNING, HE CREEPS UP BEHIND HIS VICTIM...
IS THIS THE FRONT OR THE BACK?
© 1994 United Feature Syndicate, Inc.
4-1
SCHULZ

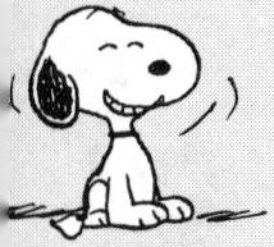

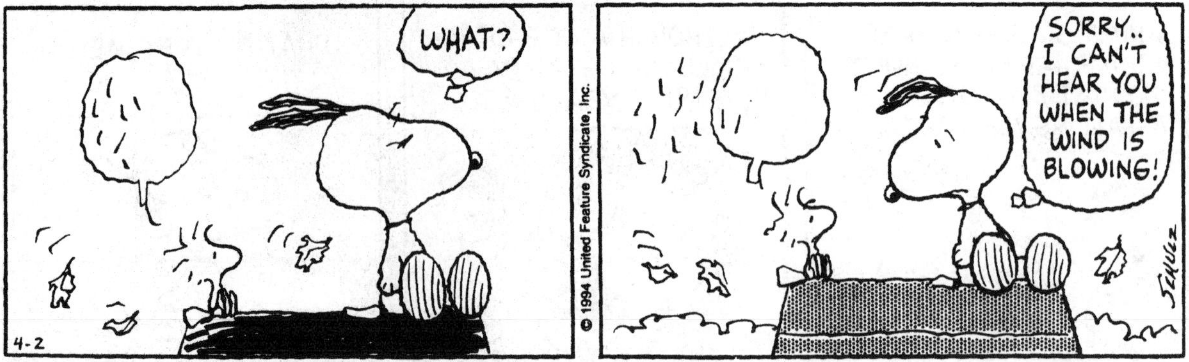
4-2
WHAT?
© 1994 United Feature Syndicate, Inc.
SORRY.. I CAN'T HEAR YOU WHEN THE WIND IS BLOWING!
SCHULZ

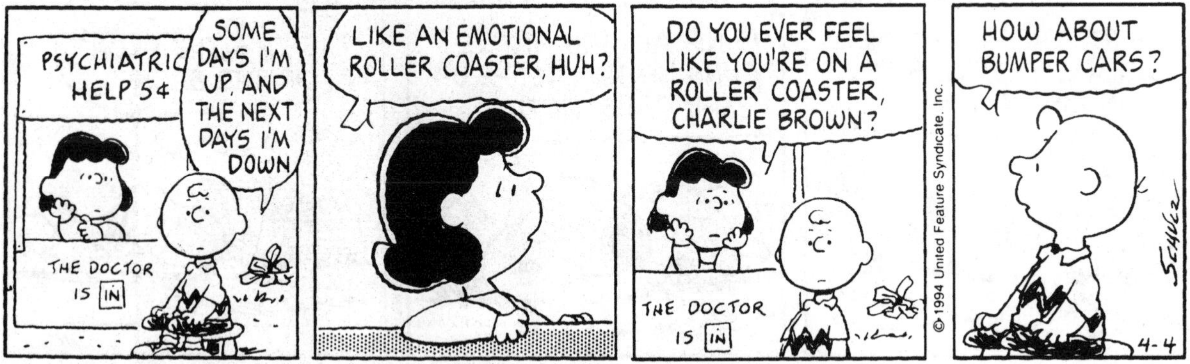
PSYCHIATRIC HELP 5¢
THE DOCTOR IS IN
SOME DAYS I'M UP, AND THE NEXT DAYS I'M DOWN
LIKE AN EMOTIONAL ROLLER COASTER, HUH?
DO YOU EVER FEEL LIKE YOU'RE ON A ROLLER COASTER, CHARLIE BROWN?
THE DOCTOR IS IN
© 1994 United Feature Syndicate, Inc.
HOW ABOUT BUMPER CARS?
SCHULZ
4-4

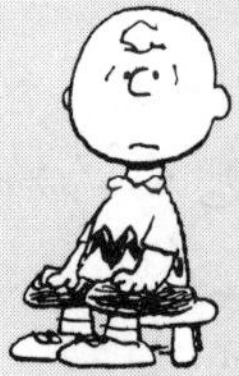

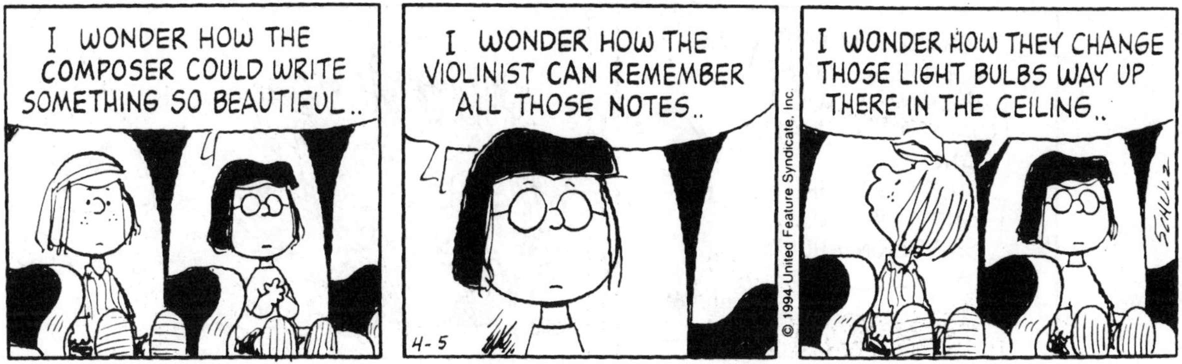
I WONDER HOW THE COMPOSER COULD WRITE SOMETHING SO BEAUTIFUL..
I WONDER HOW THE VIOLINIST CAN REMEMBER ALL THOSE NOTES..
4-5
© 1994 United Feature Syndicate, Inc.
I WONDER HOW THEY CHANGE THOSE LIGHT BULBS WAY UP THERE IN THE CEILING..
SCHULZ

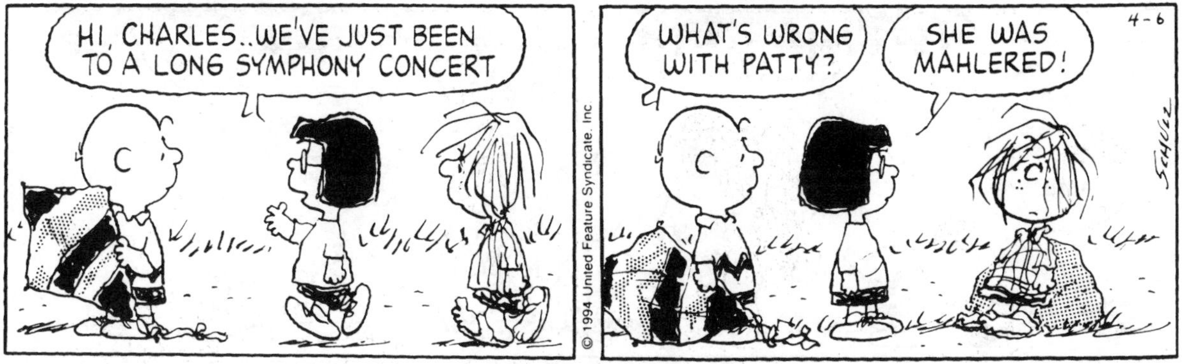
HI, CHARLES..WE'VE JUST BEEN TO A LONG SYMPHONY CONCERT
© 1994 United Feature Syndicate, Inc.
WHAT'S WRONG WITH PATTY?
SHE WAS MAHLERED!
4-6
SCHULZ

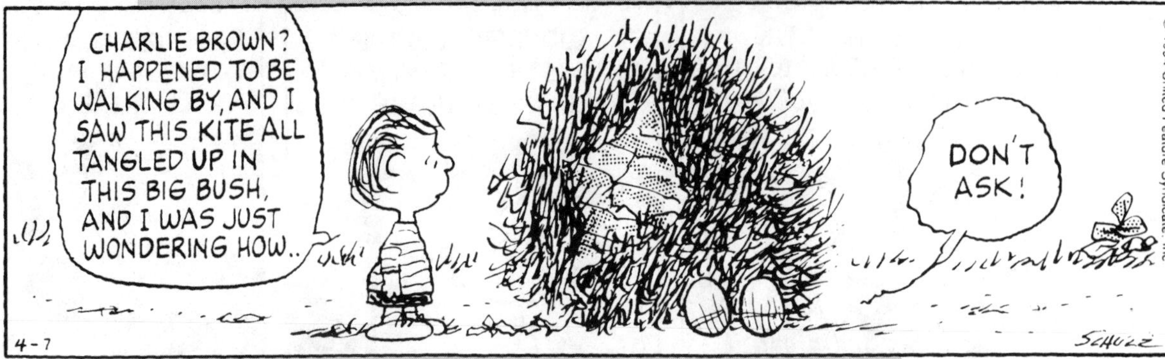
CHARLIE BROWN? I HAPPENED TO BE WALKING BY, AND I SAW THIS KITE ALL TANGLED UP IN THIS BIG BUSH, AND I WAS JUST WONDERING HOW..
DON'T ASK!
4-7
SCHULZ
© 1994 United Feature Syndicate, Inc

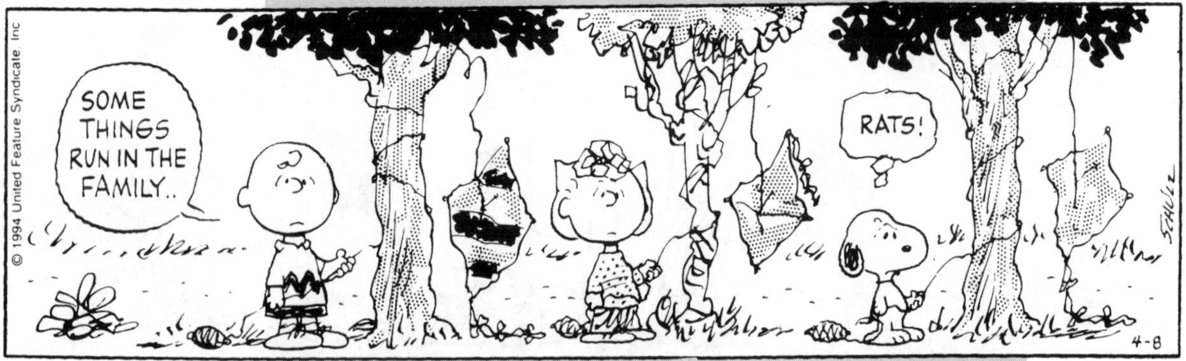
SOME THINGS RUN IN THE FAMILY..
RATS!
SCHULZ
4-8
© 1994 United Feature Syndicate, Inc

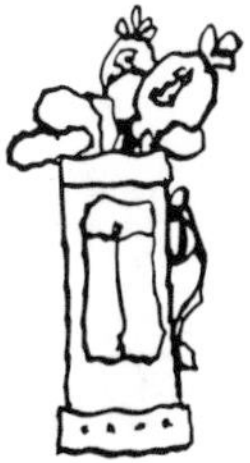

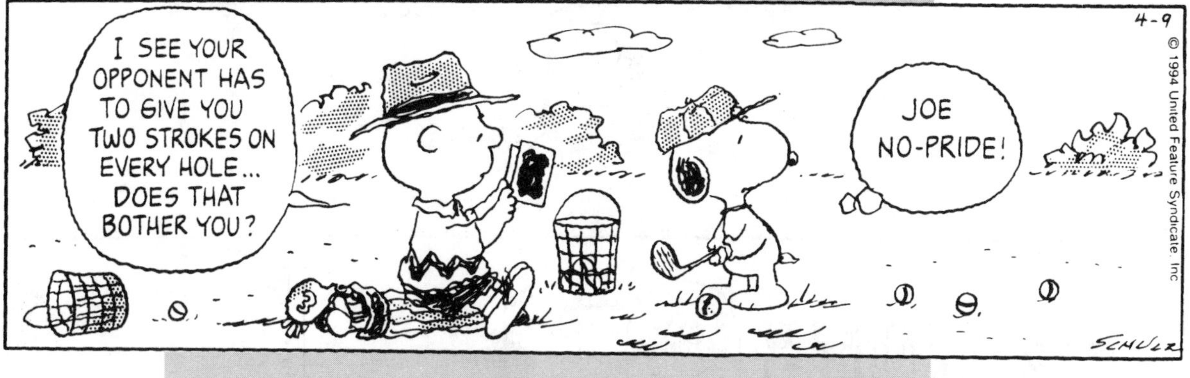
4-9
© 1994 United Feature Syndicate, Inc
I SEE YOUR OPPONENT HAS TO GIVE YOU TWO STROKES ON EVERY HOLE... DOES THAT BOTHER YOU?
JOE NO-PRIDE!
SCHULZ

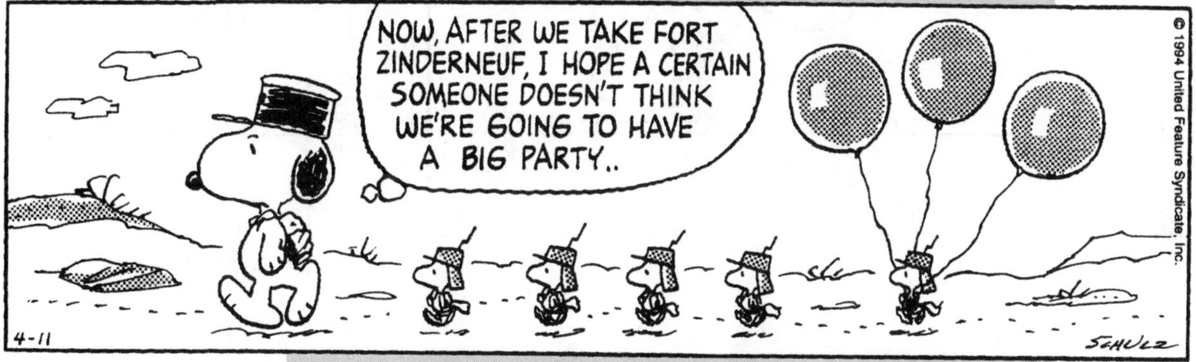
© 1994 United Feature Syndicate, Inc.
NOW, AFTER WE TAKE FORT ZINDERNEUF, I HOPE A CERTAIN SOMEONE DOESN'T THINK WE'RE GOING TO HAVE A BIG PARTY..
4-11
SCHULZ

PEANUTS. *by SCHULZ*

I LOVE MEETINGS ON THE MOUND!

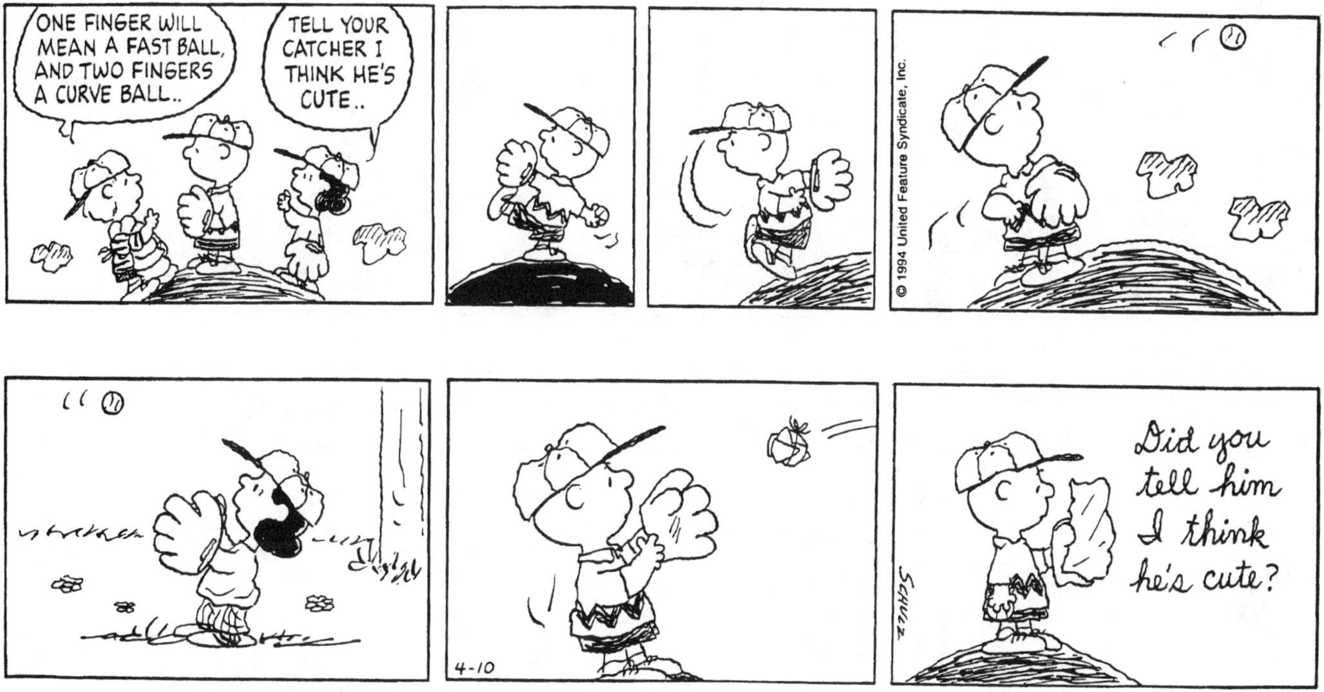
ONE FINGER WILL MEAN A FAST BALL, AND TWO FINGERS A CURVE BALL..
TELL YOUR CATCHER I THINK HE'S CUTE..
© 1994 United Feature Syndicate, Inc.
4-10
SCHULZ
Did you tell him I think he's cute?

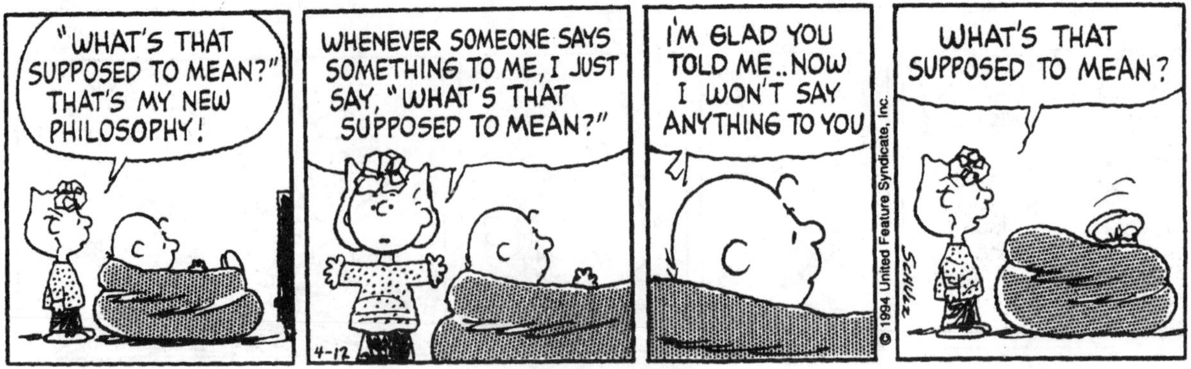
"WHAT'S THAT SUPPOSED TO MEAN?" THAT'S MY NEW PHILOSOPHY!
WHENEVER SOMEONE SAYS SOMETHING TO ME, I JUST SAY, "WHAT'S THAT SUPPOSED TO MEAN?"
4-12
I'M GLAD YOU TOLD ME..NOW I WON'T SAY ANYTHING TO YOU
© 1994 United Feature Syndicate, Inc.
SCHULZ
WHAT'S THAT SUPPOSED TO MEAN?

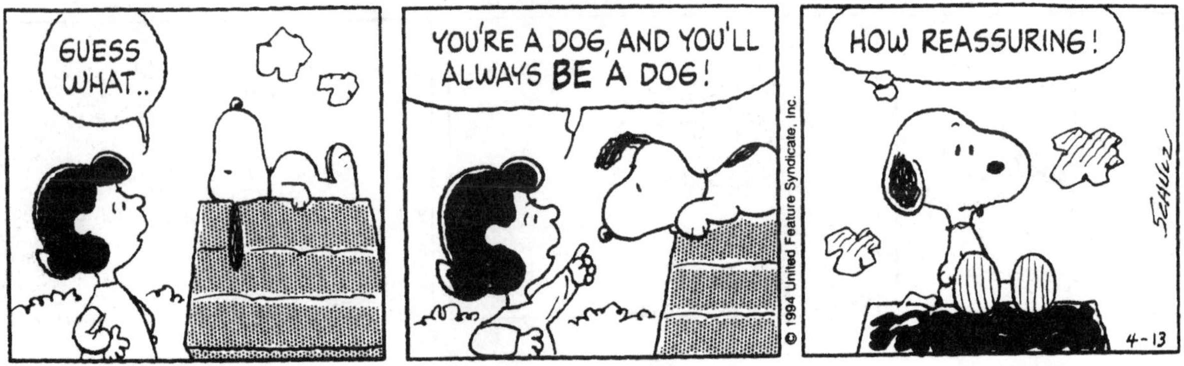
GUESS WHAT..
YOU'RE A DOG, AND YOU'LL ALWAYS **BE** A DOG!
© 1994 United Feature Syndicate, Inc.
HOW REASSURING!
SCHULZ
4-13

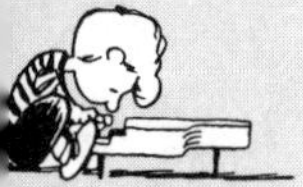

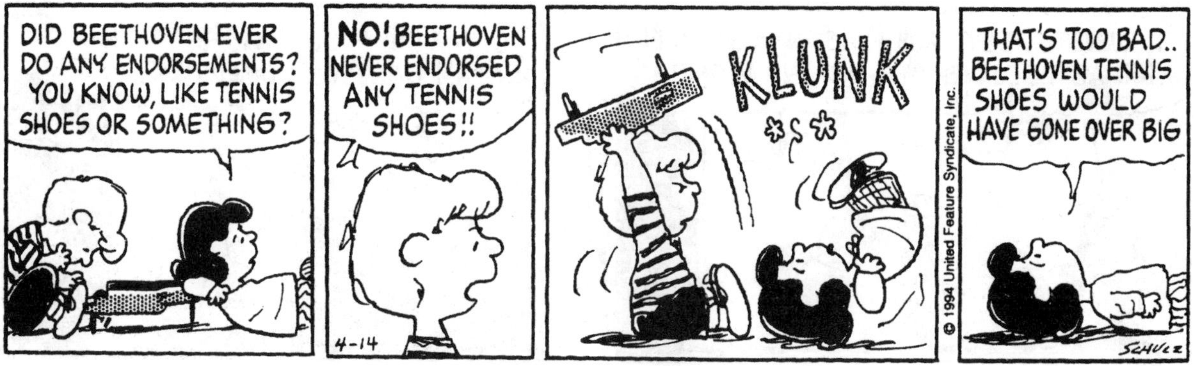
DID BEETHOVEN EVER DO ANY ENDORSEMENTS? YOU KNOW, LIKE TENNIS SHOES OR SOMETHING?
NO! BEETHOVEN NEVER ENDORSED ANY TENNIS SHOES!!
4-14
KLUNK
© 1994 United Feature Syndicate, Inc.
THAT'S TOO BAD.. BEETHOVEN TENNIS SHOES WOULD HAVE GONE OVER BIG
SCHULZ

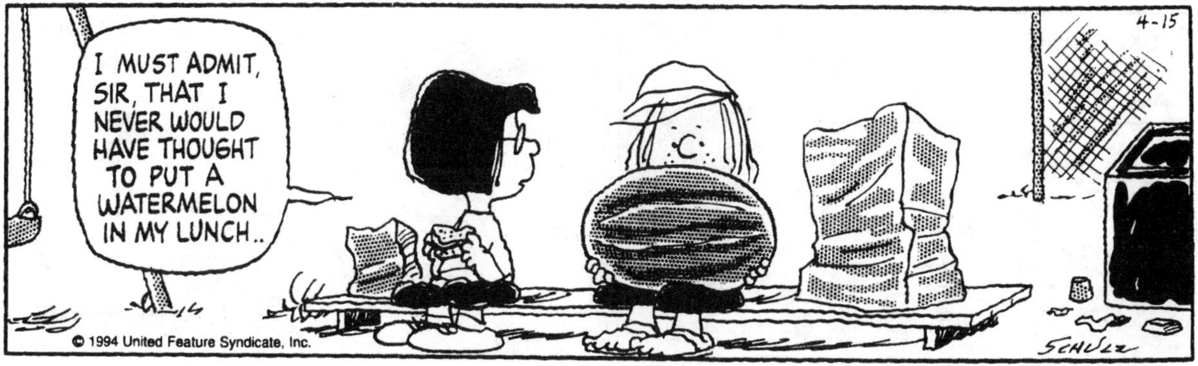
4-15
I MUST ADMIT, SIR, THAT I NEVER WOULD HAVE THOUGHT TO PUT A WATERMELON IN MY LUNCH..
© 1994 United Feature Syndicate, Inc.
SCHULZ

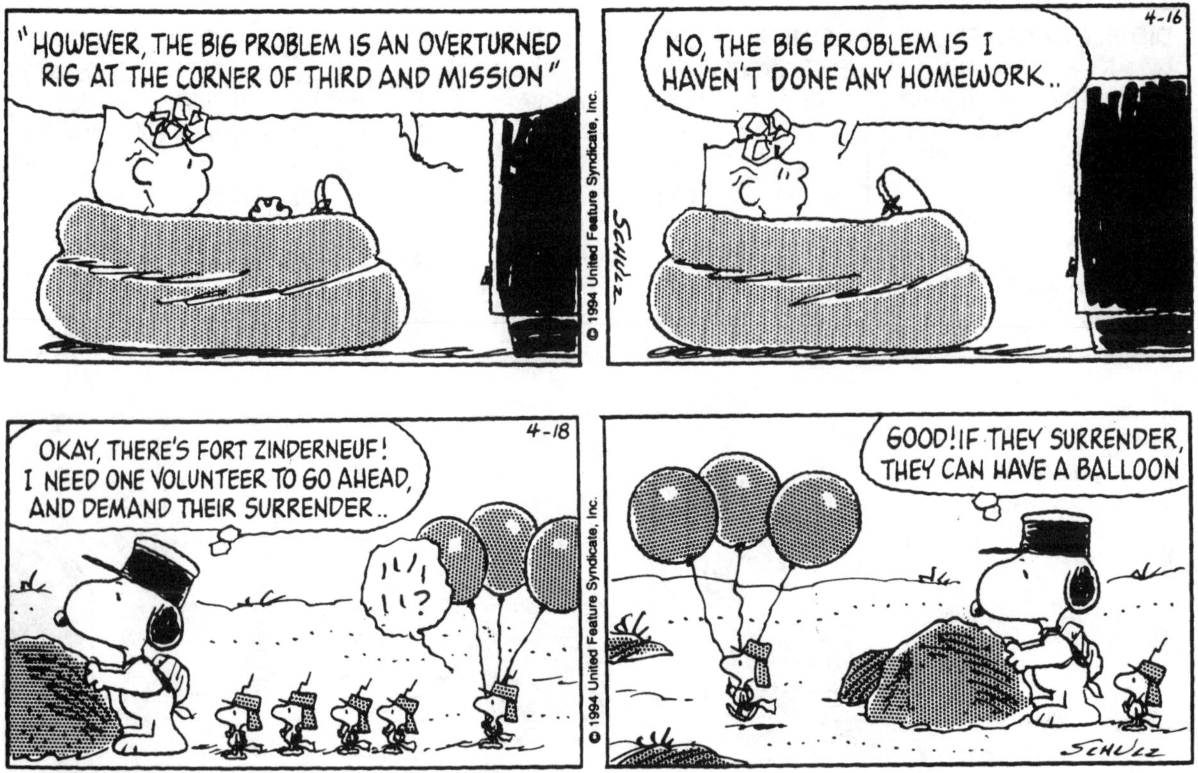
"HOWEVER, THE BIG PROBLEM IS AN OVERTURNED RIG AT THE CORNER OF THIRD AND MISSION"
© 1994 United Feature Syndicate, Inc.
SCHULZ
4-16
NO, THE BIG PROBLEM IS I HAVEN'T DONE ANY HOMEWORK..
4-18
OKAY, THERE'S FORT ZINDERNEUF! I NEED ONE VOLUNTEER TO GO AHEAD, AND DEMAND THEIR SURRENDER..
!!?
© 1994 United Feature Syndicate, Inc.
GOOD! IF THEY SURRENDER, THEY CAN HAVE A BALLOON
SCHULZ

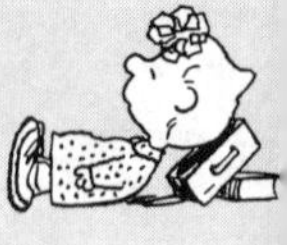

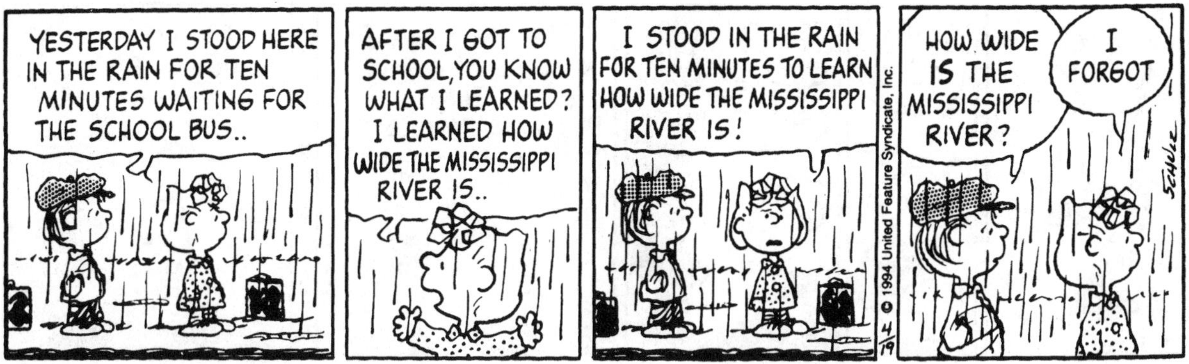
YESTERDAY I STOOD HERE IN THE RAIN FOR TEN MINUTES WAITING FOR THE SCHOOL BUS..
AFTER I GOT TO SCHOOL, YOU KNOW WHAT I LEARNED? I LEARNED HOW WIDE THE MISSISSIPPI RIVER IS..
I STOOD IN THE RAIN FOR TEN MINUTES TO LEARN HOW WIDE THE MISSISSIPPI RIVER IS!
© 1994 United Feature Syndicate, Inc.
4/19
HOW WIDE IS THE MISSISSIPPI RIVER?
I FORGOT
SCHULZ

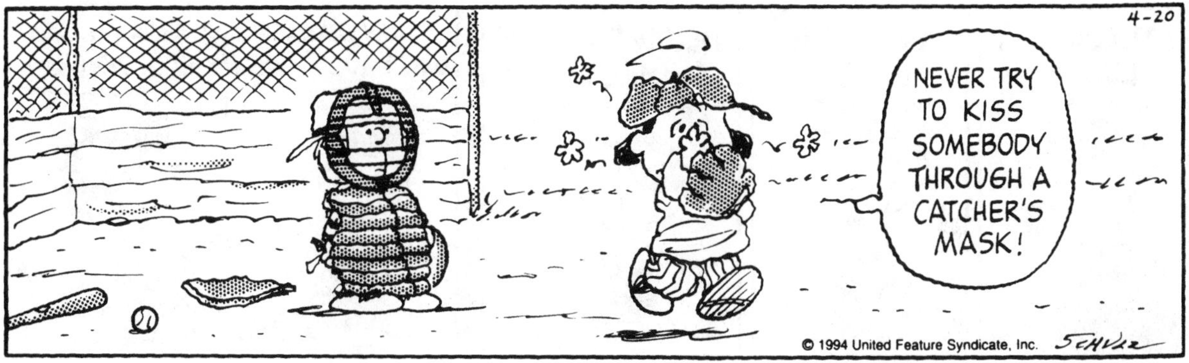
4-20
NEVER TRY TO KISS SOMEBODY THROUGH A CATCHER'S MASK!
© 1994 United Feature Syndicate, Inc.
SCHULZ

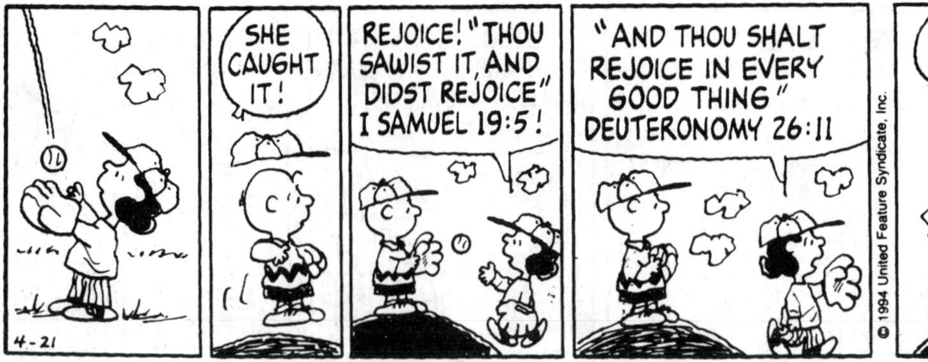
4-21
SHE CAUGHT IT!
REJOICE! "THOU SAWIST IT, AND DIDST REJOICE" I SAMUEL 19:5!
"AND THOU SHALT REJOICE IN EVERY GOOD THING" DEUTERONOMY 26:11
© 1994 United Feature Syndicate, Inc.
I HAVE A WEIRD TEAM..
SCHULZ

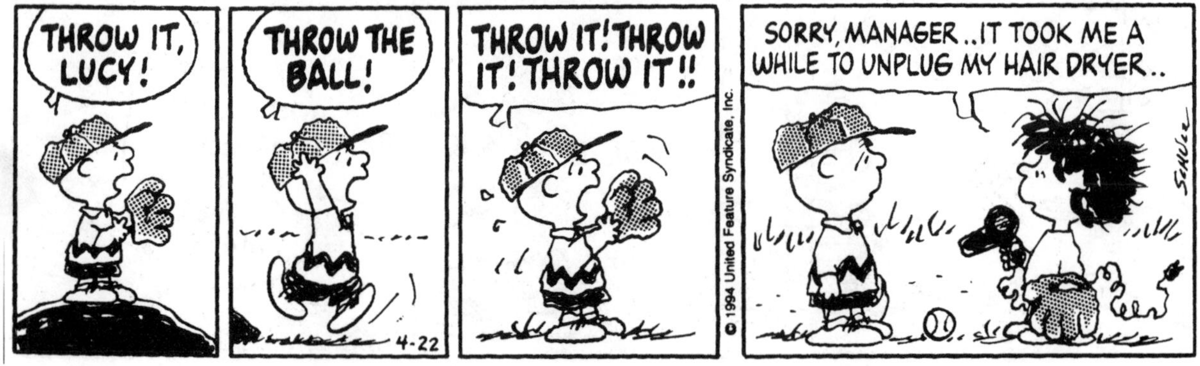
THROW IT, LUCY!
THROW THE BALL!
4-22
THROW IT! THROW IT! THROW IT!!
© 1994 United Feature Syndicate, Inc.
SORRY, MANAGER..IT TOOK ME A WHILE TO UNPLUG MY HAIR DRYER..
SCHULZ

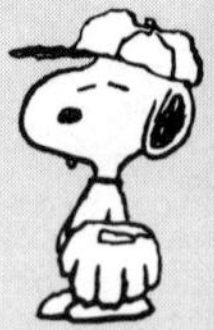

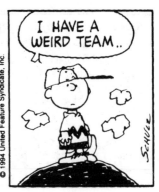

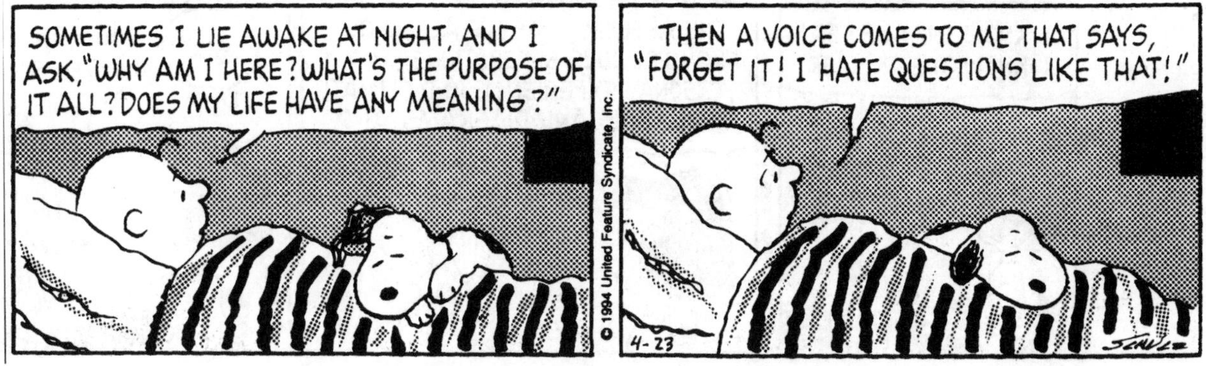
SOMETIMES I LIE AWAKE AT NIGHT, AND I ASK, "WHY AM I HERE? WHAT'S THE PURPOSE OF IT ALL? DOES MY LIFE HAVE ANY MEANING?"
© 1994 United Feature Syndicate, Inc.
THEN A VOICE COMES TO ME THAT SAYS, "FORGET IT! I HATE QUESTIONS LIKE THAT!"
4-23

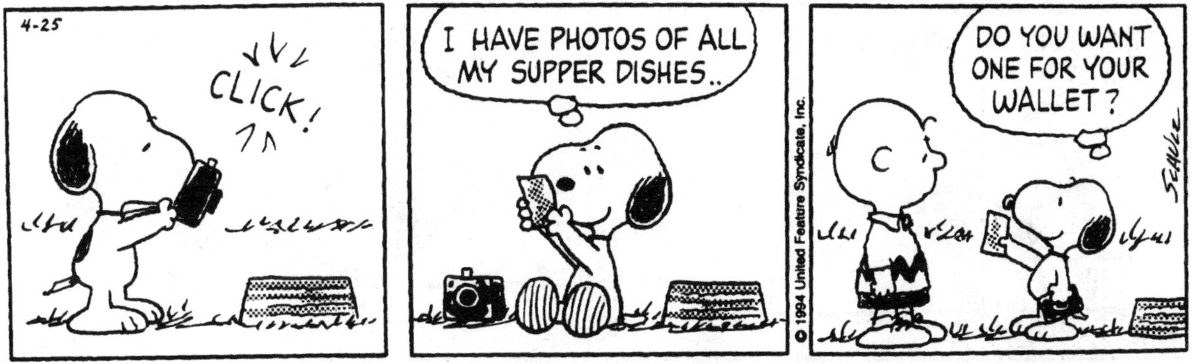
4-25
CLICK!
I HAVE PHOTOS OF ALL MY SUPPER DISHES..
© 1994 United Feature Syndicate, Inc.
DO YOU WANT ONE FOR YOUR WALLET?

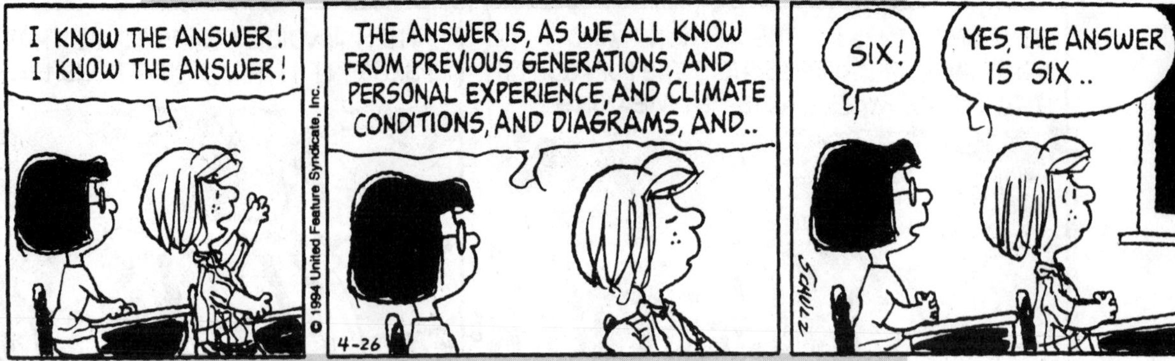
I KNOW THE ANSWER! I KNOW THE ANSWER!
THE ANSWER IS, AS WE ALL KNOW FROM PREVIOUS GENERATIONS, AND PERSONAL EXPERIENCE, AND CLIMATE CONDITIONS, AND DIAGRAMS, AND..
SIX!
YES, THE ANSWER IS SIX..
© 1994 United Feature Syndicate, Inc.
4-26
SCHULZ

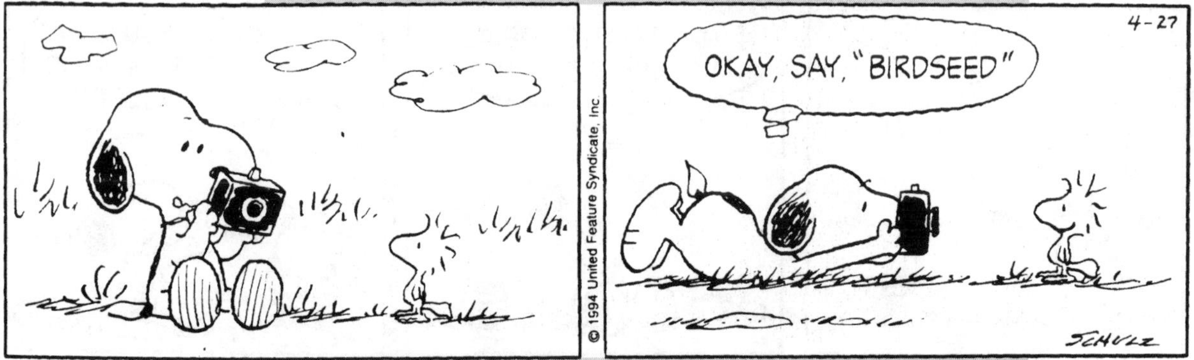
© 1994 United Feature Syndicate, Inc.
4-27
OKAY, SAY, "BIRDSEED"
SCHULZ

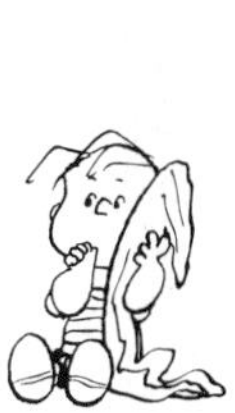

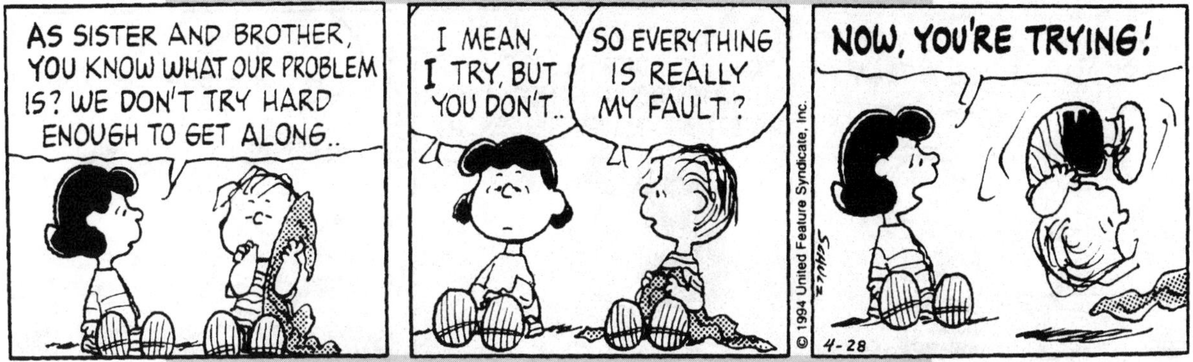
AS SISTER AND BROTHER, YOU KNOW WHAT OUR PROBLEM IS? WE DON'T TRY HARD ENOUGH TO GET ALONG..
I MEAN, I TRY, BUT YOU DON'T..
SO EVERYTHING IS REALLY MY FAULT?
NOW, YOU'RE TRYING!
© 1994 United Feature Syndicate, Inc.
4-28

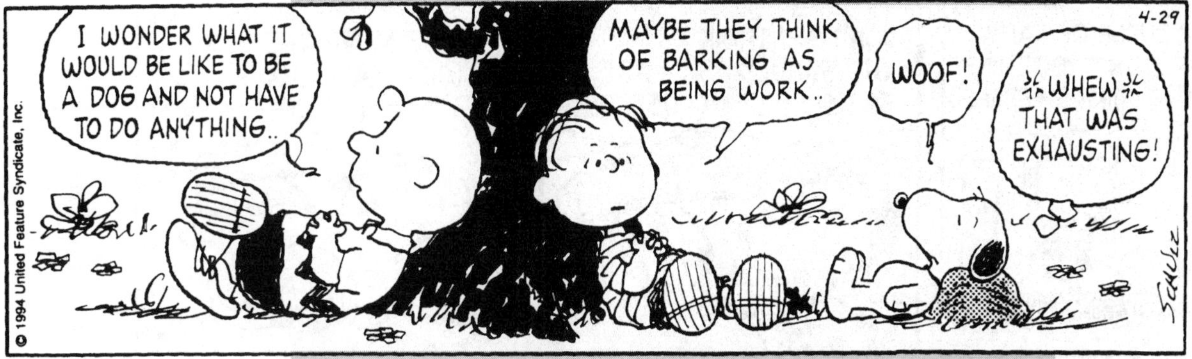
4-29
I WONDER WHAT IT WOULD BE LIKE TO BE A DOG AND NOT HAVE TO DO ANYTHING..
MAYBE THEY THINK OF BARKING AS BEING WORK..
WOOF!
WHEW THAT WAS EXHAUSTING!
© 1994 United Feature Syndicate, Inc.

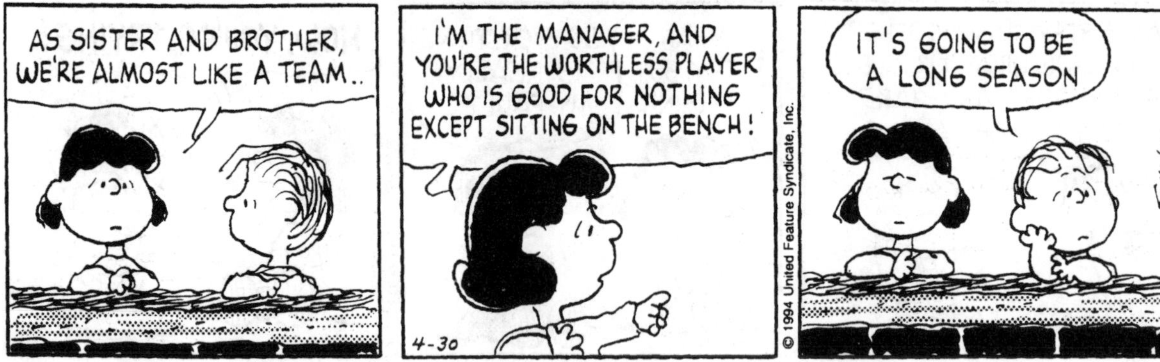
AS SISTER AND BROTHER, WE'RE ALMOST LIKE A TEAM..
I'M THE MANAGER, AND YOU'RE THE WORTHLESS PLAYER WHO IS GOOD FOR NOTHING EXCEPT SITTING ON THE BENCH!
4-30
IT'S GOING TO BE A LONG SEASON
© 1994 United Feature Syndicate, Inc.
SCHULZ

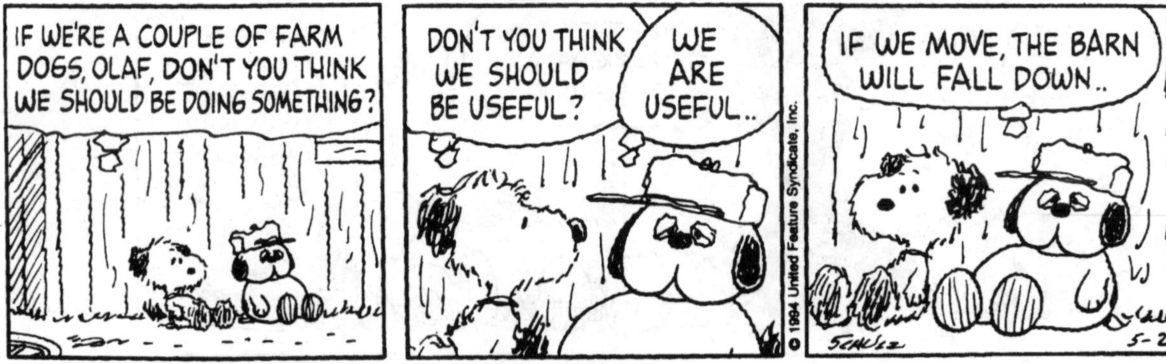
IF WE'RE A COUPLE OF FARM DOGS, OLAF, DON'T YOU THINK WE SHOULD BE DOING SOMETHING?
DON'T YOU THINK WE SHOULD BE USEFUL?
WE ARE USEFUL..
IF WE MOVE, THE BARN WILL FALL DOWN..
© 1994 United Feature Syndicate, Inc.
SCHULZ
5-2

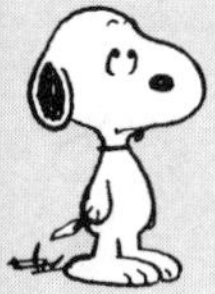

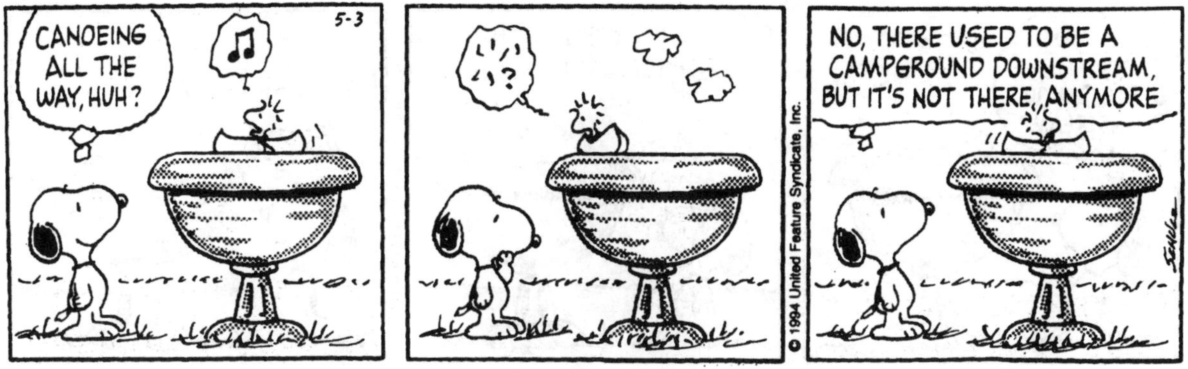
5-3
CANOEING ALL THE WAY, HUH?
NO, THERE USED TO BE A CAMPGROUND DOWNSTREAM, BUT IT'S NOT THERE ANYMORE
© 1994 United Feature Syndicate, Inc.
SCHULZ

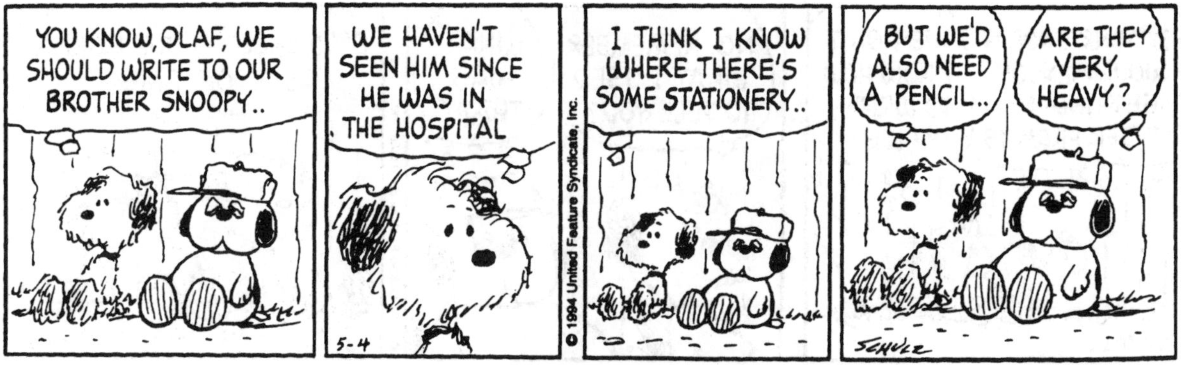
YOU KNOW, OLAF, WE SHOULD WRITE TO OUR BROTHER SNOOPY..
WE HAVEN'T SEEN HIM SINCE HE WAS IN THE HOSPITAL
5-4
© 1994 United Feature Syndicate, Inc.
I THINK I KNOW WHERE THERE'S SOME STATIONERY..
BUT WE'D ALSO NEED A PENCIL..
ARE THEY VERY HEAVY?
SCHULZ

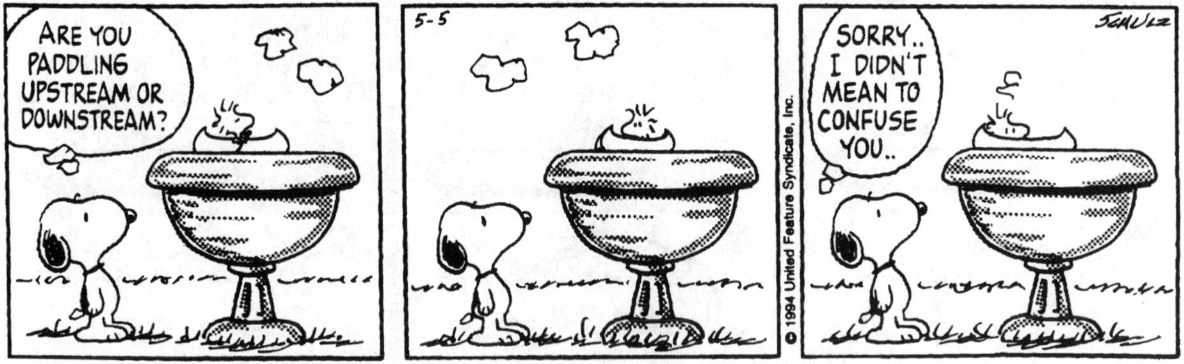
ARE YOU PADDLING UPSTREAM OR DOWNSTREAM?
5-5
© 1994 United Feature Syndicate, Inc.
SORRY.. I DIDN'T MEAN TO CONFUSE YOU..
SCHULZ

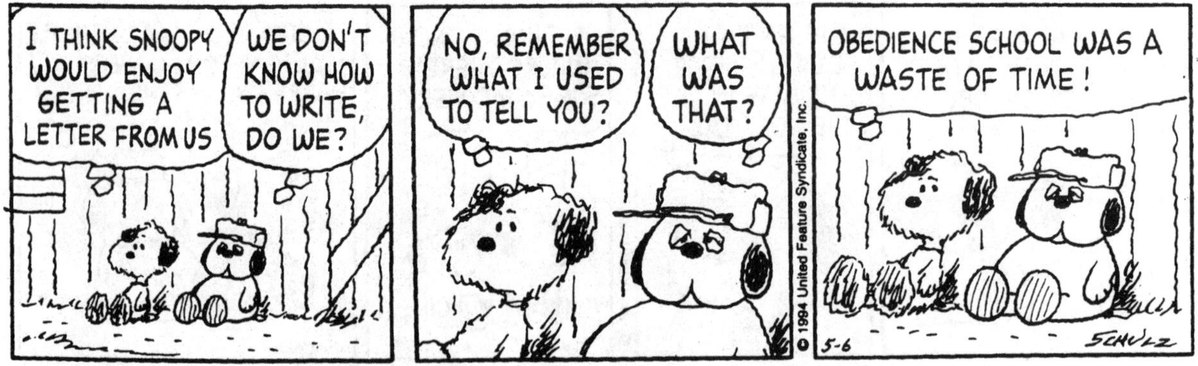
I THINK SNOOPY WOULD ENJOY GETTING A LETTER FROM US
WE DON'T KNOW HOW TO WRITE, DO WE?
NO, REMEMBER WHAT I USED TO TELL YOU?
WHAT WAS THAT?
© 1994 United Feature Syndicate, Inc.
OBEDIENCE SCHOOL WAS A WASTE OF TIME!
5-6
SCHULZ

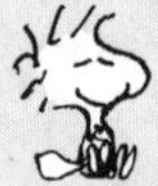

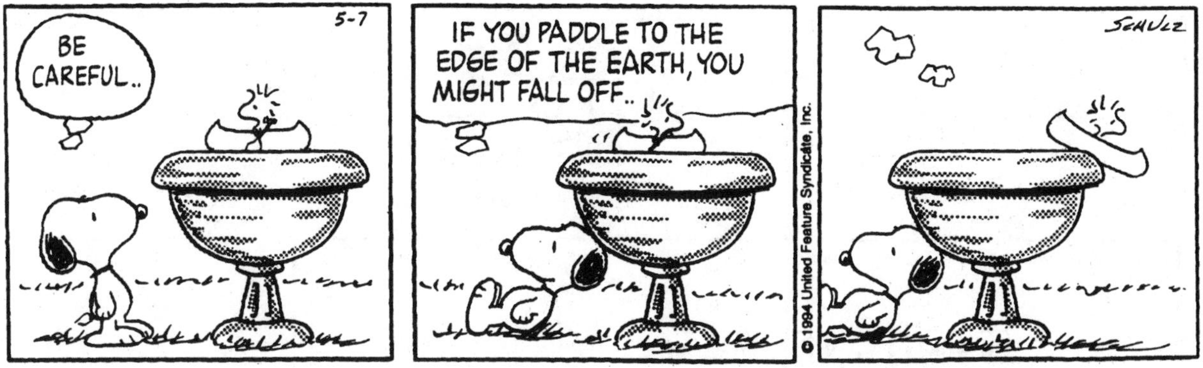
5-7
BE CAREFUL..
IF YOU PADDLE TO THE EDGE OF THE EARTH, YOU MIGHT FALL OFF..
SCHULZ
© 1994 United Feature Syndicate, Inc.

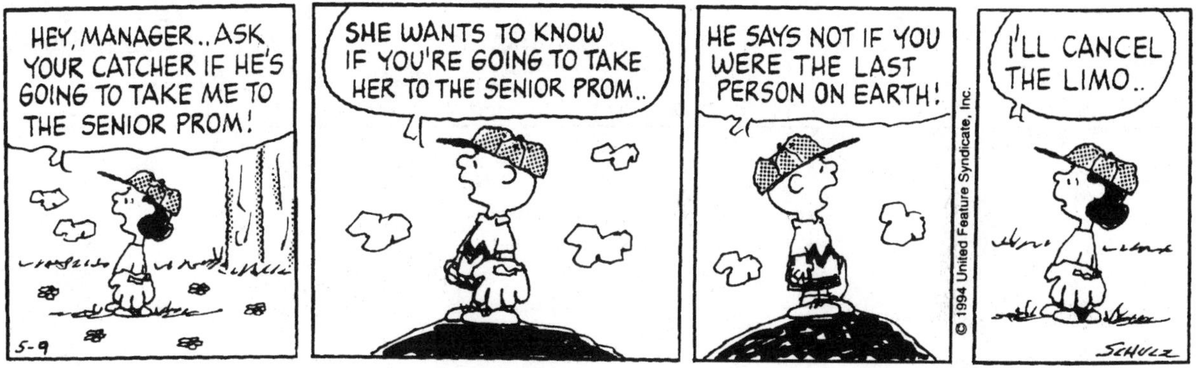
HEY, MANAGER..ASK YOUR CATCHER IF HE'S GOING TO TAKE ME TO THE SENIOR PROM!
5-9
SHE WANTS TO KNOW IF YOU'RE GOING TO TAKE HER TO THE SENIOR PROM..
HE SAYS NOT IF YOU WERE THE LAST PERSON ON EARTH!
© 1994 United Feature Syndicate, Inc.
I'LL CANCEL THE LIMO..
SCHULZ

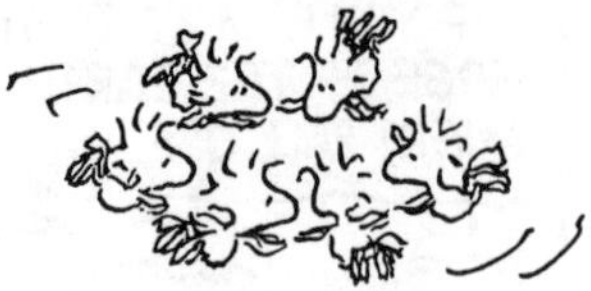

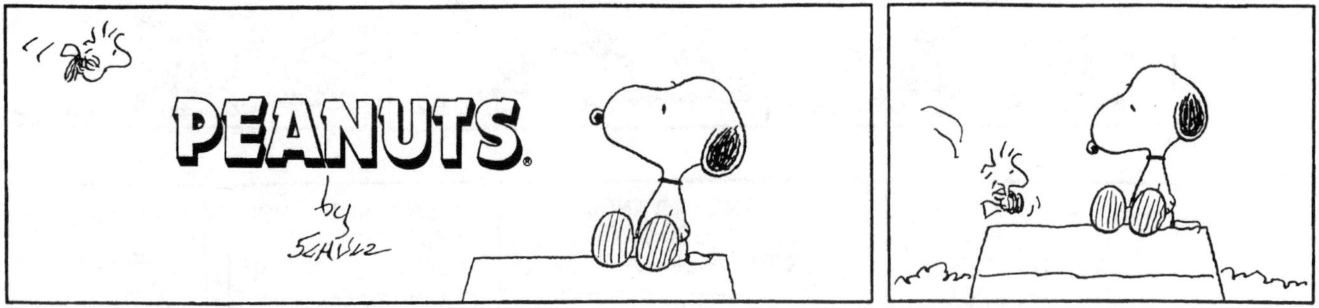
PEANUTS®
by
SCHULZ

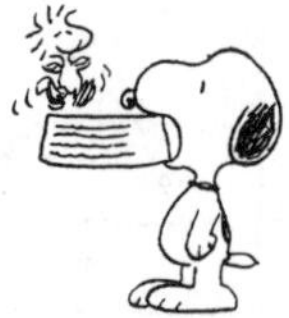

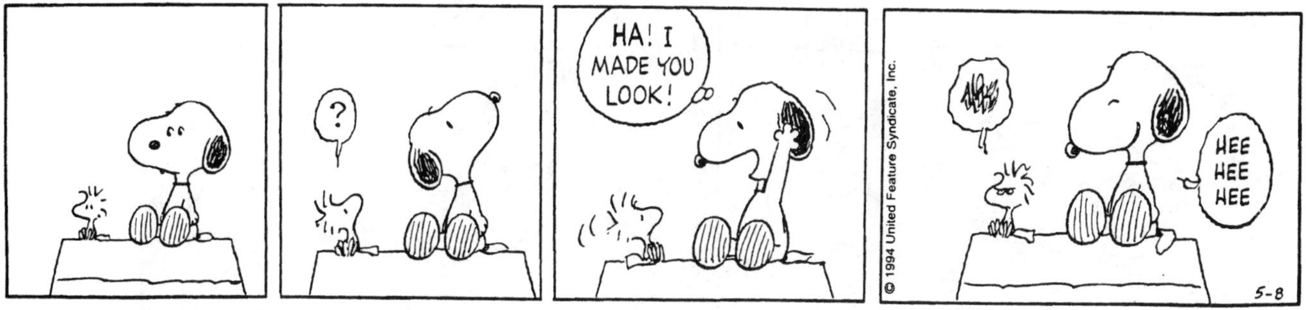
?
HA! I MADE YOU LOOK!
© 1994 United Feature Syndicate, Inc.
HEE HEE HEE
5-8

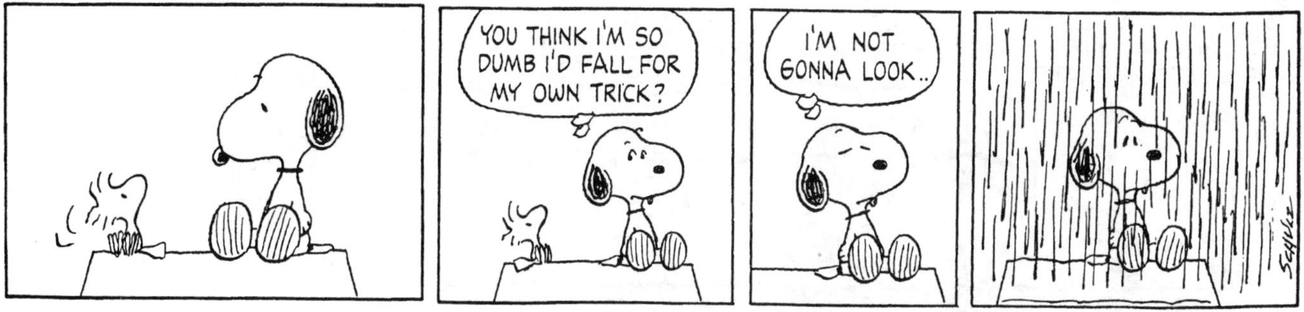
YOU THINK I'M SO DUMB I'D FALL FOR MY OWN TRICK?
I'M NOT GONNA LOOK..
SCHULZ

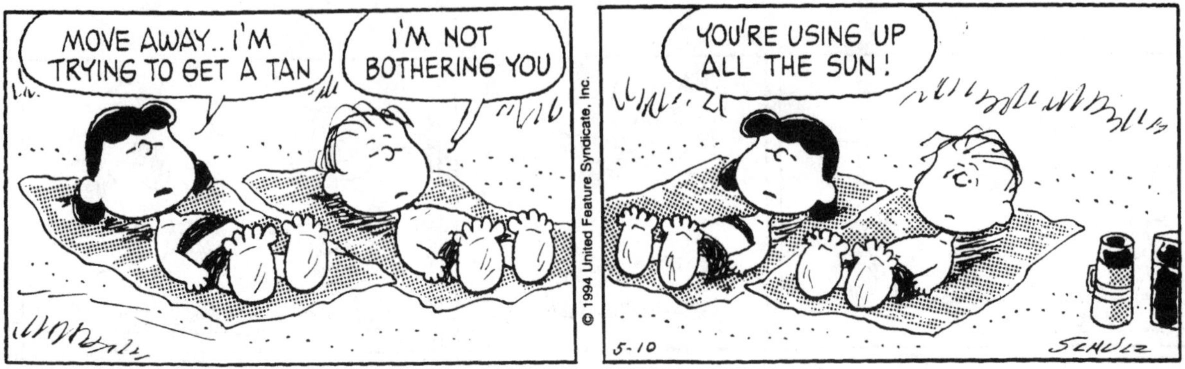
MOVE AWAY.. I'M TRYING TO GET A TAN
I'M NOT BOTHERING YOU
© 1994 United Feature Syndicate, Inc.
YOU'RE USING UP ALL THE SUN!
5-10
SCHULZ

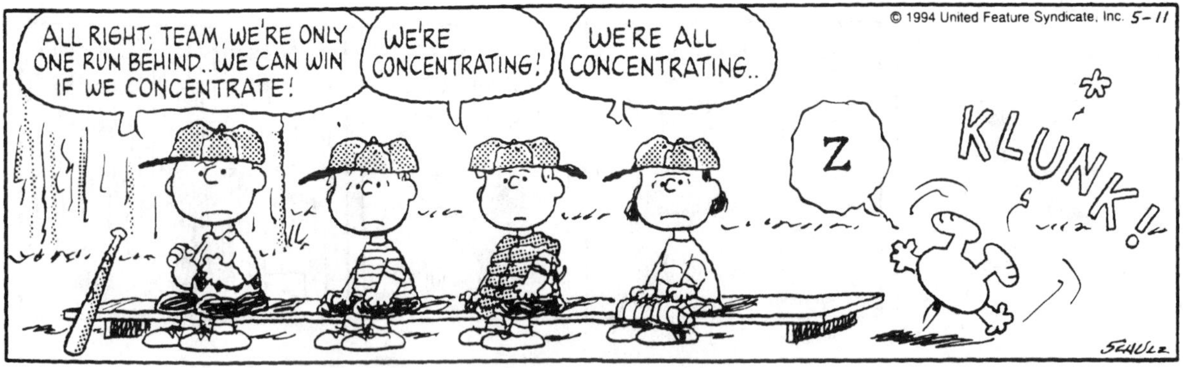
© 1994 United Feature Syndicate, Inc. 5-11
ALL RIGHT, TEAM, WE'RE ONLY ONE RUN BEHIND.. WE CAN WIN IF WE CONCENTRATE!
WE'RE CONCENTRATING!
WE'RE ALL CONCENTRATING..
Z
KLUNK!
SCHULZ

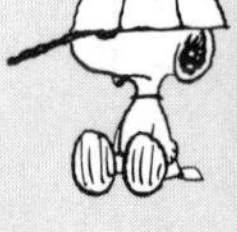

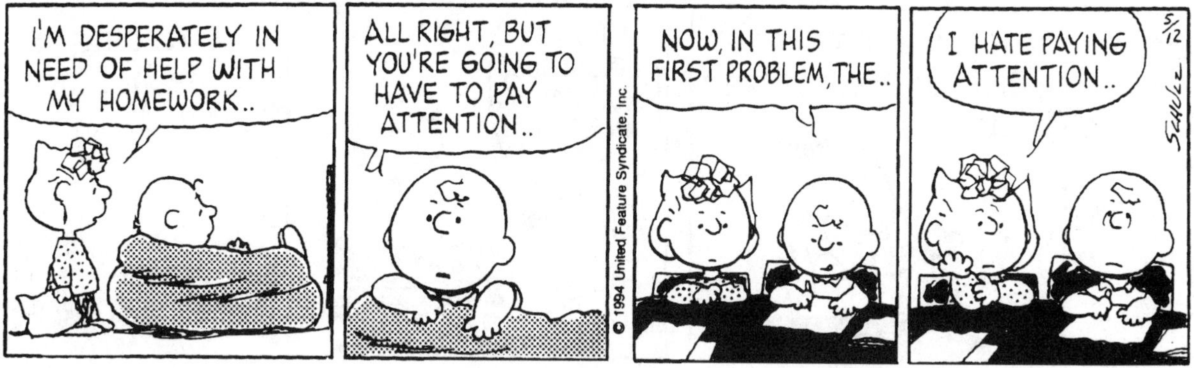
I'M DESPERATELY IN NEED OF HELP WITH MY HOMEWORK..
ALL RIGHT, BUT YOU'RE GOING TO HAVE TO PAY ATTENTION..
NOW, IN THIS FIRST PROBLEM, THE..
I HATE PAYING ATTENTION..
5/12
SCHULZ
© 1994 United Feature Syndicate, Inc.

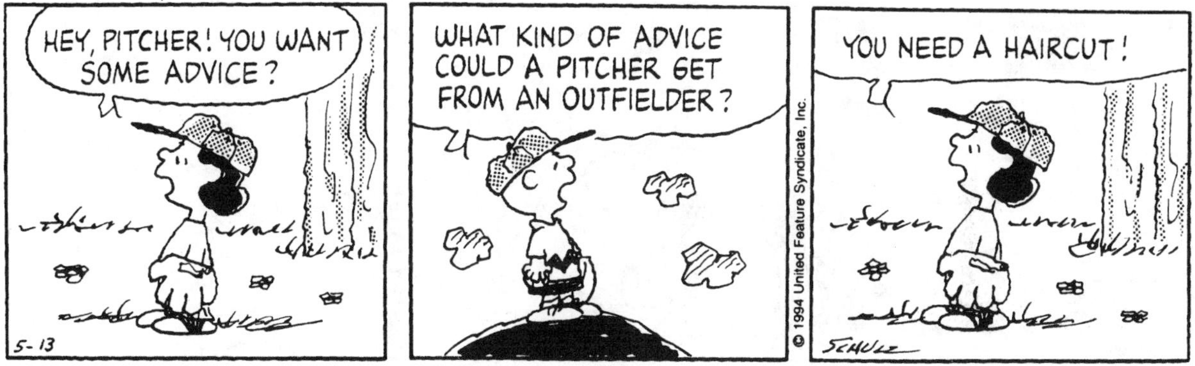
HEY, PITCHER! YOU WANT SOME ADVICE?
WHAT KIND OF ADVICE COULD A PITCHER GET FROM AN OUTFIELDER?
YOU NEED A HAIRCUT!
5-13
SCHULZ
© 1994 United Feature Syndicate, Inc.

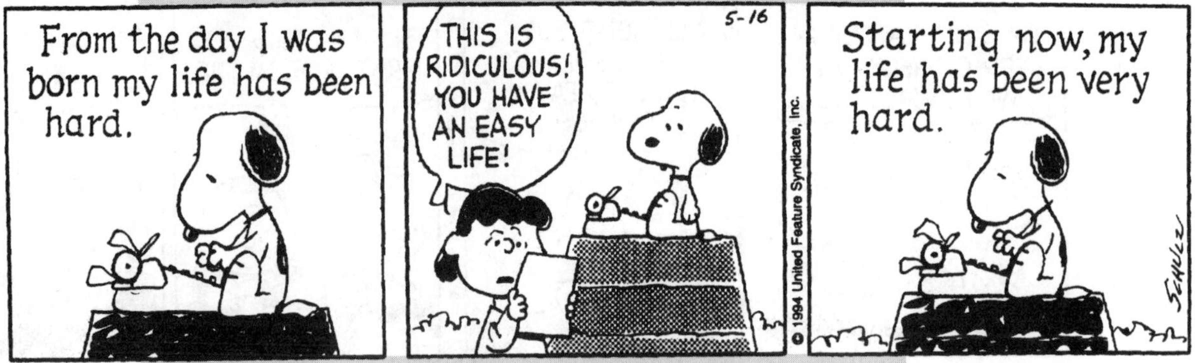
5-16
From the day I was born my life has been hard.
THIS IS RIDICULOUS! YOU HAVE AN EASY LIFE!
© 1994 United Feature Syndicate, Inc.
Starting now, my life has been very hard.
SCHULZ

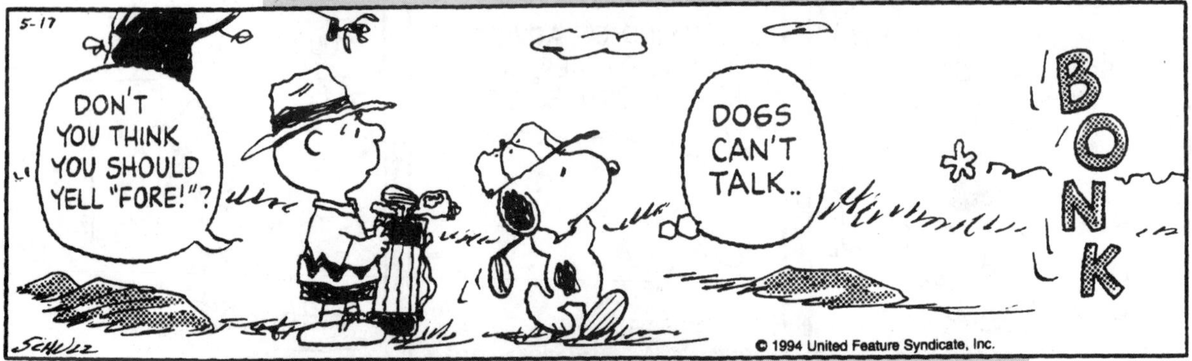
5-17
DON'T YOU THINK YOU SHOULD YELL "FORE!"?
DOGS CAN'T TALK..
BONK
SCHULZ
© 1994 United Feature Syndicate, Inc.

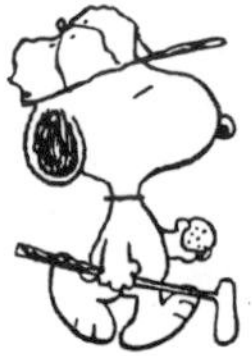

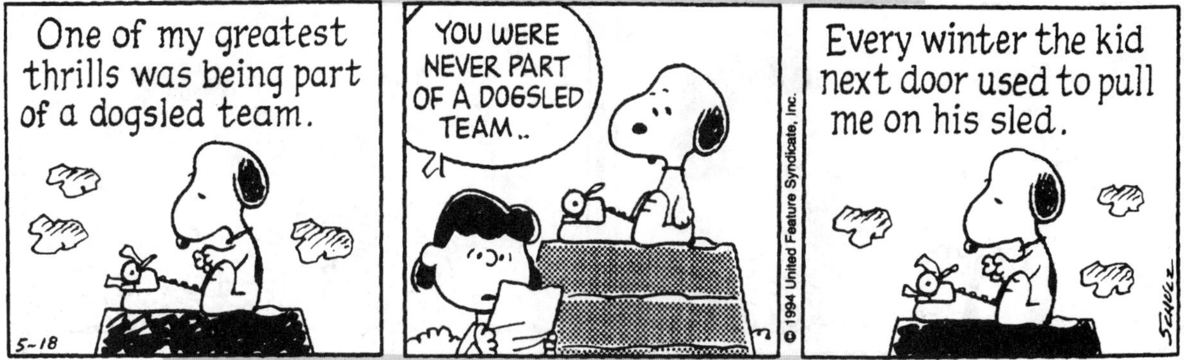
One of my greatest thrills was being part of a dogsled team.
5-18
YOU WERE NEVER PART OF A DOGSLED TEAM..
© 1994 United Feature Syndicate, Inc.
Every winter the kid next door used to pull me on his sled.
SCHULZ

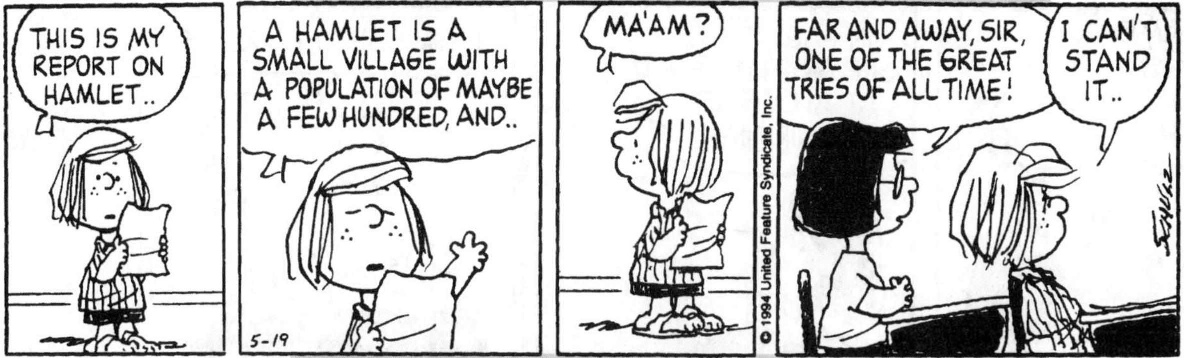
THIS IS MY REPORT ON HAMLET..
A HAMLET IS A SMALL VILLAGE WITH A POPULATION OF MAYBE A FEW HUNDRED, AND..
5-19
MA'AM?
© 1994 United Feature Syndicate, Inc.
FAR AND AWAY, SIR, ONE OF THE GREAT TRIES OF ALL TIME!
I CAN'T STAND IT..
SCHULZ

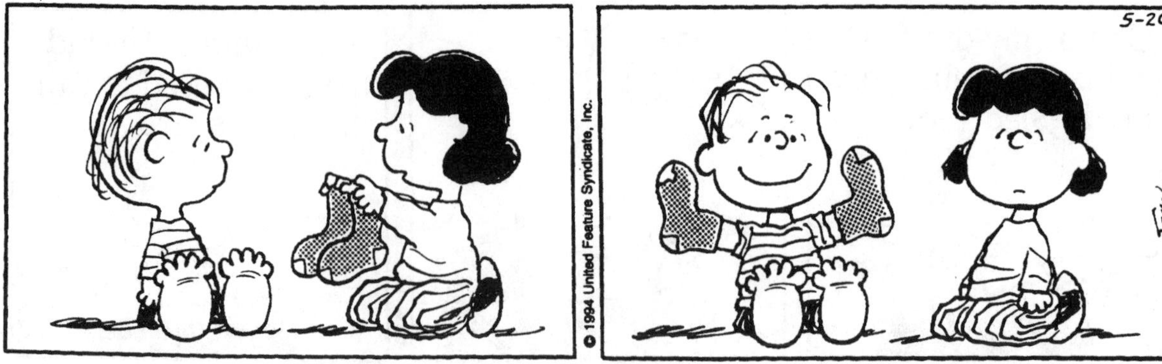
5-20
© 1994 United Feature Syndicate, Inc.
SCHULZ

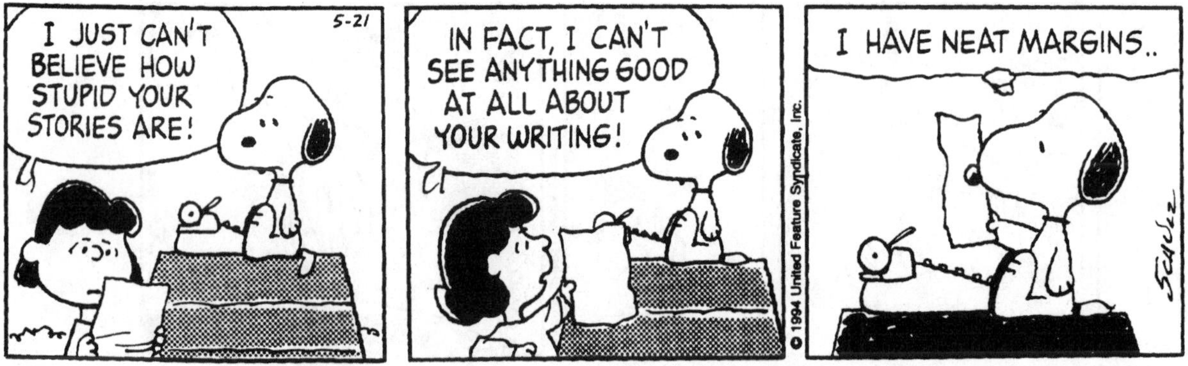
5-21
I JUST CAN'T BELIEVE HOW STUPID YOUR STORIES ARE!
IN FACT, I CAN'T SEE ANYTHING GOOD AT ALL ABOUT YOUR WRITING!
© 1994 United Feature Syndicate, Inc.
I HAVE NEAT MARGINS..
SCHULZ

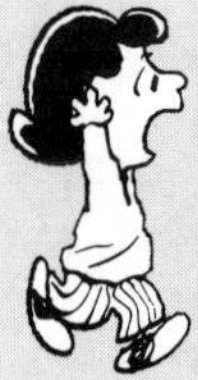

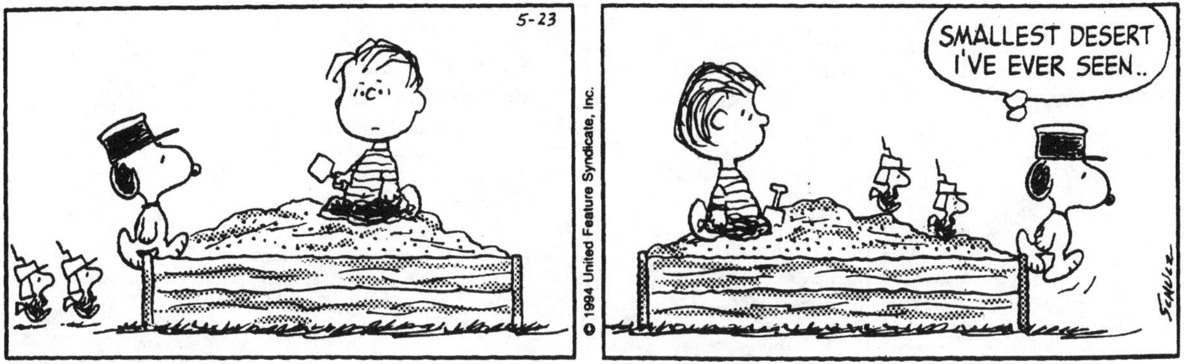
5-23
© 1994 United Feature Syndicate, Inc.
SMALLEST DESERT I'VE EVER SEEN..
SCHULZ

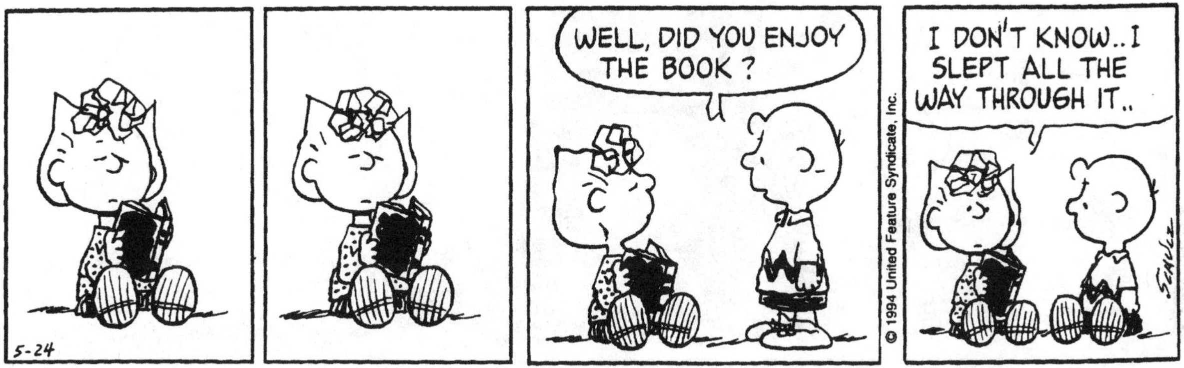
5-24
WELL, DID YOU ENJOY THE BOOK ?
© 1994 United Feature Syndicate, Inc.
I DON'T KNOW.. I SLEPT ALL THE WAY THROUGH IT..
SCHULZ

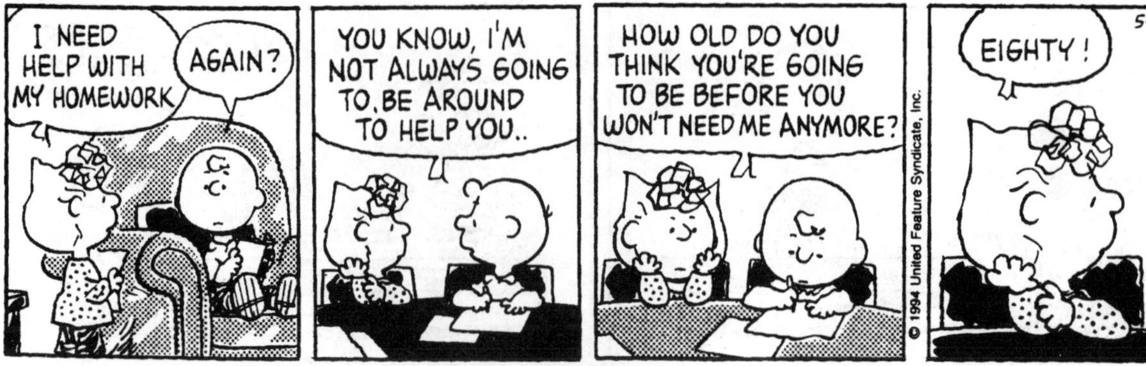
I NEED HELP WITH MY HOMEWORK
AGAIN?
YOU KNOW, I'M NOT ALWAYS GOING TO BE AROUND TO HELP YOU..
HOW OLD DO YOU THINK YOU'RE GOING TO BE BEFORE YOU WON'T NEED ME ANYMORE?
EIGHTY!
5-25
© 1994 United Feature Syndicate, Inc.
SCHULZ

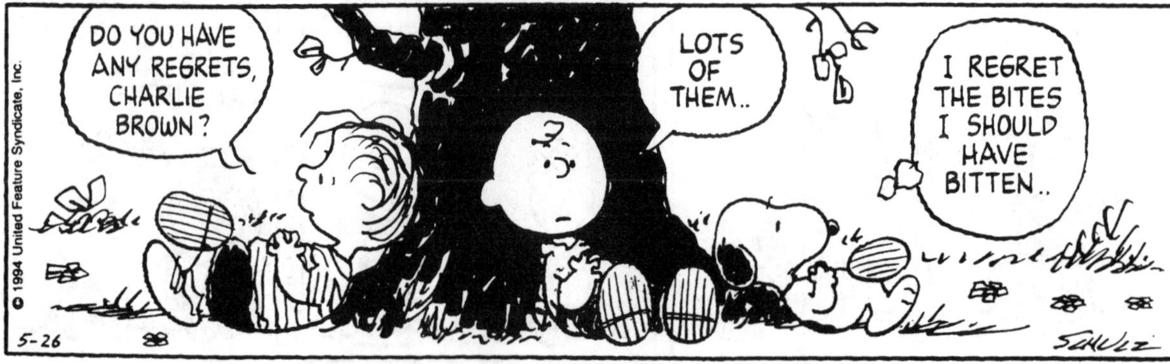
DO YOU HAVE ANY REGRETS, CHARLIE BROWN?
LOTS OF THEM..
I REGRET THE BITES I SHOULD HAVE BITTEN..
© 1994 United Feature Syndicate, Inc.
5-26
SCHULZ

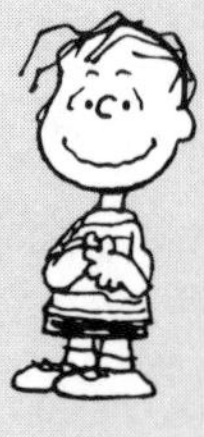

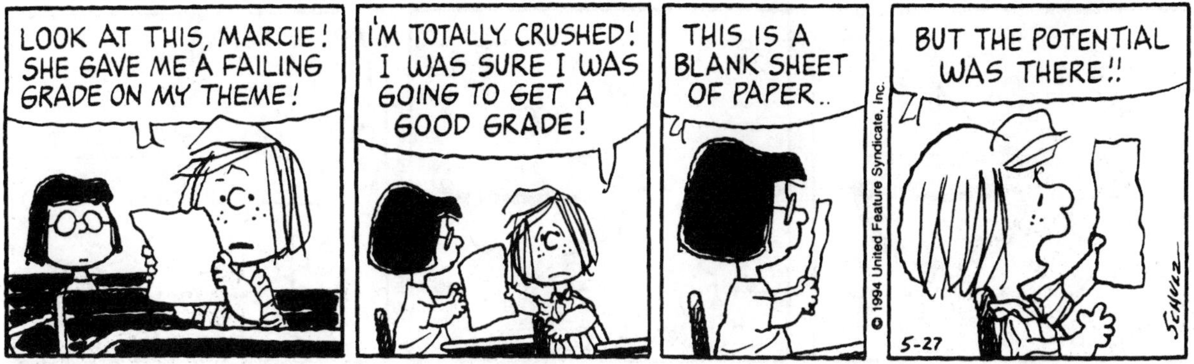
LOOK AT THIS, MARCIE! SHE GAVE ME A FAILING GRADE ON MY THEME!
I'M TOTALLY CRUSHED! I WAS SURE I WAS GOING TO GET A GOOD GRADE!
THIS IS A BLANK SHEET OF PAPER..
BUT THE POTENTIAL WAS THERE!!
© 1994 United Feature Syndicate, Inc.
5-27
SCHULZ

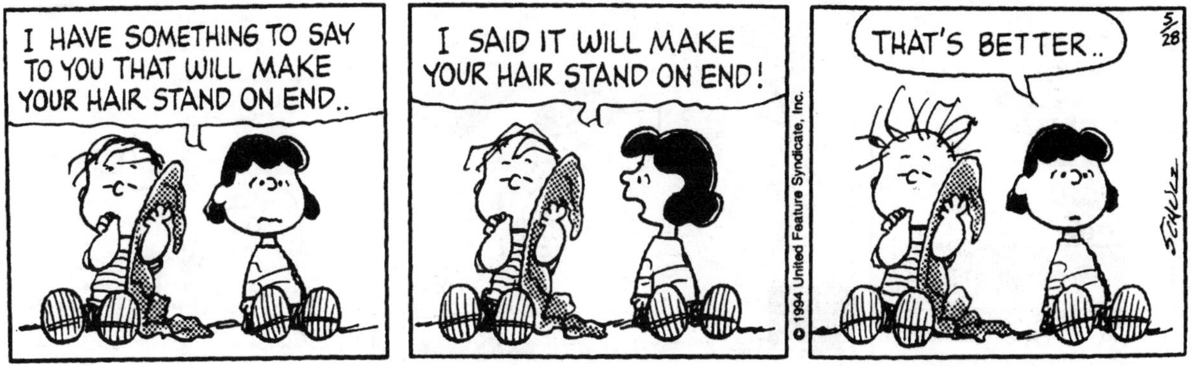
I HAVE SOMETHING TO SAY TO YOU THAT WILL MAKE YOUR HAIR STAND ON END..
I SAID IT WILL MAKE YOUR HAIR STAND ON END!
© 1994 United Feature Syndicate, Inc.
THAT'S BETTER..
5/28
SCHULZ

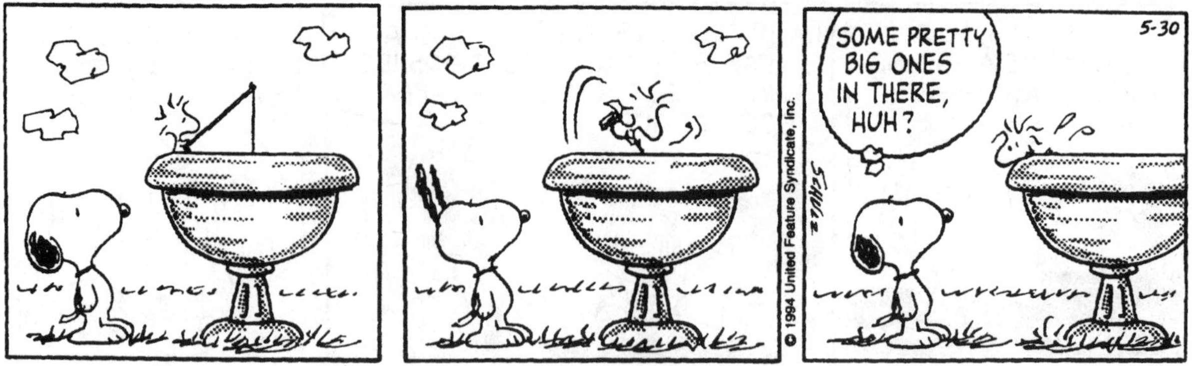
SOME PRETTY BIG ONES IN THERE, HUH?
5-30
© 1994 United Feature Syndicate, Inc.
SCHULZ

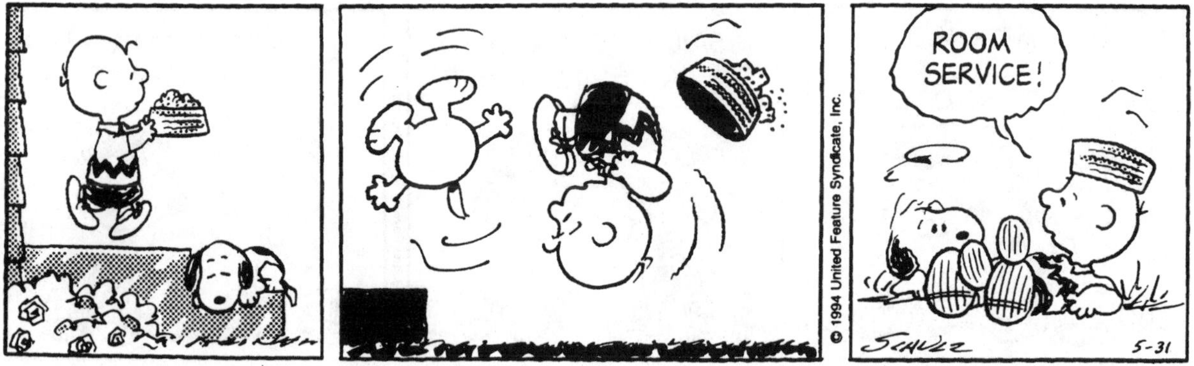
ROOM SERVICE!
© 1994 United Feature Syndicate, Inc.
SCHULZ
5-31

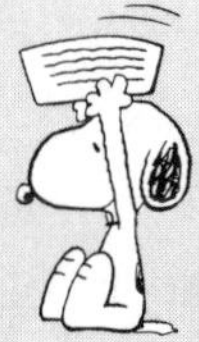

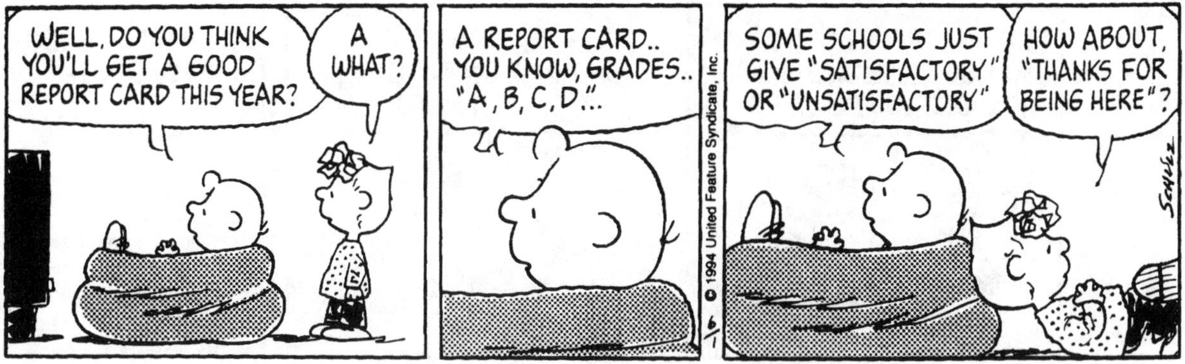
WELL, DO YOU THINK YOU'LL GET A GOOD REPORT CARD THIS YEAR?
A WHAT?
A REPORT CARD.. YOU KNOW, GRADES.. "A, B, C, D"..
SOME SCHOOLS JUST GIVE "SATISFACTORY" OR "UNSATISFACTORY"
HOW ABOUT, "THANKS FOR BEING HERE"?
© 1994 United Feature Syndicate, Inc.
SCHULZ

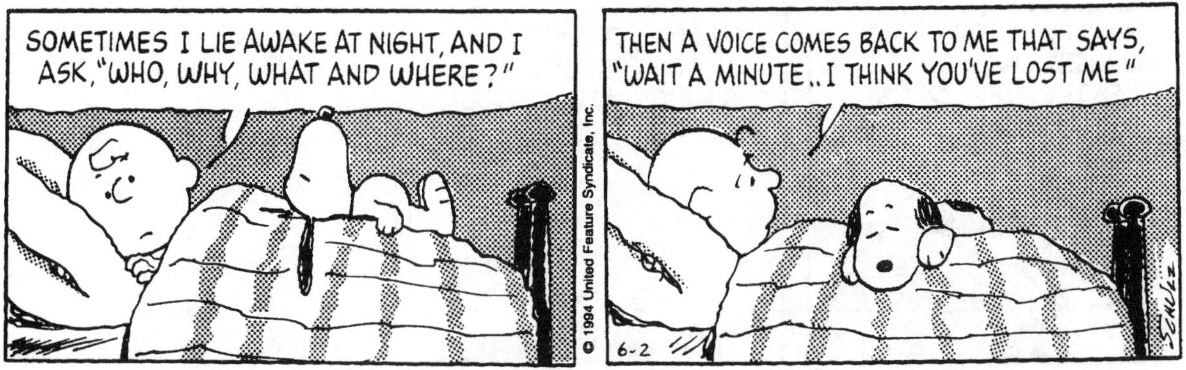
SOMETIMES I LIE AWAKE AT NIGHT, AND I ASK, "WHO, WHY, WHAT AND WHERE?"
THEN A VOICE COMES BACK TO ME THAT SAYS, "WAIT A MINUTE.. I THINK YOU'VE LOST ME"
© 1994 United Feature Syndicate, Inc.
6-2
SCHULZ

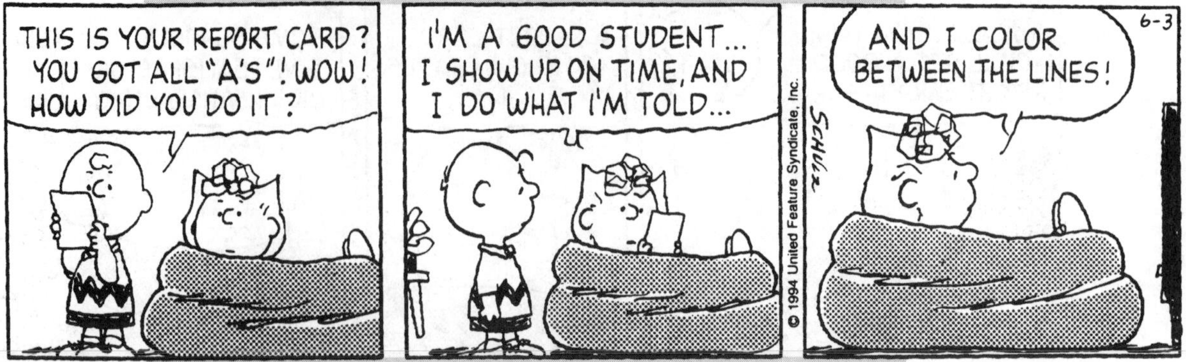
THIS IS YOUR REPORT CARD? YOU GOT ALL "A'S"! WOW! HOW DID YOU DO IT?
I'M A GOOD STUDENT... I SHOW UP ON TIME, AND I DO WHAT I'M TOLD...
AND I COLOR BETWEEN THE LINES!
6-3
© 1994 United Feature Syndicate, Inc.
SCHULZ

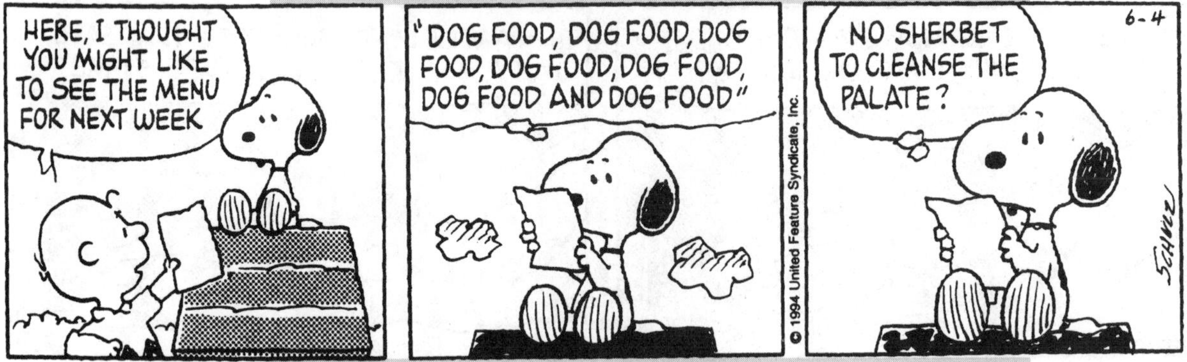
HERE, I THOUGHT YOU MIGHT LIKE TO SEE THE MENU FOR NEXT WEEK
"DOG FOOD, DOG FOOD, DOG FOOD, DOG FOOD, DOG FOOD, DOG FOOD AND DOG FOOD"
NO SHERBET TO CLEANSE THE PALATE?
6-4
© 1994 United Feature Syndicate, Inc.
SCHULZ

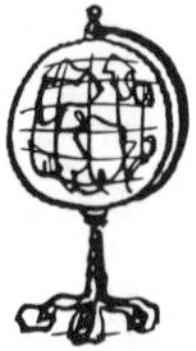

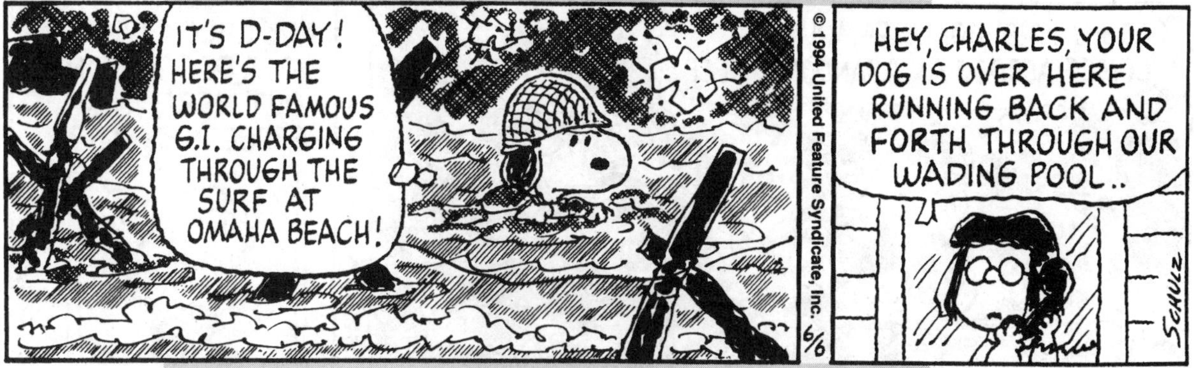
IT'S D-DAY! HERE'S THE WORLD FAMOUS G.I. CHARGING THROUGH THE SURF AT OMAHA BEACH!
© 1994 United Feature Syndicate, Inc.
6/6
HEY, CHARLES, YOUR DOG IS OVER HERE RUNNING BACK AND FORTH THROUGH OUR WADING POOL..
SCHULZ

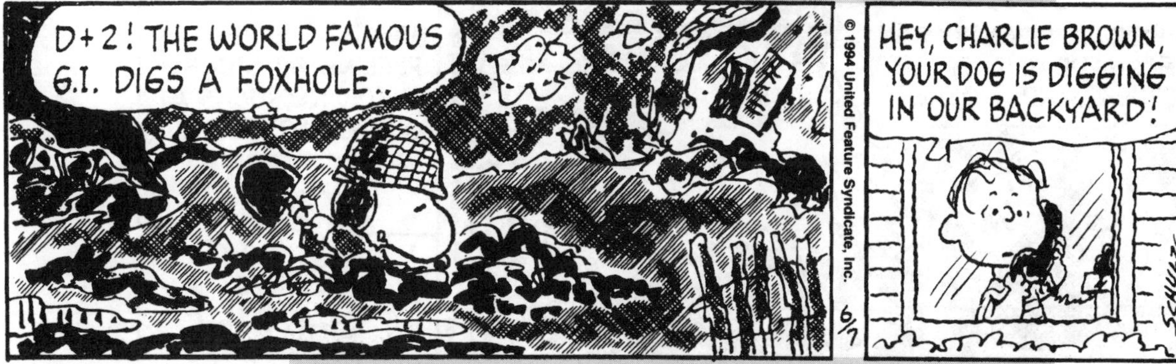
D+2! THE WORLD FAMOUS G.I. DIGS A FOXHOLE..
© 1994 United Feature Syndicate, Inc.
6/7
HEY, CHARLIE BROWN, YOUR DOG IS DIGGING IN OUR BACKYARD!
SCHULZ

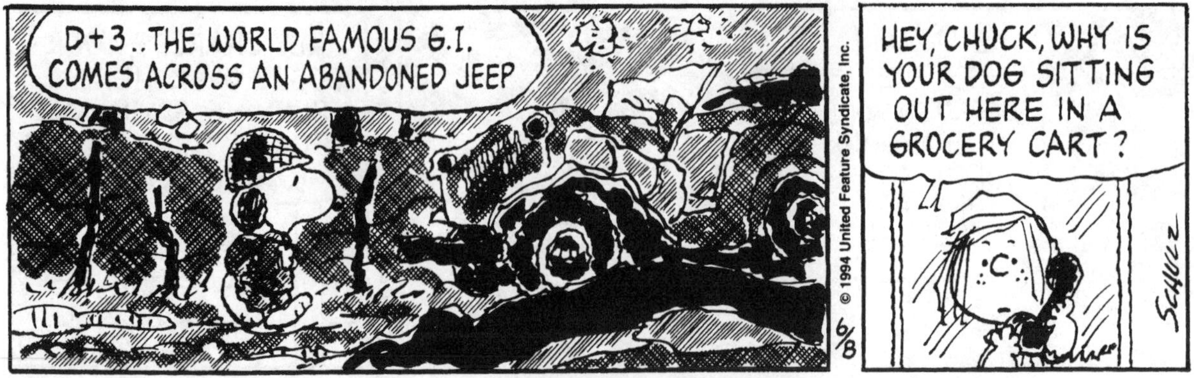
D+3..THE WORLD FAMOUS G.I. COMES ACROSS AN ABANDONED JEEP
© 1994 United Feature Syndicate, Inc.
6/8
HEY, CHUCK, WHY IS YOUR DOG SITTING OUT HERE IN A GROCERY CART?
SCHULZ

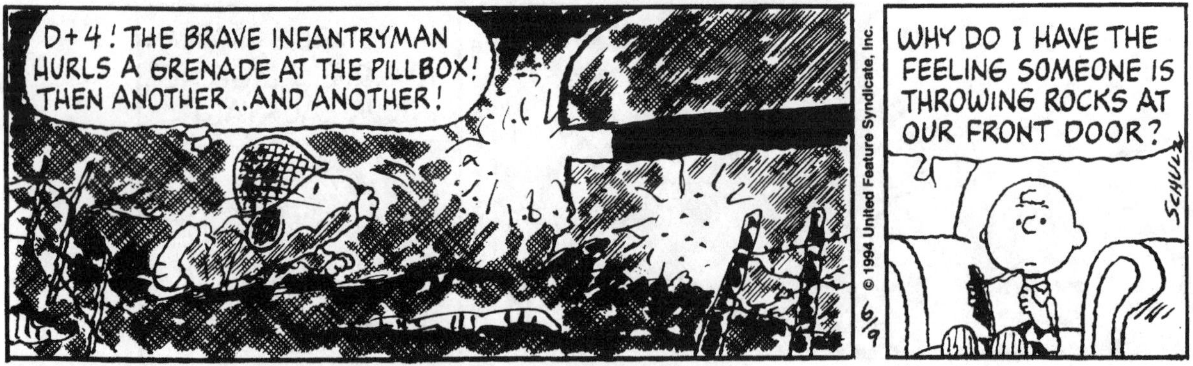
D+4! THE BRAVE INFANTRYMAN HURLS A GRENADE AT THE PILLBOX! THEN ANOTHER..AND ANOTHER!
© 1994 United Feature Syndicate, Inc.
6/9
WHY DO I HAVE THE FEELING SOMEONE IS THROWING ROCKS AT OUR FRONT DOOR?
SCHULZ

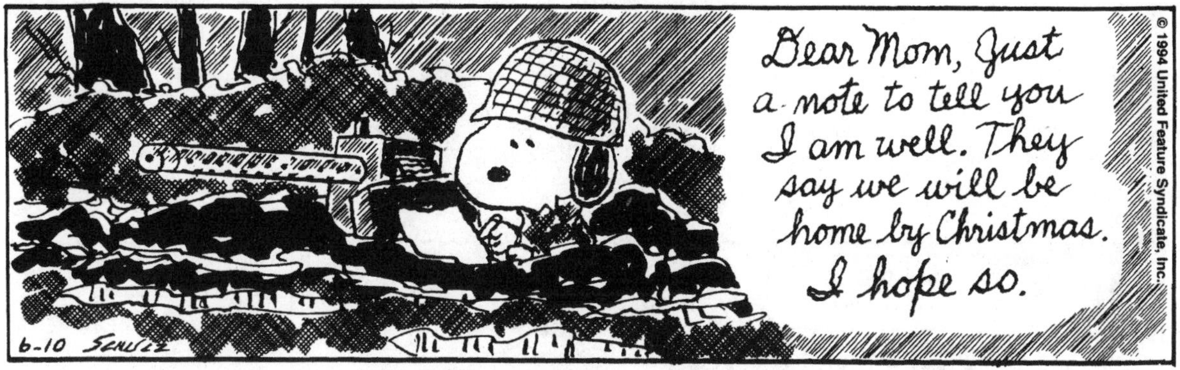
Dear Mom, Just a note to tell you I am well. They say we will be home by Christmas. I hope so.
6-10 SCHULZ
© 1994 United Feature Syndicate, Inc.

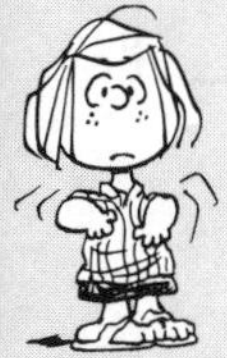

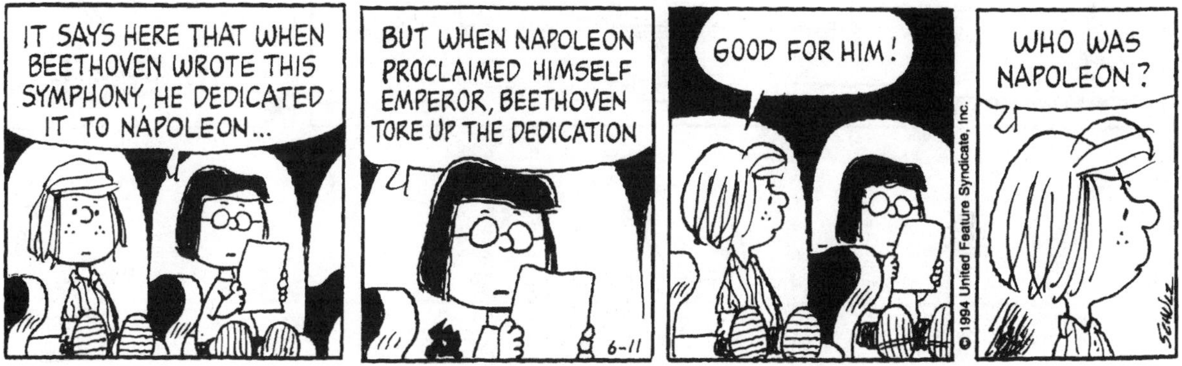
IT SAYS HERE THAT WHEN BEETHOVEN WROTE THIS SYMPHONY, HE DEDICATED IT TO NAPOLEON...
BUT WHEN NAPOLEON PROCLAIMED HIMSELF EMPEROR, BEETHOVEN TORE UP THE DEDICATION
6-11
GOOD FOR HIM!
© 1994 United Feature Syndicate, Inc.
WHO WAS NAPOLEON?
SCHULZ

PEANUTS
by SCHULZ

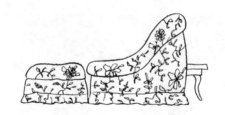

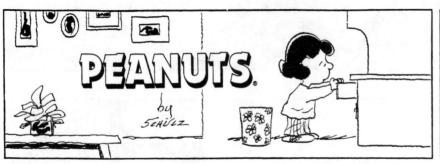

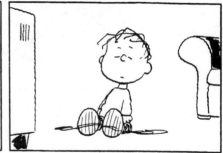

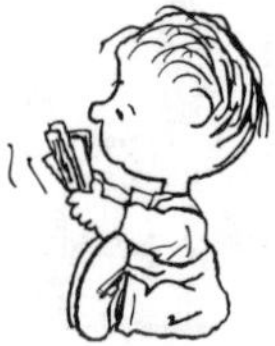

THIS IS A GOOD GAME, RERUN..

HERE, YOU TAKE THIS PACK OF CARDS..

AND I'LL PUT THIS BASKET OVER HERE...

6-12

NOW, SEE HOW MANY CARDS YOU CAN THROW INTO THE BASKET..

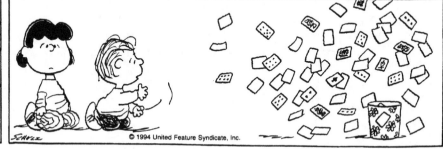

© 1994 United Feature Syndicate, Inc.

81

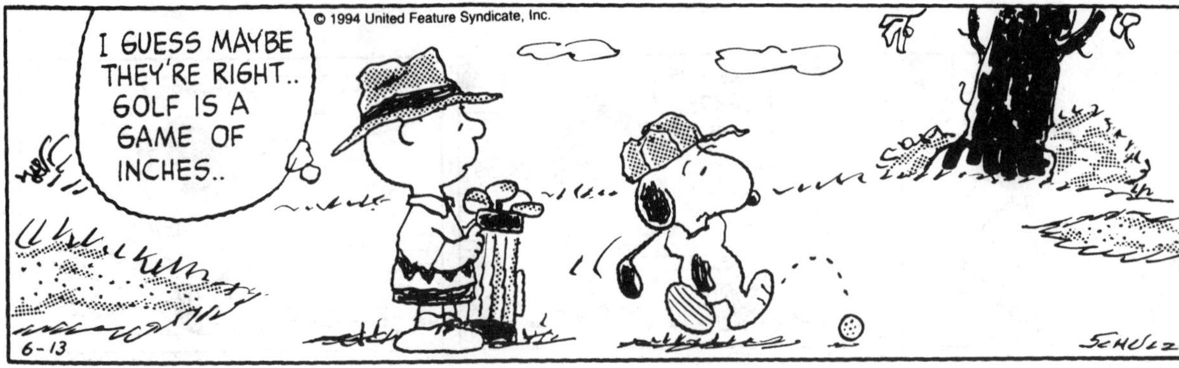
I GUESS MAYBE THEY'RE RIGHT.. GOLF IS A GAME OF INCHES..
© 1994 United Feature Syndicate, Inc.
6-13
SCHULZ

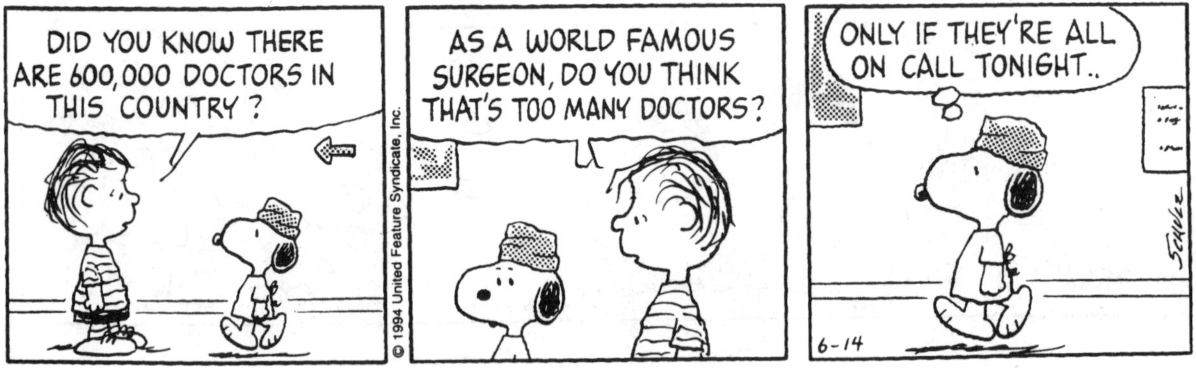
DID YOU KNOW THERE ARE 600,000 DOCTORS IN THIS COUNTRY ?
AS A WORLD FAMOUS SURGEON, DO YOU THINK THAT'S TOO MANY DOCTORS?
ONLY IF THEY'RE ALL ON CALL TONIGHT..
© 1994 United Feature Syndicate, Inc.
6-14
SCHULZ

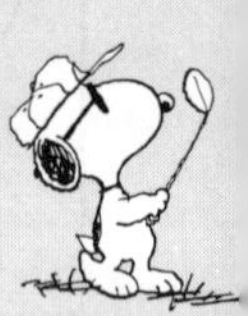

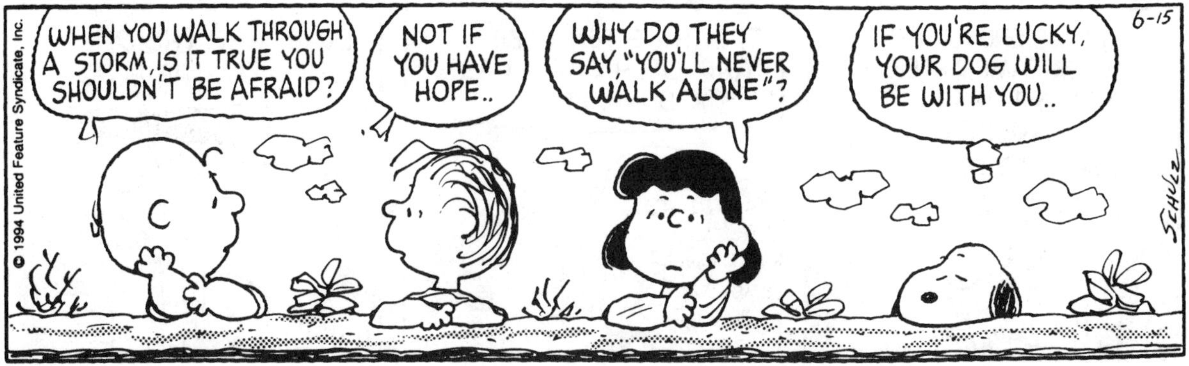
WHEN YOU WALK THROUGH A STORM, IS IT TRUE YOU SHOULDN'T BE AFRAID?
NOT IF YOU HAVE HOPE..
WHY DO THEY SAY, "YOU'LL NEVER WALK ALONE"?
IF YOU'RE LUCKY, YOUR DOG WILL BE WITH YOU..
6-15
© 1994 United Feature Syndicate, Inc.
SCHULZ

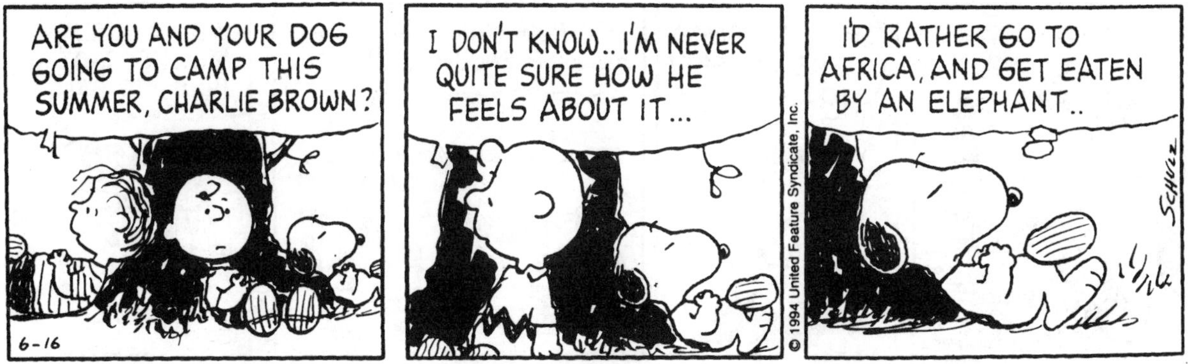
ARE YOU AND YOUR DOG GOING TO CAMP THIS SUMMER, CHARLIE BROWN?
6-16
I DON'T KNOW.. I'M NEVER QUITE SURE HOW HE FEELS ABOUT IT...
© 1994 United Feature Syndicate, Inc.
I'D RATHER GO TO AFRICA, AND GET EATEN BY AN ELEPHANT..
SCHULZ

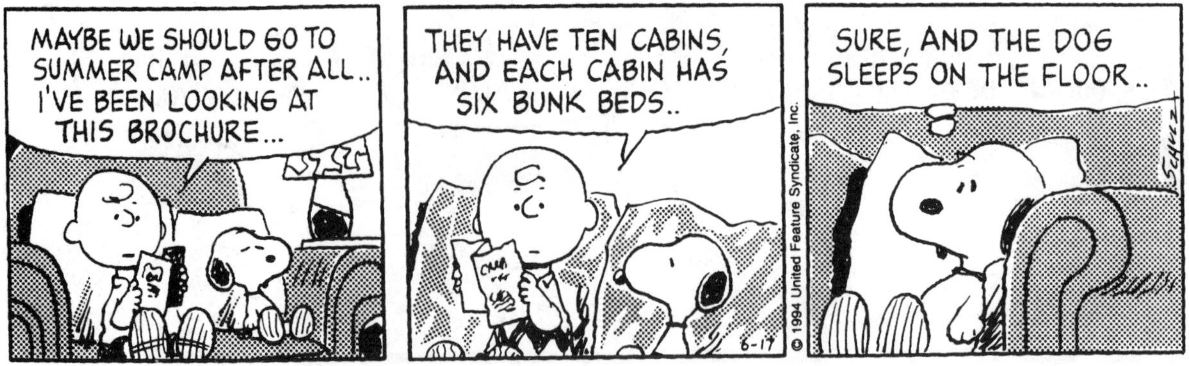
MAYBE WE SHOULD GO TO SUMMER CAMP AFTER ALL.. I'VE BEEN LOOKING AT THIS BROCHURE...
THEY HAVE TEN CABINS, AND EACH CABIN HAS SIX BUNK BEDS..
© 1994 United Feature Syndicate, Inc.
6-17
SURE, AND THE DOG SLEEPS ON THE FLOOR..
SCHULZ

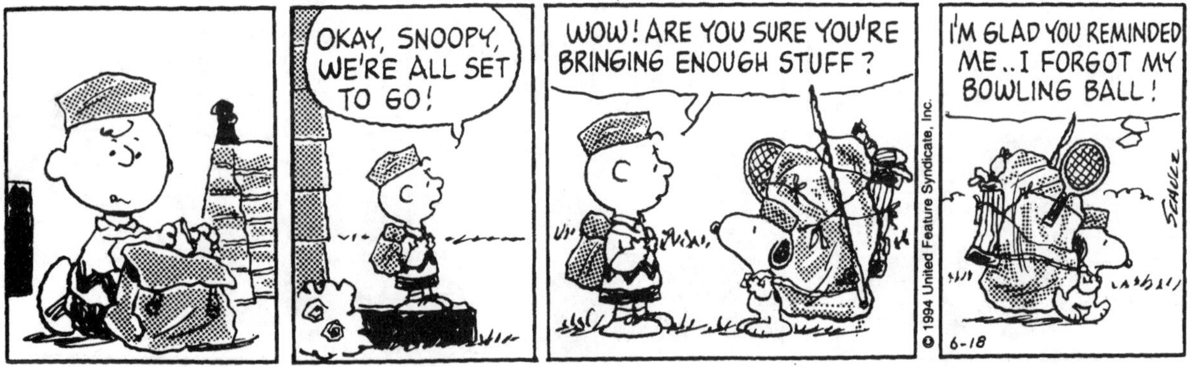
OKAY, SNOOPY, WE'RE ALL SET TO GO!
WOW! ARE YOU SURE YOU'RE BRINGING ENOUGH STUFF?
© 1994 United Feature Syndicate, Inc.
I'M GLAD YOU REMINDED ME..I FORGOT MY BOWLING BALL!
SCHULZ
6-18

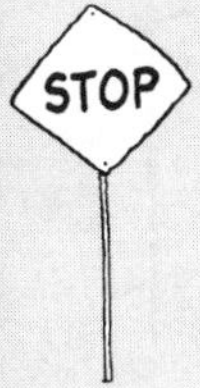
STOP

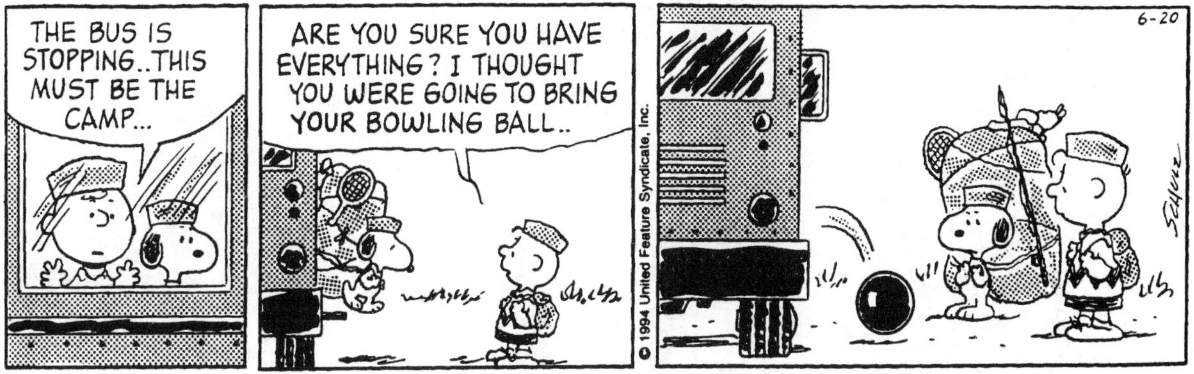
THE BUS IS STOPPING..THIS MUST BE THE CAMP...
ARE YOU SURE YOU HAVE EVERYTHING? I THOUGHT YOU WERE GOING TO BRING YOUR BOWLING BALL..
© 1994 United Feature Syndicate, Inc.
6-20
SCHULZ

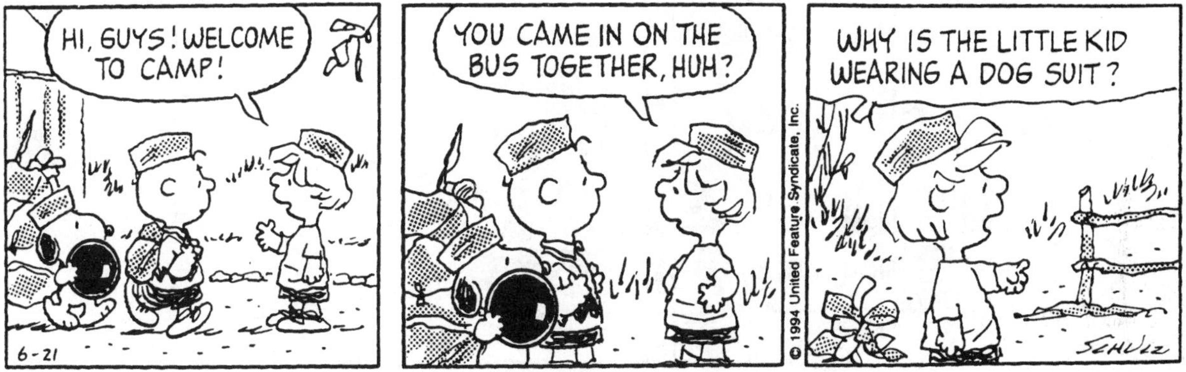
HI, GUYS! WELCOME TO CAMP!
6-21
YOU CAME IN ON THE BUS TOGETHER, HUH?
© 1994 United Feature Syndicate, Inc.
WHY IS THE LITTLE KID WEARING A DOG SUIT?
SCHULZ

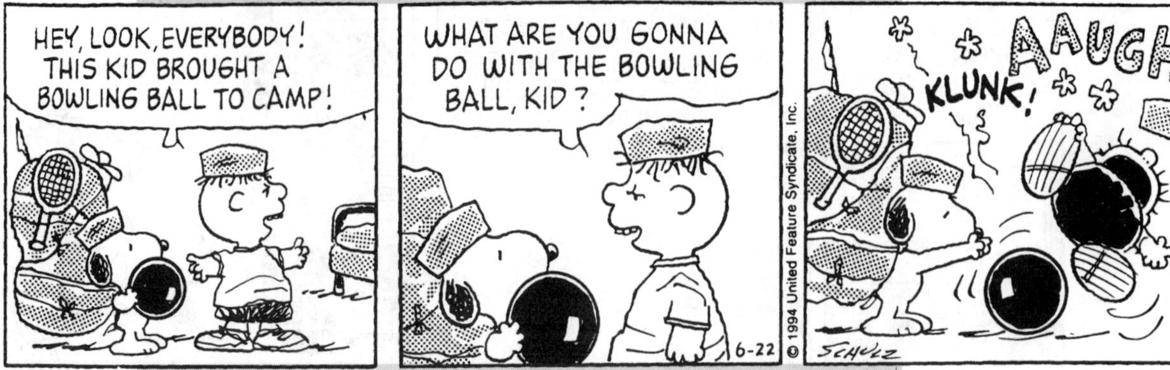
HEY, LOOK, EVERYBODY! THIS KID BROUGHT A BOWLING BALL TO CAMP!
WHAT ARE YOU GONNA DO WITH THE BOWLING BALL, KID?
6-22
© 1994 United Feature Syndicate, Inc.
KLUNK!
AAUGH
SCHULZ

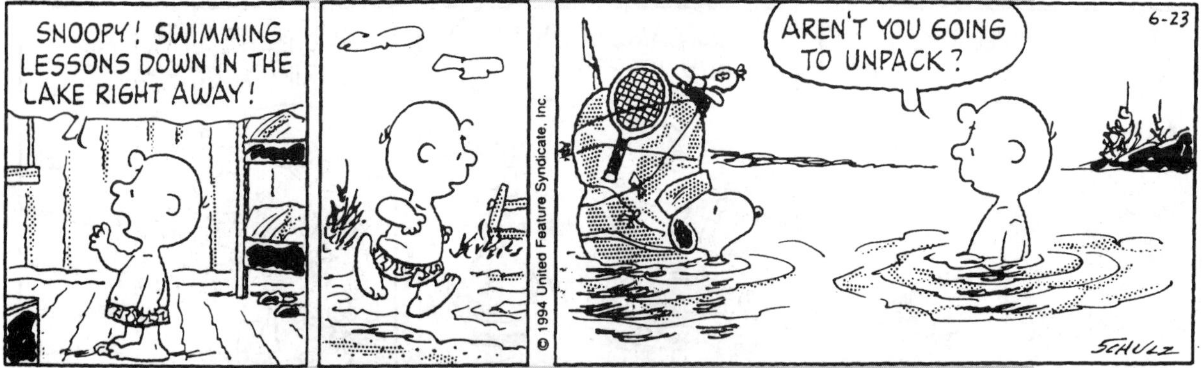
SNOOPY! SWIMMING LESSONS DOWN IN THE LAKE RIGHT AWAY!
© 1994 United Feature Syndicate, Inc.
6-23
AREN'T YOU GOING TO UNPACK?
SCHULZ

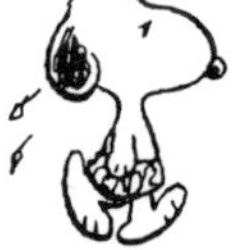

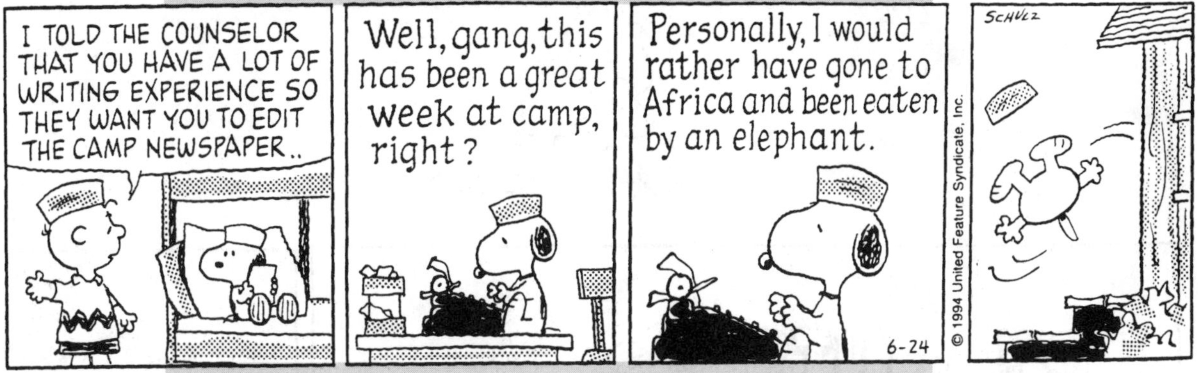
I TOLD THE COUNSELOR THAT YOU HAVE A LOT OF WRITING EXPERIENCE SO THEY WANT YOU TO EDIT THE CAMP NEWSPAPER..
Well, gang, this has been a great week at camp, right?
Personally, I would rather have gone to Africa and been eaten by an elephant.
6-24
© 1994 United Feature Syndicate, Inc.
SCHULZ

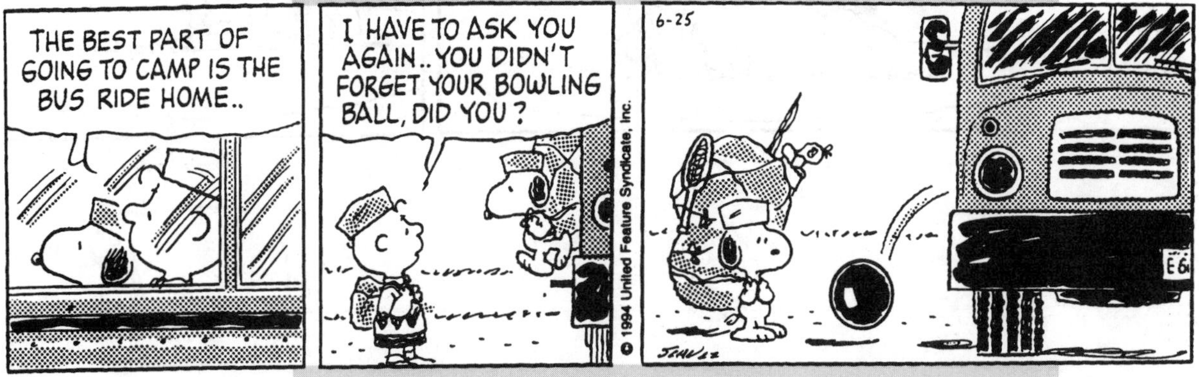
THE BEST PART OF GOING TO CAMP IS THE BUS RIDE HOME..
I HAVE TO ASK YOU AGAIN.. YOU DIDN'T FORGET YOUR BOWLING BALL, DID YOU?
© 1994 United Feature Syndicate, Inc.
6-25
SCHULZ

PEANUTS
by SCHULZ

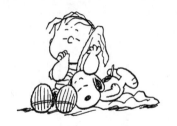

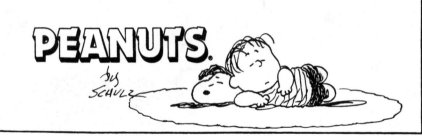

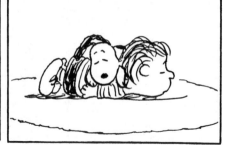

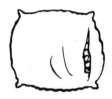

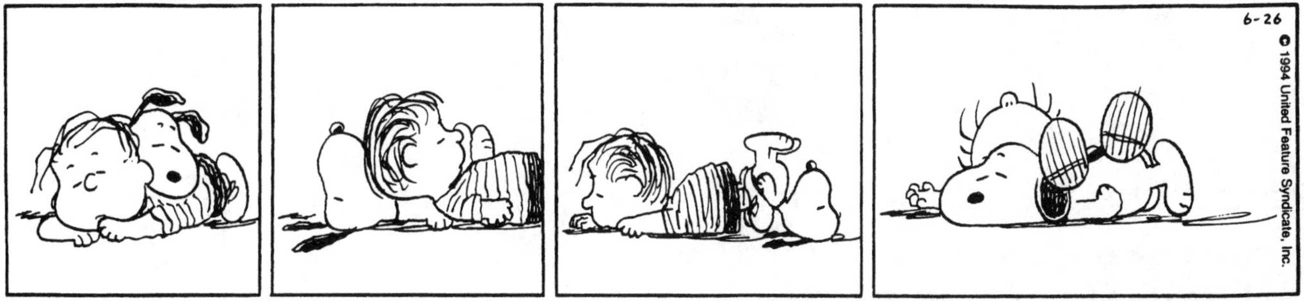
6-26
© 1994 United Feature Syndicate, Inc.

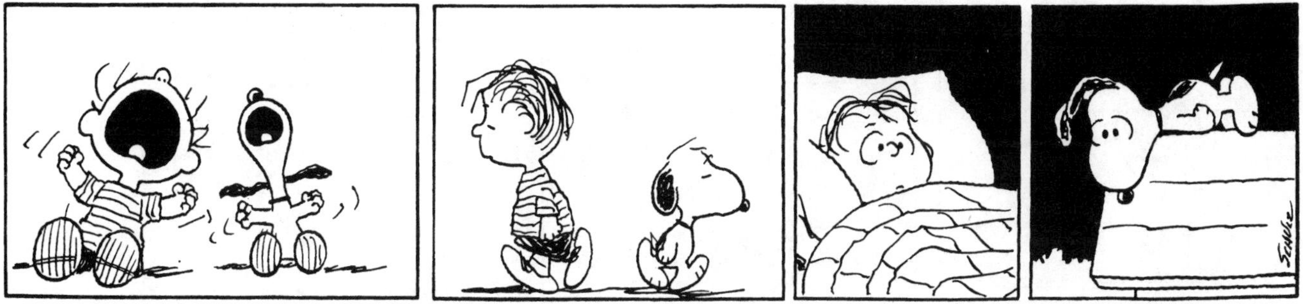
SCHULZ

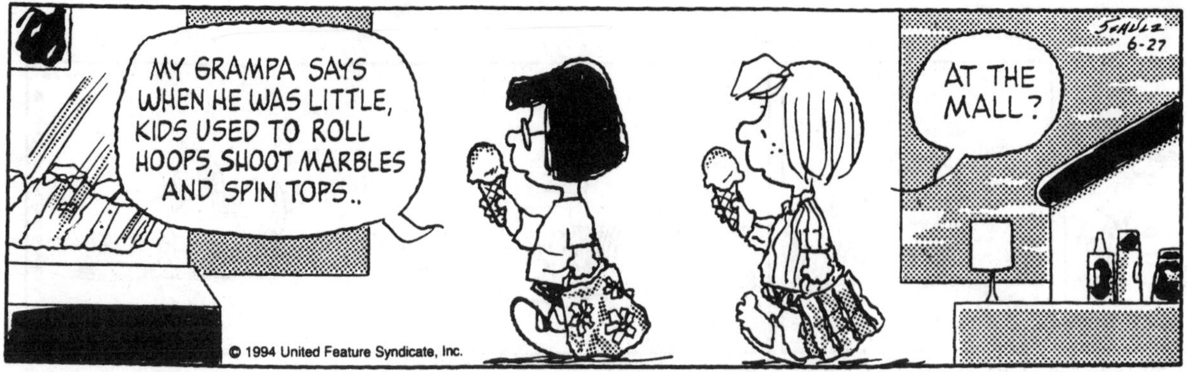
SCHULZ 6-27
MY GRAMPA SAYS WHEN HE WAS LITTLE, KIDS USED TO ROLL HOOPS, SHOOT MARBLES AND SPIN TOPS..
AT THE MALL?
© 1994 United Feature Syndicate, Inc.

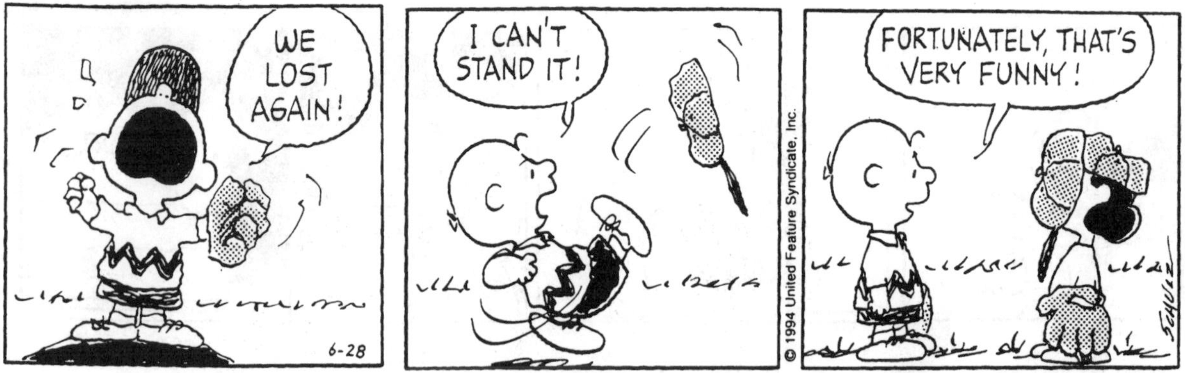
WE LOST AGAIN!
6-28
I CAN'T STAND IT!
© 1994 United Feature Syndicate, Inc.
FORTUNATELY, THAT'S VERY FUNNY!
SCHULZ

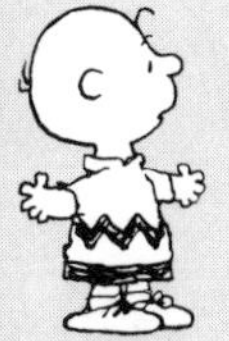

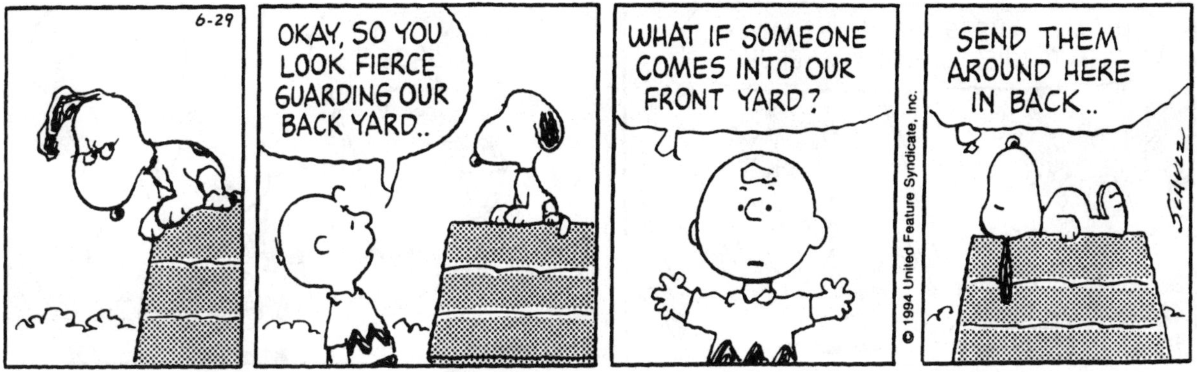
6-29
OKAY, SO YOU LOOK FIERCE GUARDING OUR BACK YARD..
WHAT IF SOMEONE COMES INTO OUR FRONT YARD?
© 1994 United Feature Syndicate, Inc.
SEND THEM AROUND HERE IN BACK..
SCHULZ

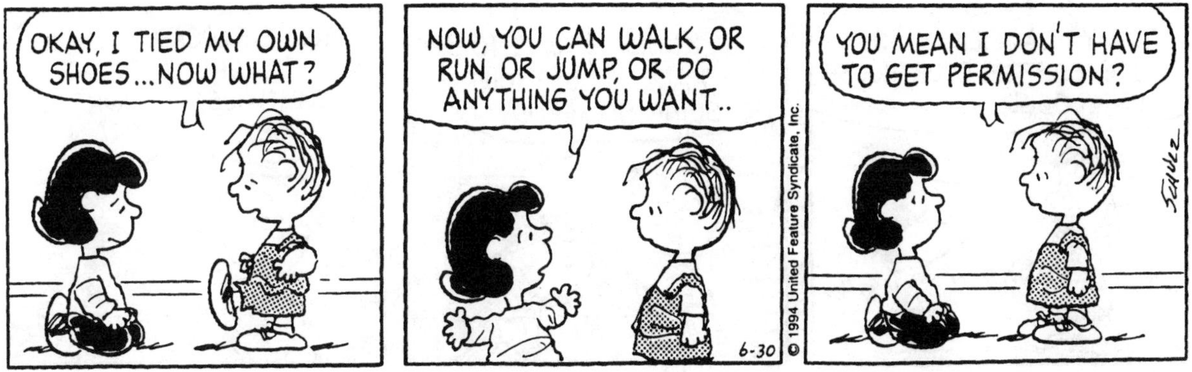
OKAY, I TIED MY OWN SHOES...NOW WHAT?
NOW, YOU CAN WALK, OR RUN, OR JUMP, OR DO ANYTHING YOU WANT..
6-30
© 1994 United Feature Syndicate, Inc.
YOU MEAN I DON'T HAVE TO GET PERMISSION?
SCHULZ

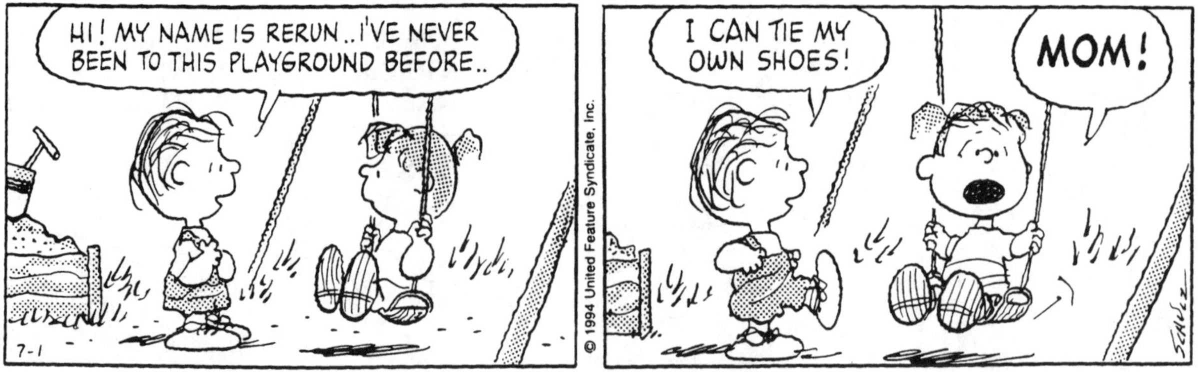
HI! MY NAME IS RERUN.. I'VE NEVER BEEN TO THIS PLAYGROUND BEFORE..
I CAN TIE MY OWN SHOES!
MOM!
7-1
© 1994 United Feature Syndicate, Inc.
SCHULZ

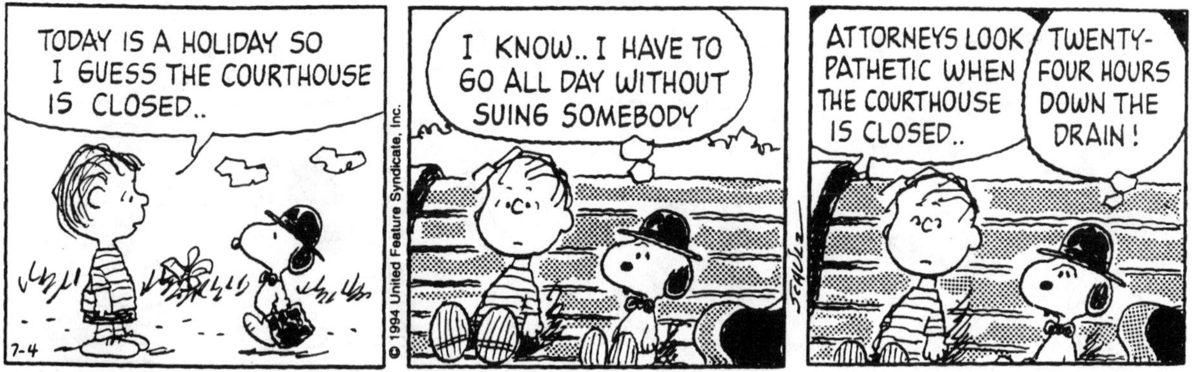
TODAY IS A HOLIDAY SO I GUESS THE COURTHOUSE IS CLOSED..
I KNOW.. I HAVE TO GO ALL DAY WITHOUT SUING SOMEBODY
ATTORNEYS LOOK PATHETIC WHEN THE COURTHOUSE IS CLOSED..
TWENTY-FOUR HOURS DOWN THE DRAIN!
7-4
© 1994 United Feature Syndicate, Inc.
SCHULZ

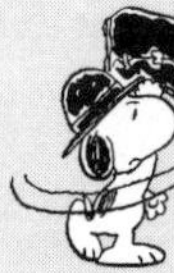

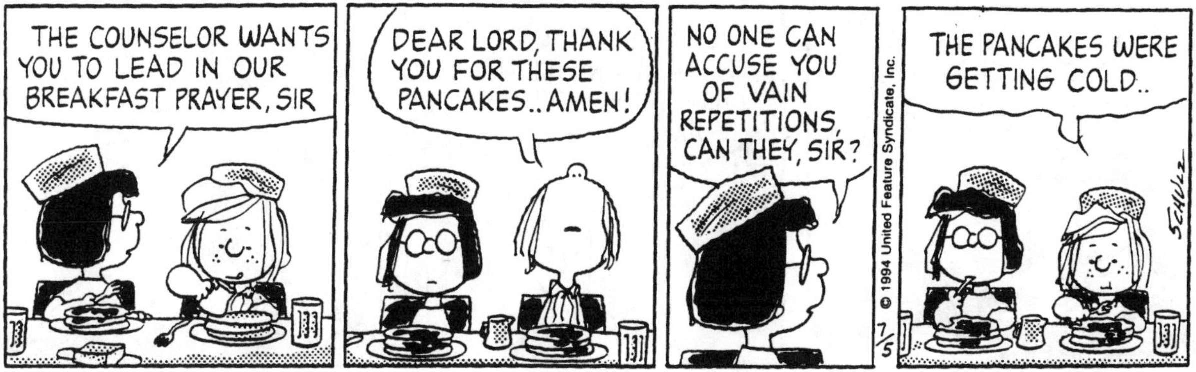
THE COUNSELOR WANTS YOU TO LEAD IN OUR BREAKFAST PRAYER, SIR
DEAR LORD, THANK YOU FOR THESE PANCAKES..AMEN!
NO ONE CAN ACCUSE YOU OF VAIN REPETITIONS, CAN THEY, SIR?
© 1994 United Feature Syndicate, Inc.
7/5
THE PANCAKES WERE GETTING COLD..
SCHULZ

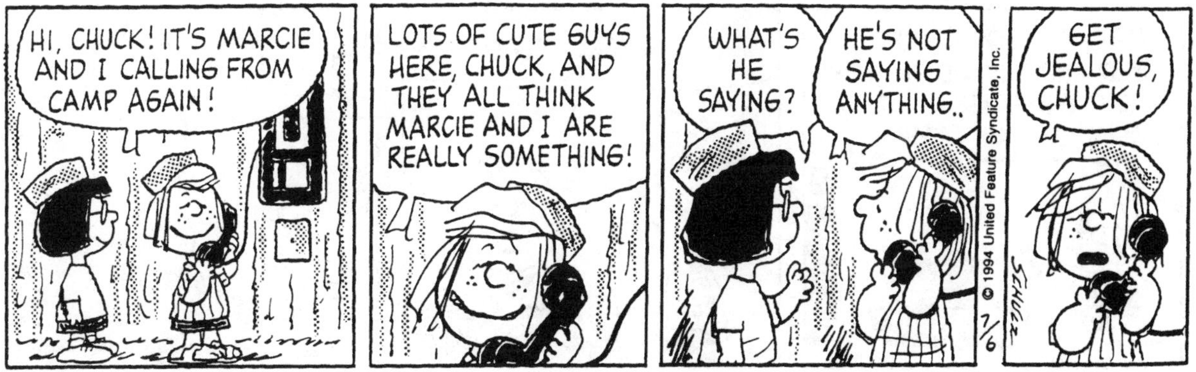
HI, CHUCK! IT'S MARCIE AND I CALLING FROM CAMP AGAIN!
LOTS OF CUTE GUYS HERE, CHUCK, AND THEY ALL THINK MARCIE AND I ARE REALLY SOMETHING!
WHAT'S HE SAYING?
HE'S NOT SAYING ANYTHING..
© 1994 United Feature Syndicate, Inc.
7/6
SCHULZ
GET JEALOUS, CHUCK!

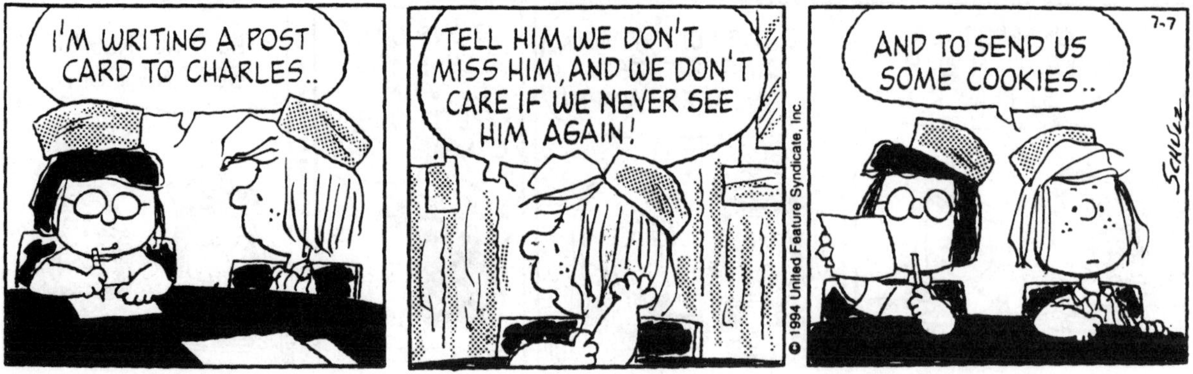
I'M WRITING A POST CARD TO CHARLES..
TELL HIM WE DON'T MISS HIM, AND WE DON'T CARE IF WE NEVER SEE HIM AGAIN!
AND TO SEND US SOME COOKIES..
7-7
SCHULZ
© 1994 United Feature Syndicate, Inc.

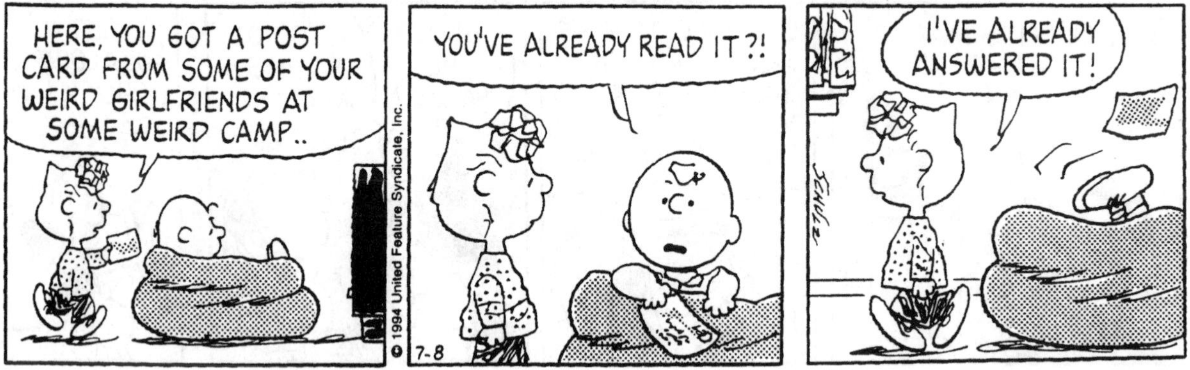
HERE, YOU GOT A POST CARD FROM SOME OF YOUR WEIRD GIRLFRIENDS AT SOME WEIRD CAMP..
YOU'VE ALREADY READ IT?!
I'VE ALREADY ANSWERED IT!
7-8
SCHULZ
© 1994 United Feature Syndicate, Inc.

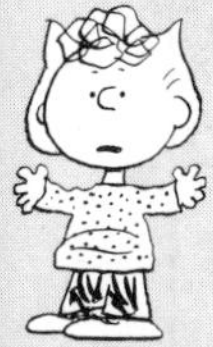

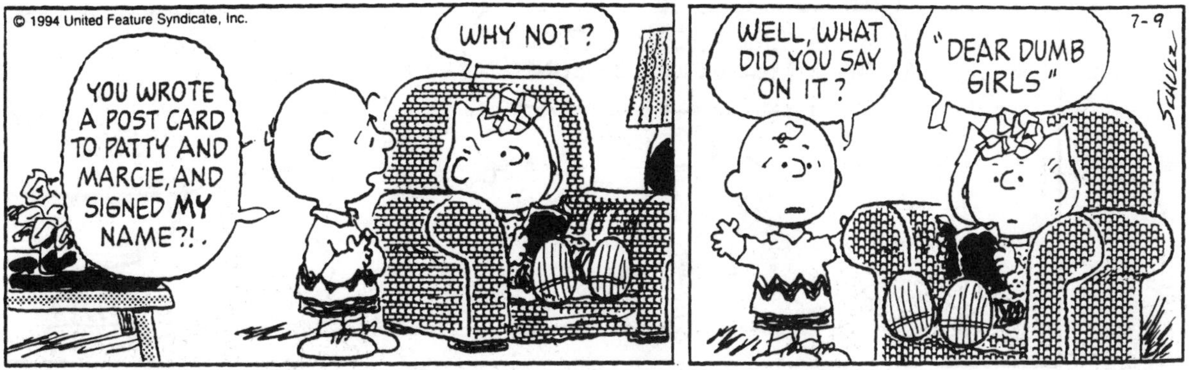
© 1994 United Feature Syndicate, Inc.
YOU WROTE A POST CARD TO PATTY AND MARCIE, AND SIGNED MY NAME?!..
WHY NOT?
7-9
WELL, WHAT DID YOU SAY ON IT?
"DEAR DUMB GIRLS"
SCHULZ

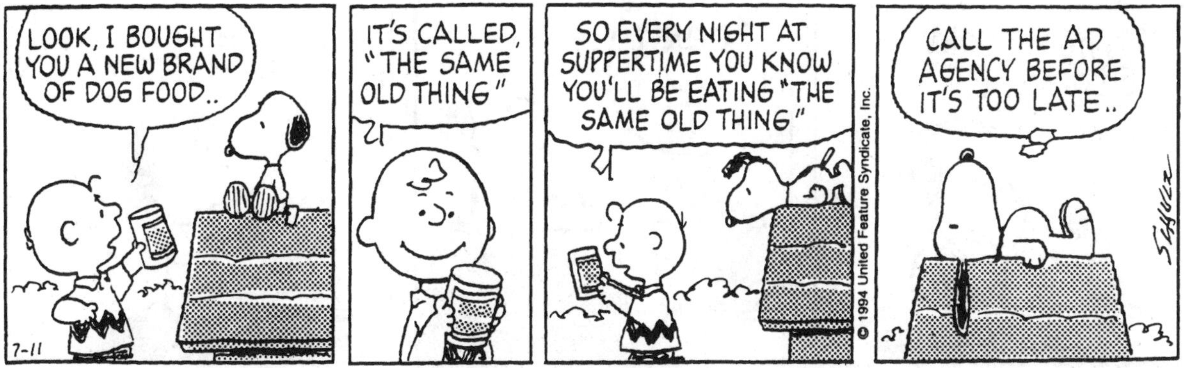
LOOK, I BOUGHT YOU A NEW BRAND OF DOG FOOD..
7-11
IT'S CALLED, "THE SAME OLD THING"
SO EVERY NIGHT AT SUPPERTIME YOU KNOW YOU'LL BE EATING "THE SAME OLD THING"
© 1994 United Feature Syndicate, Inc.
CALL THE AD AGENCY BEFORE IT'S TOO LATE..
SCHULZ

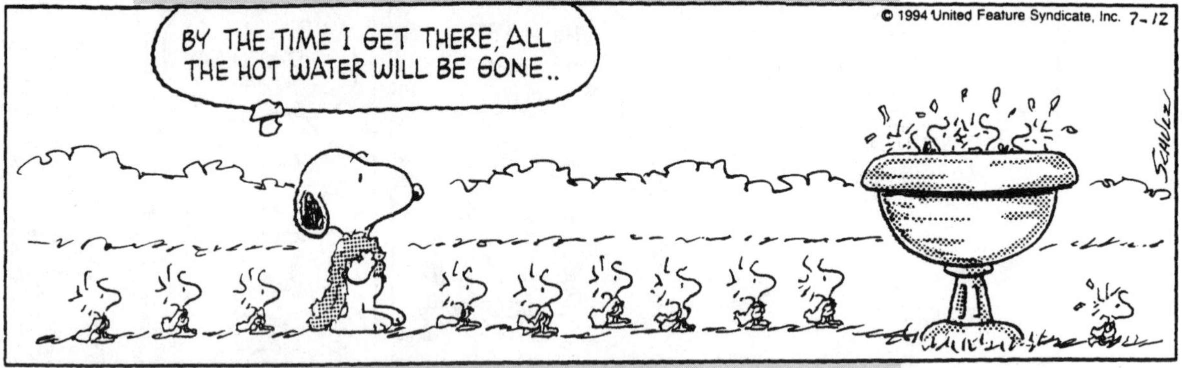
© 1994 United Feature Syndicate, Inc. 7-12
BY THE TIME I GET THERE, ALL THE HOT WATER WILL BE GONE..
SCHULZ

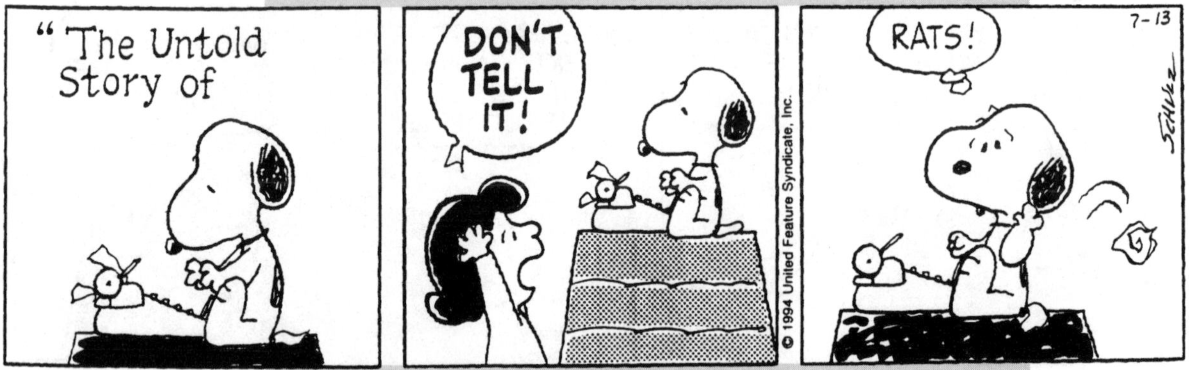
"The Untold Story of
DON'T TELL IT!
© 1994 United Feature Syndicate, Inc.
7-13
RATS!
SCHULZ

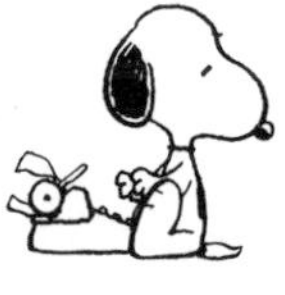

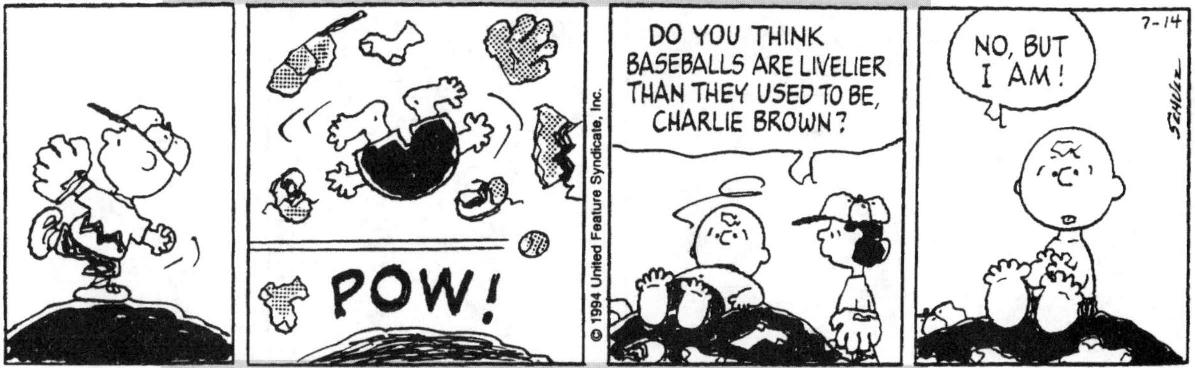
DO YOU THINK BASEBALLS ARE LIVELIER THAN THEY USED TO BE, CHARLIE BROWN?
NO, BUT I AM!
POW!
7-14
SCHULZ
© 1994 United Feature Syndicate, Inc.

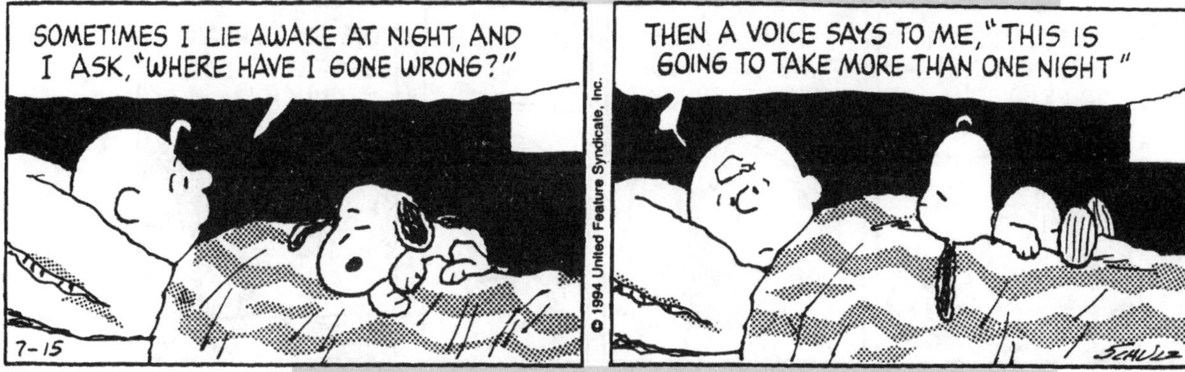
SOMETIMES I LIE AWAKE AT NIGHT, AND I ASK, "WHERE HAVE I GONE WRONG?"
THEN A VOICE SAYS TO ME, "THIS IS GOING TO TAKE MORE THAN ONE NIGHT"
7-15
SCHULZ
© 1994 United Feature Syndicate, Inc.

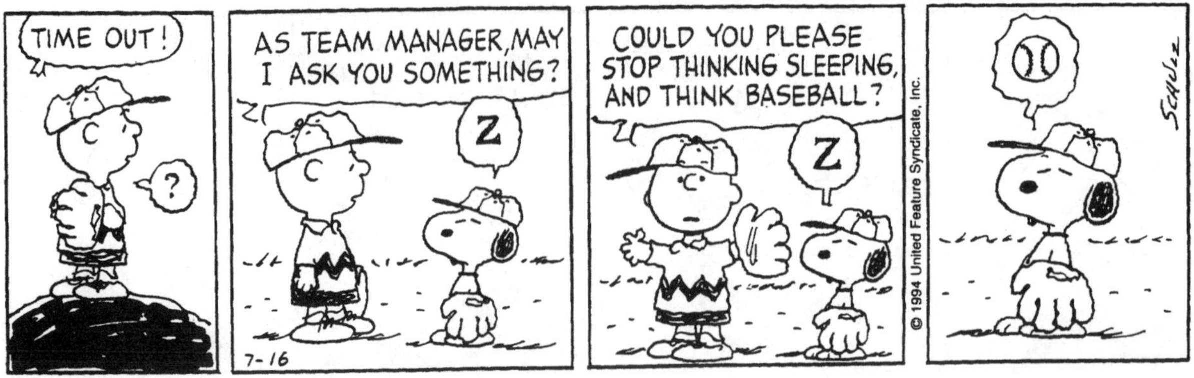
TIME OUT!
?
AS TEAM MANAGER, MAY I ASK YOU SOMETHING?
Z
7-16
COULD YOU PLEASE STOP THINKING SLEEPING, AND THINK BASEBALL?
Z
© 1994 United Feature Syndicate, Inc.
SCHULZ

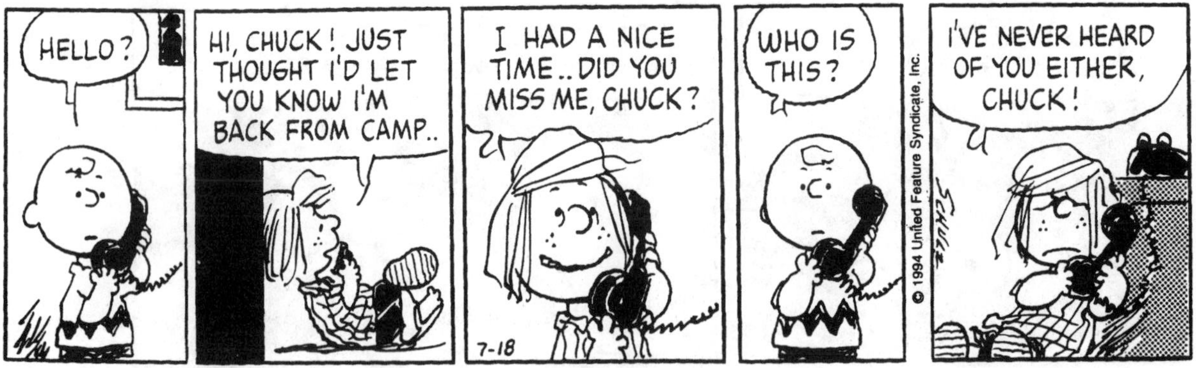
HELLO?
HI, CHUCK! JUST THOUGHT I'D LET YOU KNOW I'M BACK FROM CAMP..
I HAD A NICE TIME.. DID YOU MISS ME, CHUCK?
7-18
WHO IS THIS?
© 1994 United Feature Syndicate, Inc.
SCHULZ
I'VE NEVER HEARD OF YOU EITHER, CHUCK!

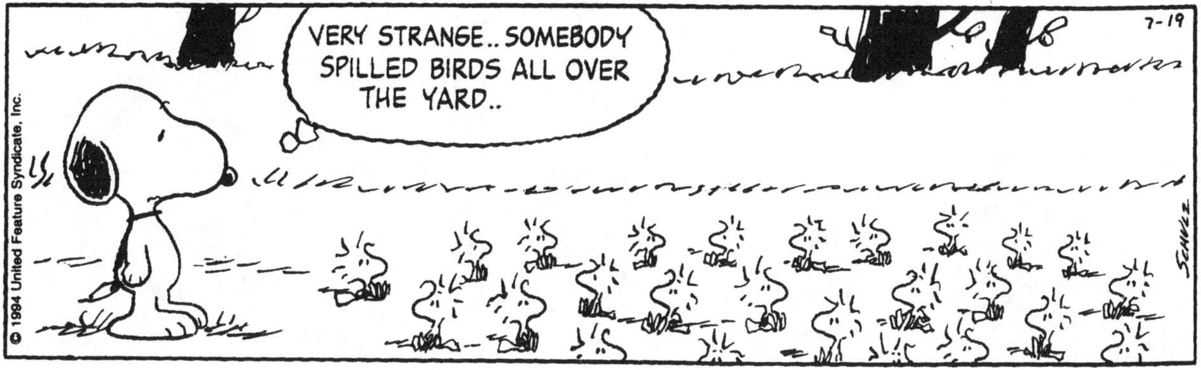
7-19
VERY STRANGE.. SOMEBODY SPILLED BIRDS ALL OVER THE YARD..
© 1994 United Feature Syndicate, Inc.
SCHULZ

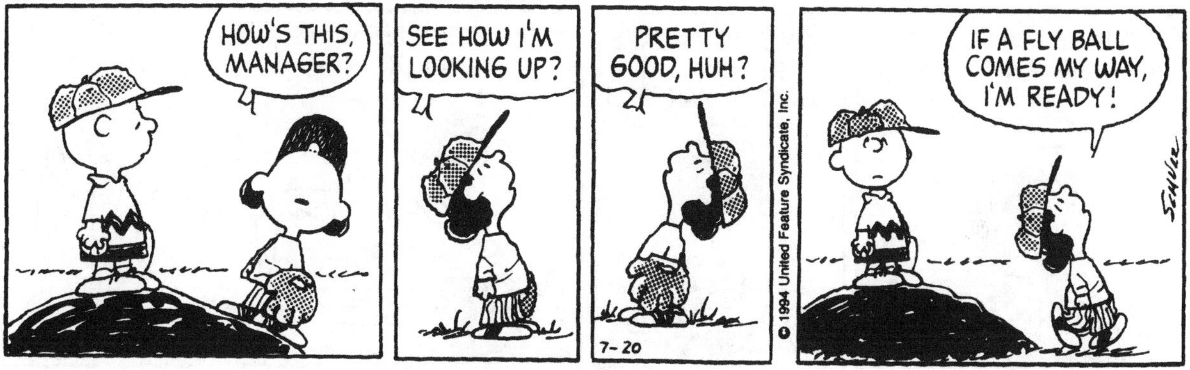
HOW'S THIS, MANAGER?
SEE HOW I'M LOOKING UP?
PRETTY GOOD, HUH?
7-20
© 1994 United Feature Syndicate, Inc.
IF A FLY BALL COMES MY WAY, I'M READY!
SCHULZ

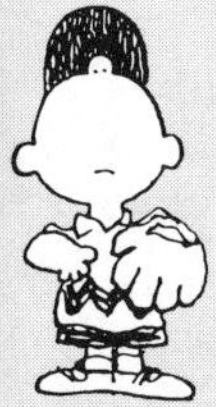

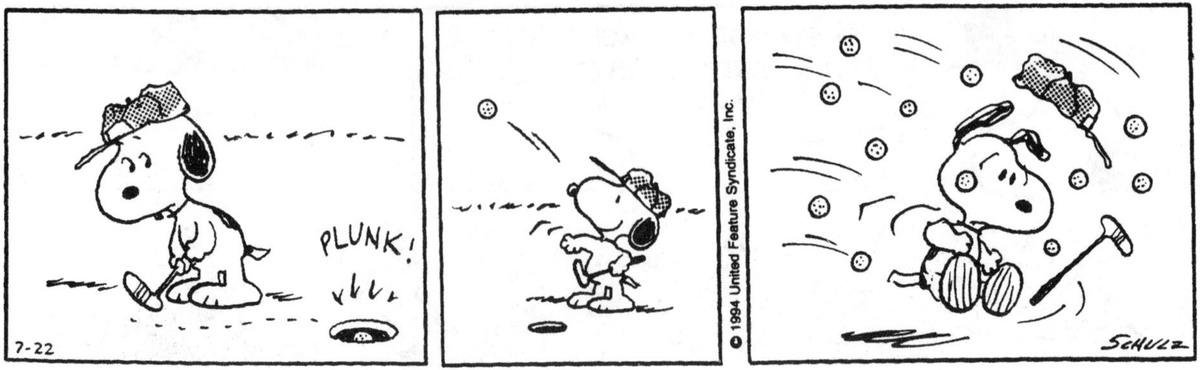
7-22
PLUNK!
© 1994 United Feature Syndicate, Inc.
SCHULZ

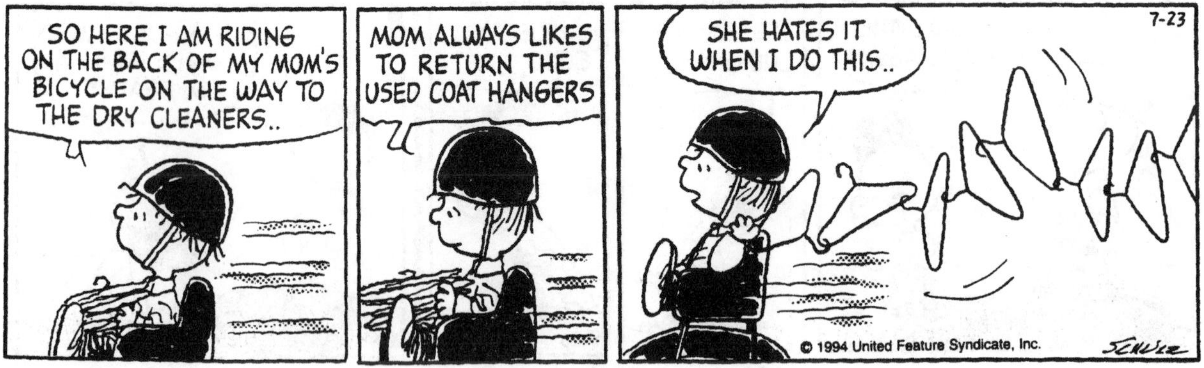
SO HERE I AM RIDING ON THE BACK OF MY MOM'S BICYCLE ON THE WAY TO THE DRY CLEANERS..
MOM ALWAYS LIKES TO RETURN THE USED COAT HANGERS
7-23
SHE HATES IT WHEN I DO THIS..
© 1994 United Feature Syndicate, Inc.
SCHULZ

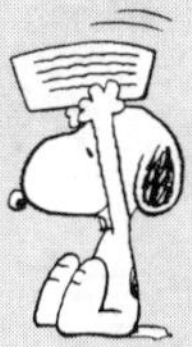

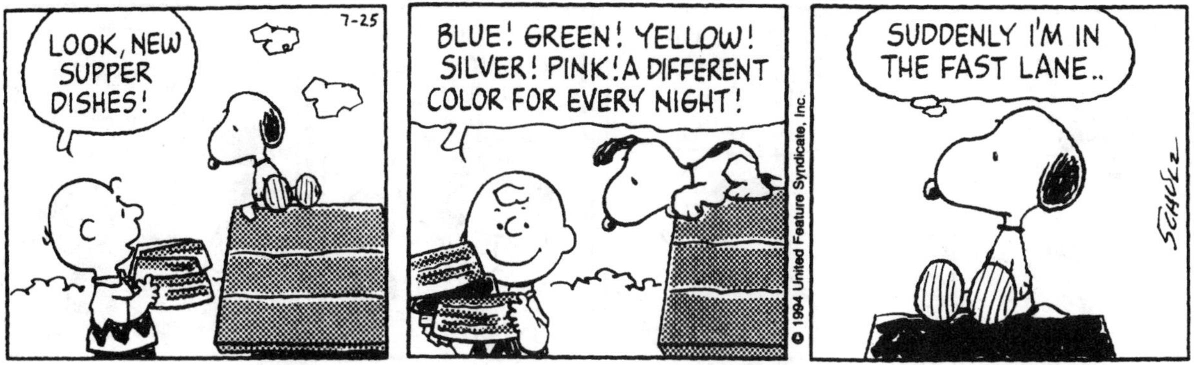

7-25
LOOK, NEW SUPPER DISHES!
BLUE! GREEN! YELLOW! SILVER! PINK! A DIFFERENT COLOR FOR EVERY NIGHT!
© 1994 United Feature Syndicate, Inc.
SUDDENLY I'M IN THE FAST LANE..
SCHULZ

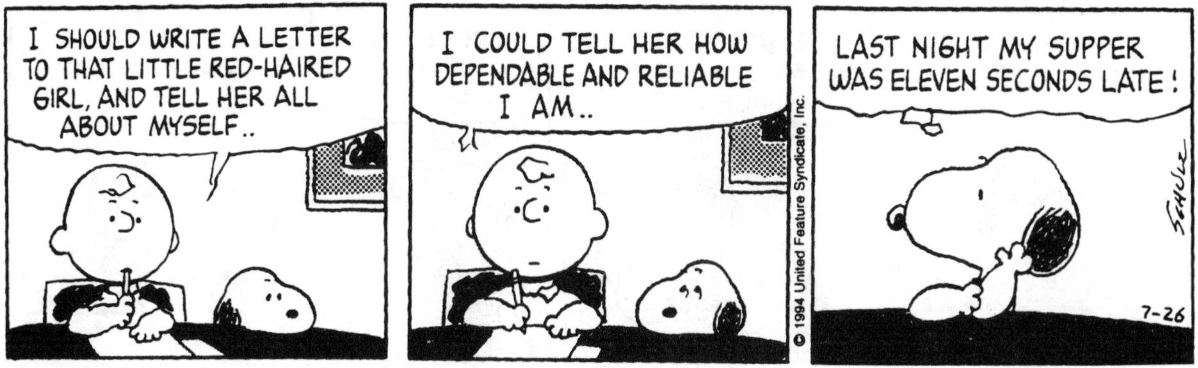

I SHOULD WRITE A LETTER TO THAT LITTLE RED-HAIRED GIRL, AND TELL HER ALL ABOUT MYSELF..
I COULD TELL HER HOW DEPENDABLE AND RELIABLE I AM..
© 1994 United Feature Syndicate, Inc.
LAST NIGHT MY SUPPER WAS ELEVEN SECONDS LATE!
SCHULZ
7-26

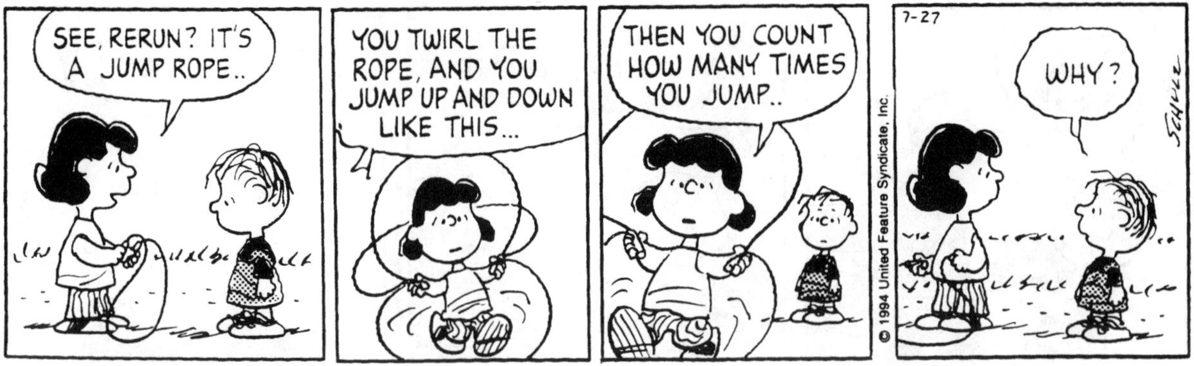
SEE, RERUN? IT'S A JUMP ROPE..
YOU TWIRL THE ROPE, AND YOU JUMP UP AND DOWN LIKE THIS...
THEN YOU COUNT HOW MANY TIMES YOU JUMP..
© 1994 United Feature Syndicate, Inc.
7-27
WHY?
SCHULZ

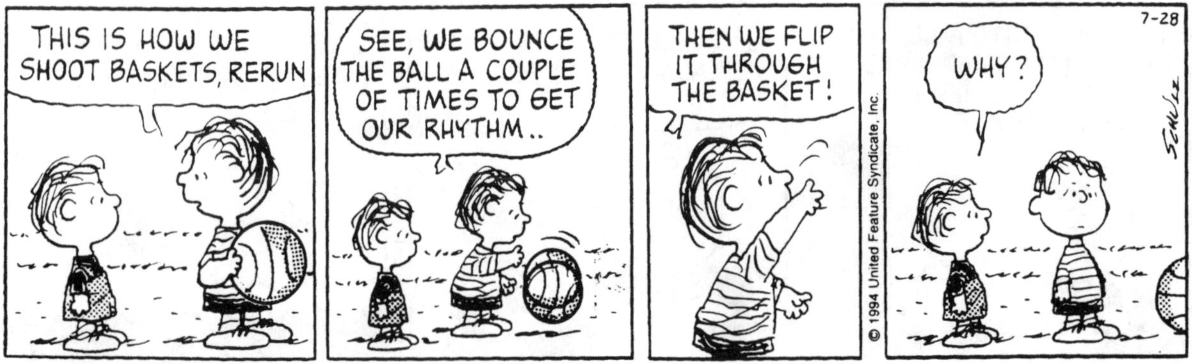
THIS IS HOW WE SHOOT BASKETS, RERUN
SEE, WE BOUNCE THE BALL A COUPLE OF TIMES TO GET OUR RHYTHM..
THEN WE FLIP IT THROUGH THE BASKET!
© 1994 United Feature Syndicate, Inc.
7-28
WHY?
SCHULZ

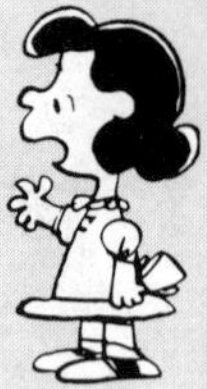

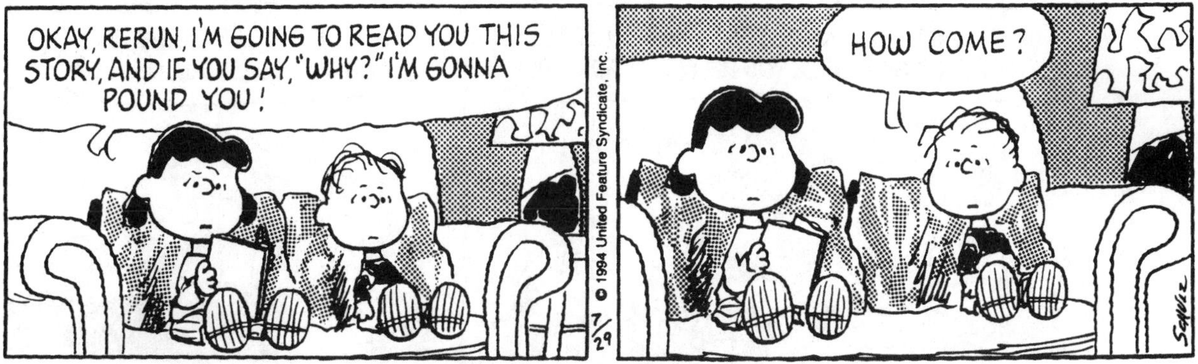
OKAY, RERUN, I'M GOING TO READ YOU THIS STORY, AND IF YOU SAY, "WHY?" I'M GONNA POUND YOU!
HOW COME?
© 1994 United Feature Syndicate, Inc.
7/29
SCHULZ

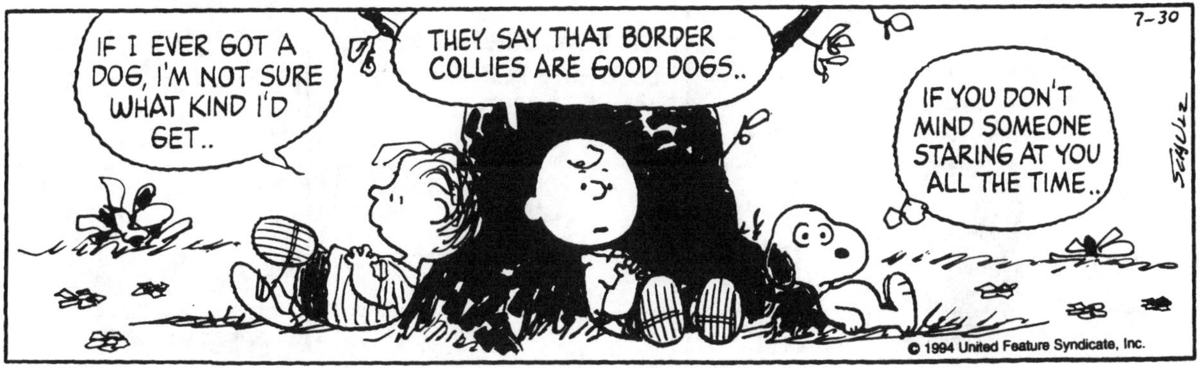
7-30
IF I EVER GOT A DOG, I'M NOT SURE WHAT KIND I'D GET..
THEY SAY THAT BORDER COLLIES ARE GOOD DOGS..
IF YOU DON'T MIND SOMEONE STARING AT YOU ALL THE TIME..
SCHULZ
© 1994 United Feature Syndicate, Inc.

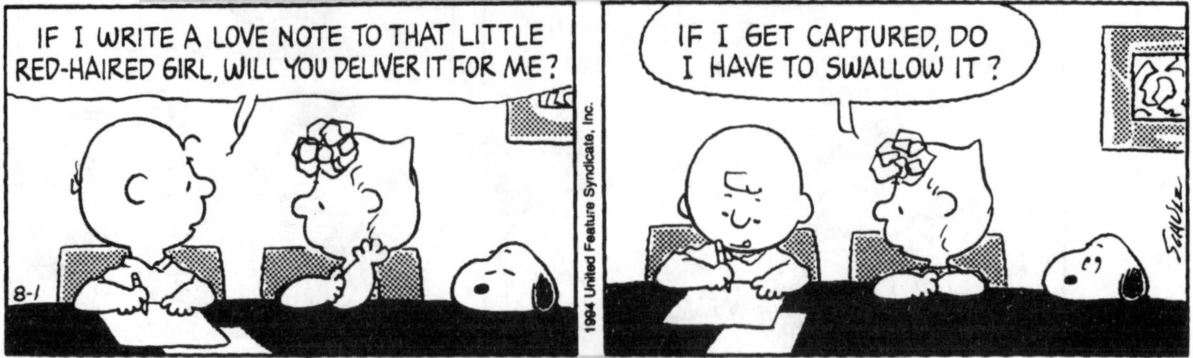
IF I WRITE A LOVE NOTE TO THAT LITTLE RED-HAIRED GIRL, WILL YOU DELIVER IT FOR ME?
8-1
1994 United Feature Syndicate, Inc.
IF I GET CAPTURED, DO I HAVE TO SWALLOW IT?
SCHULZ

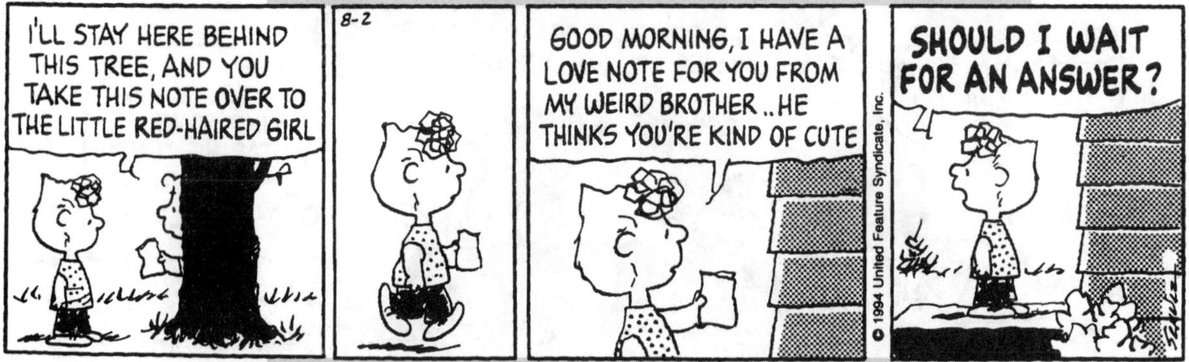
I'LL STAY HERE BEHIND THIS TREE, AND YOU TAKE THIS NOTE OVER TO THE LITTLE RED-HAIRED GIRL
8-2
GOOD MORNING, I HAVE A LOVE NOTE FOR YOU FROM MY WEIRD BROTHER..HE THINKS YOU'RE KIND OF CUTE
© 1994 United Feature Syndicate, Inc.
SHOULD I WAIT FOR AN ANSWER?
SCHULZ

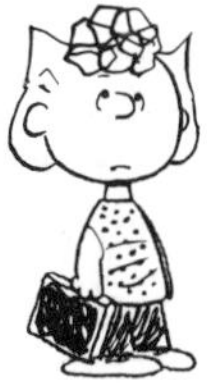

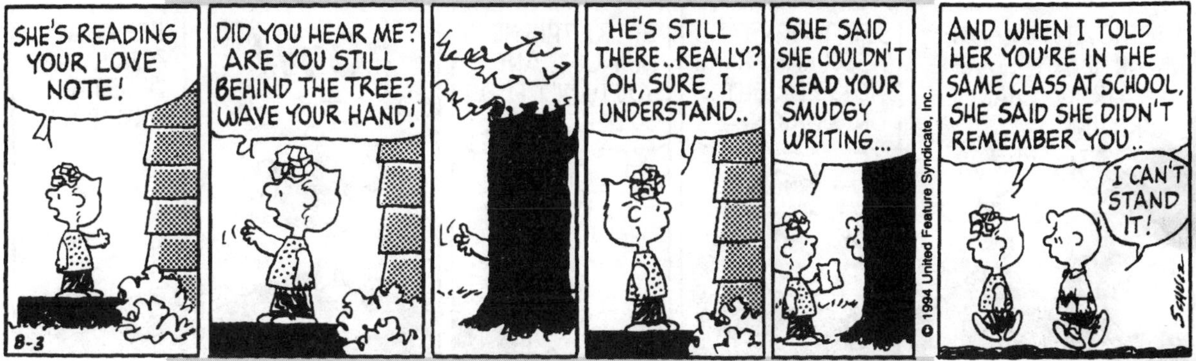
SHE'S READING YOUR LOVE NOTE!
8-3
DID YOU HEAR ME? ARE YOU STILL BEHIND THE TREE? WAVE YOUR HAND!
HE'S STILL THERE..REALLY? OH, SURE, I UNDERSTAND..
SHE SAID SHE COULDN'T READ YOUR SMUDGY WRITING...
© 1994 United Feature Syndicate, Inc.
AND WHEN I TOLD HER YOU'RE IN THE SAME CLASS AT SCHOOL, SHE SAID SHE DIDN'T REMEMBER YOU..
I CAN'T STAND IT!
SCHULZ

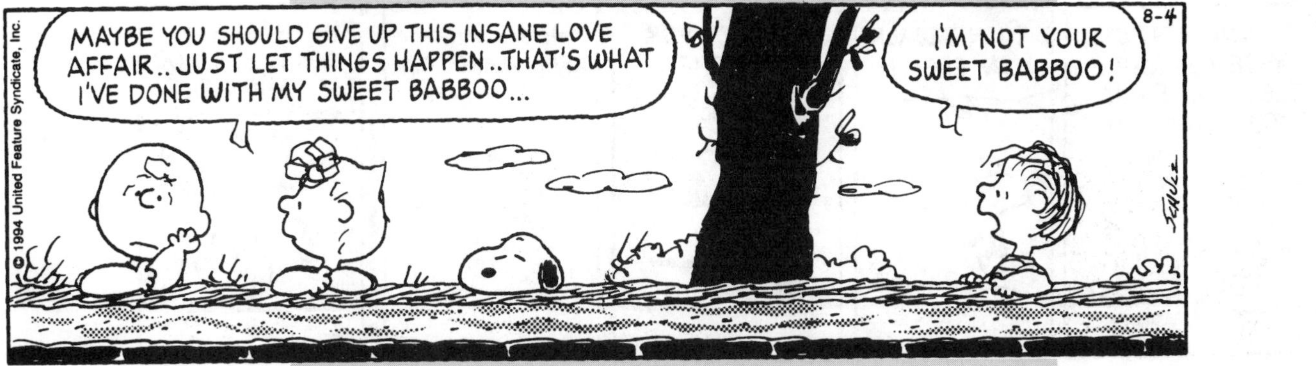
© 1994 United Feature Syndicate, Inc.
MAYBE YOU SHOULD GIVE UP THIS INSANE LOVE AFFAIR.. JUST LET THINGS HAPPEN..THAT'S WHAT I'VE DONE WITH MY SWEET BABBOO...
8-4
I'M NOT YOUR SWEET BABBOO!
SCHULZ

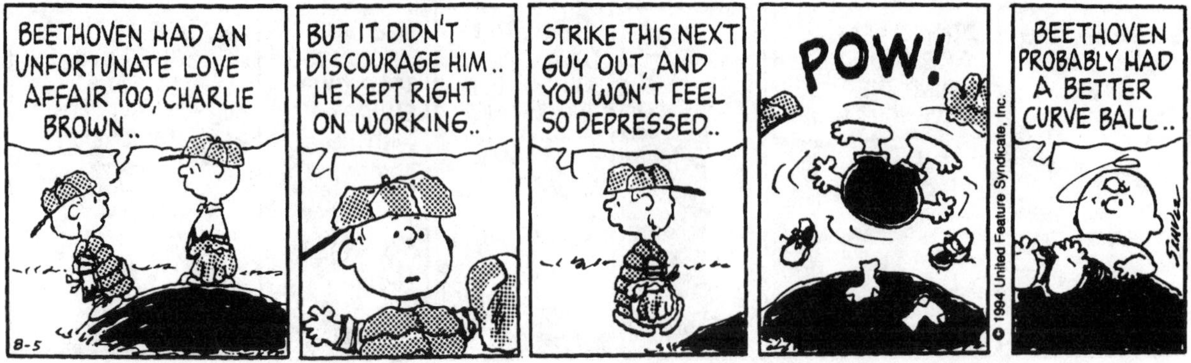
BEETHOVEN HAD AN UNFORTUNATE LOVE AFFAIR TOO, CHARLIE BROWN..
8-5
BUT IT DIDN'T DISCOURAGE HIM.. HE KEPT RIGHT ON WORKING..
STRIKE THIS NEXT GUY OUT, AND YOU WON'T FEEL SO DEPRESSED..
POW!
© 1994 United Feature Syndicate, Inc.
BEETHOVEN PROBABLY HAD A BETTER CURVE BALL..

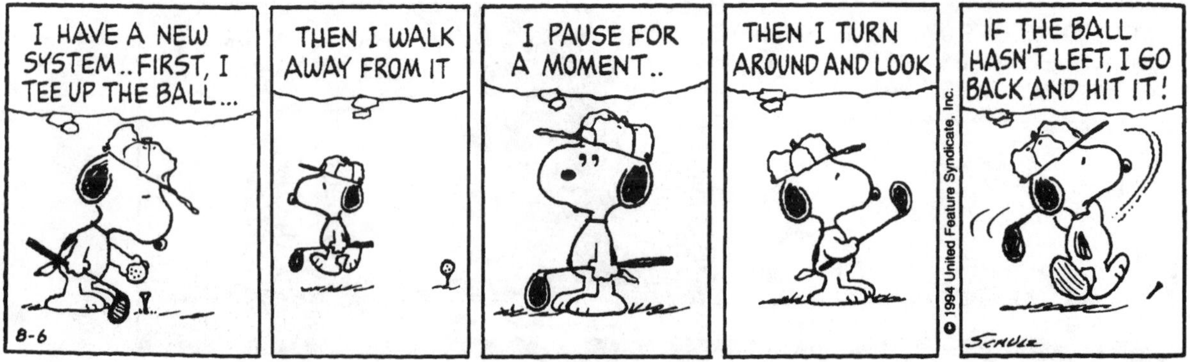
I HAVE A NEW SYSTEM.. FIRST, I TEE UP THE BALL...
8-6
THEN I WALK AWAY FROM IT
I PAUSE FOR A MOMENT..
THEN I TURN AROUND AND LOOK
© 1994 United Feature Syndicate, Inc.
IF THE BALL HASN'T LEFT, I GO BACK AND HIT IT!

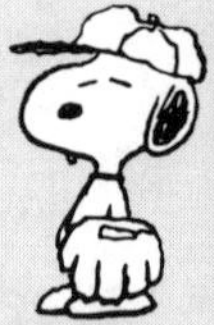

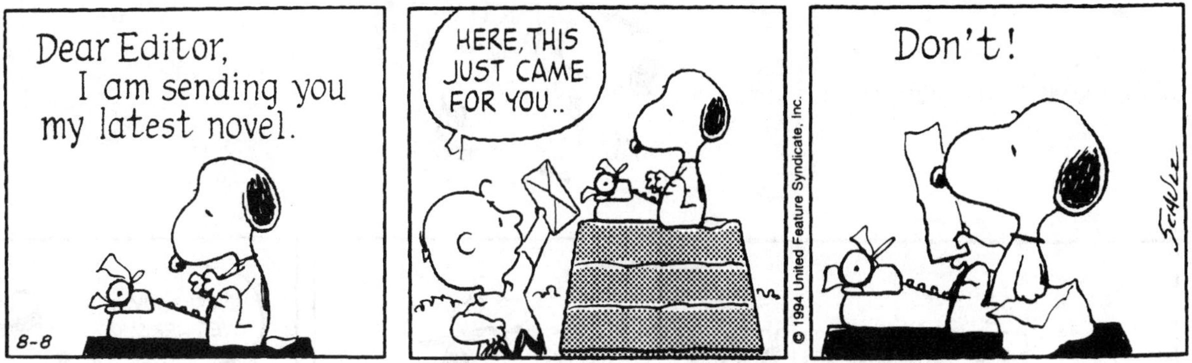
Dear Editor,
I am sending you
my latest novel.
8-8
HERE, THIS
JUST CAME
FOR YOU..
© 1994 United Feature Syndicate, Inc.
Don't!
SCHULZ

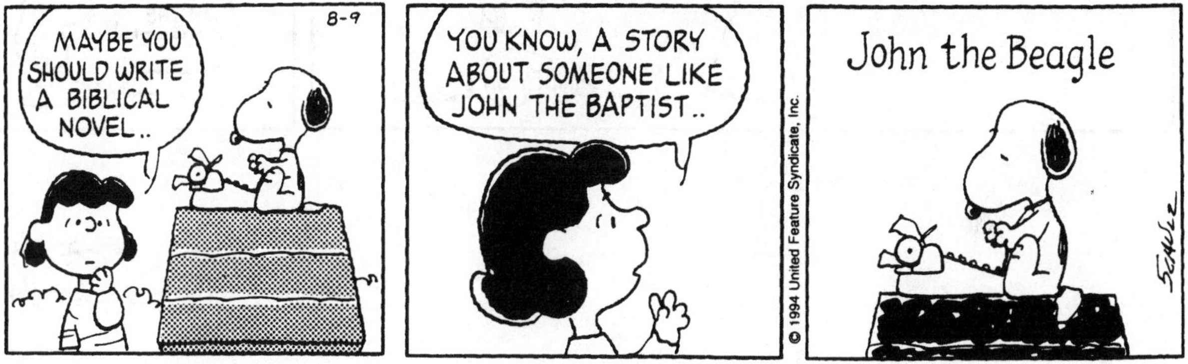
8-9
MAYBE YOU
SHOULD WRITE
A BIBLICAL
NOVEL..
YOU KNOW, A STORY
ABOUT SOMEONE LIKE
JOHN THE BAPTIST..
© 1994 United Feature Syndicate, Inc.
John the Beagle
SCHULZ

PEANUTS
by SCHULZ
EVERYBODY OVER HERE!
ON THE DOUBLE!

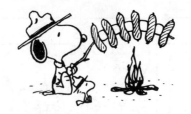

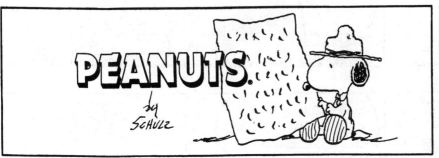

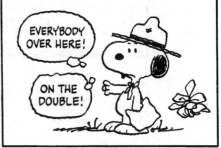

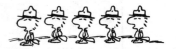

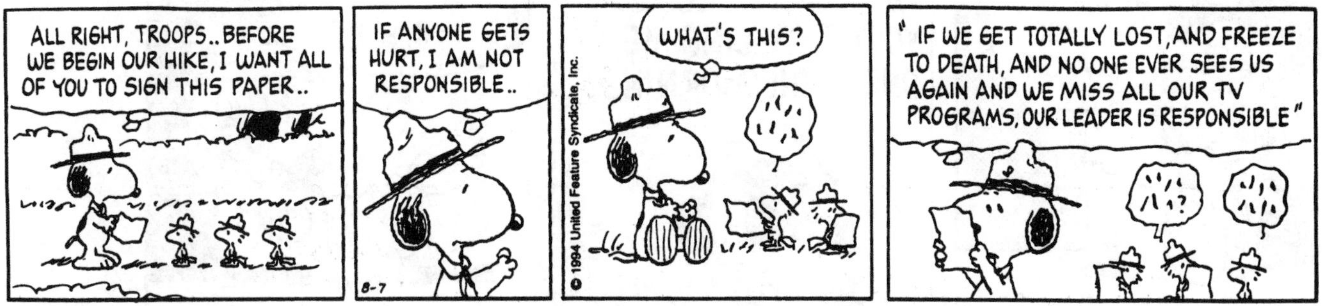
ALL RIGHT, TROOPS.. BEFORE WE BEGIN OUR HIKE, I WANT ALL OF YOU TO SIGN THIS PAPER..
IF ANYONE GETS HURT, I AM NOT RESPONSIBLE..
8-7
© 1994 United Feature Syndicate, Inc.
WHAT'S THIS?
" IF WE GET TOTALLY LOST, AND FREEZE TO DEATH, AND NO ONE EVER SEES US AGAIN AND WE MISS ALL OUR TV PROGRAMS, OUR LEADER IS RESPONSIBLE"

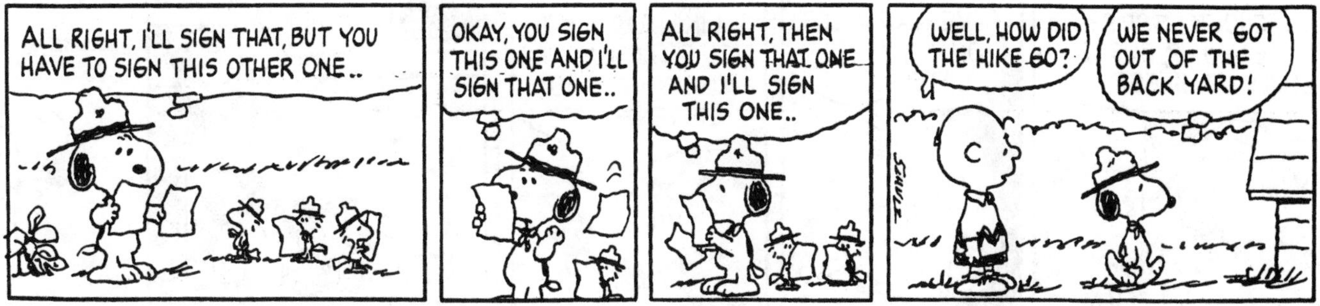
ALL RIGHT, I'LL SIGN THAT, BUT YOU HAVE TO SIGN THIS OTHER ONE..
OKAY, YOU SIGN THIS ONE AND I'LL SIGN THAT ONE..
ALL RIGHT, THEN YOU SIGN THAT ONE AND I'LL SIGN THIS ONE..
WELL, HOW DID THE HIKE GO?
WE NEVER GOT OUT OF THE BACK YARD!
SCHULZ

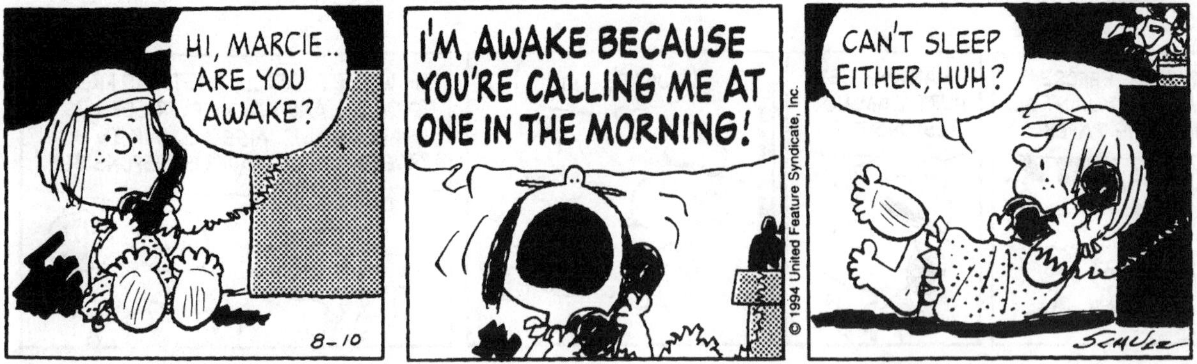

HI, MARCIE.. ARE YOU AWAKE?
8-10
I'M AWAKE BECAUSE YOU'RE CALLING ME AT ONE IN THE MORNING!
© 1994 United Feature Syndicate, Inc.
CAN'T SLEEP EITHER, HUH?
SCHULZ

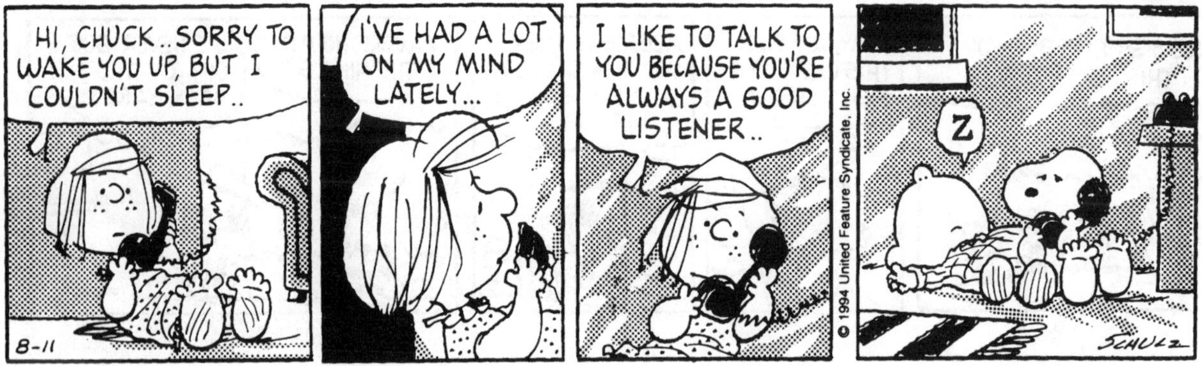

HI, CHUCK.. SORRY TO WAKE YOU UP, BUT I COULDN'T SLEEP..
8-11
I'VE HAD A LOT ON MY MIND LATELY...
I LIKE TO TALK TO YOU BECAUSE YOU'RE ALWAYS A GOOD LISTENER..
© 1994 United Feature Syndicate, Inc.
Z
SCHULZ

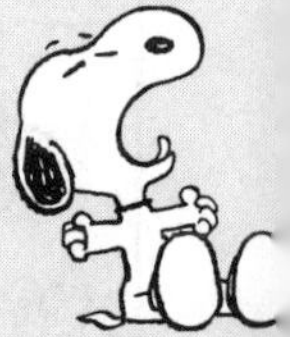

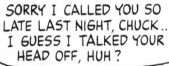
SORRY I CALLED YOU SO LATE LAST NIGHT, CHUCK.. I GUESS I TALKED YOUR HEAD OFF, HUH?

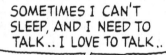
SOMETIMES I CAN'T SLEEP, AND I NEED TO TALK.. I LOVE TO TALK..

SOMETIMES I JUST NEED SOMEONE TO TALK TO..

8-12

© 1994 United Feature Syndicate, Inc.

8-13

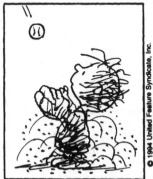

© 1994 United Feature Syndicate, Inc.

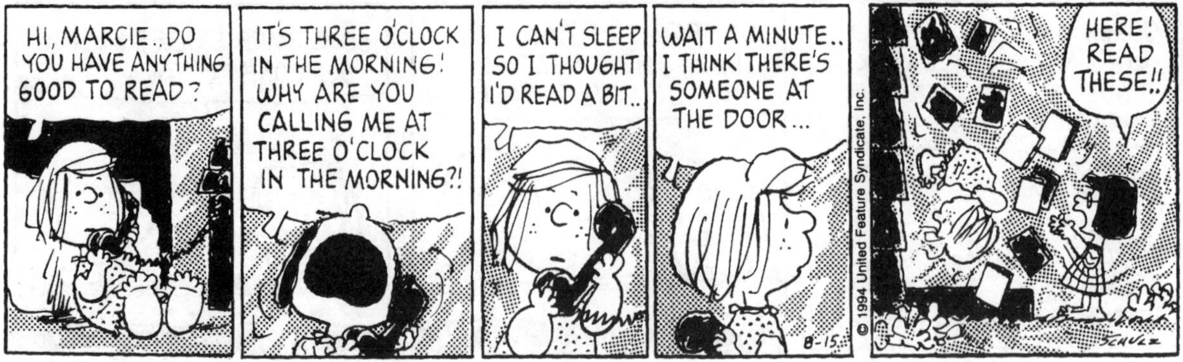
HI, MARCIE.. DO YOU HAVE ANYTHING GOOD TO READ?
IT'S THREE O'CLOCK IN THE MORNING! WHY ARE YOU CALLING ME AT THREE O'CLOCK IN THE MORNING?!
I CAN'T SLEEP SO I THOUGHT I'D READ A BIT..
WAIT A MINUTE.. I THINK THERE'S SOMEONE AT THE DOOR...
HERE! READ THESE!!
8-15
© 1994 United Feature Syndicate, Inc.
SCHULZ

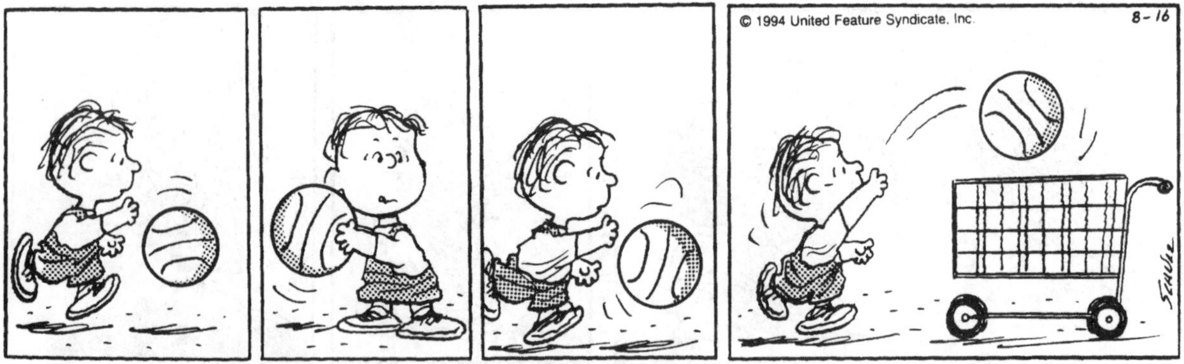
© 1994 United Feature Syndicate, Inc.
8-16
SCHULZ

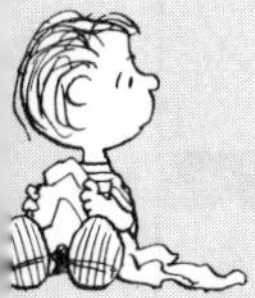

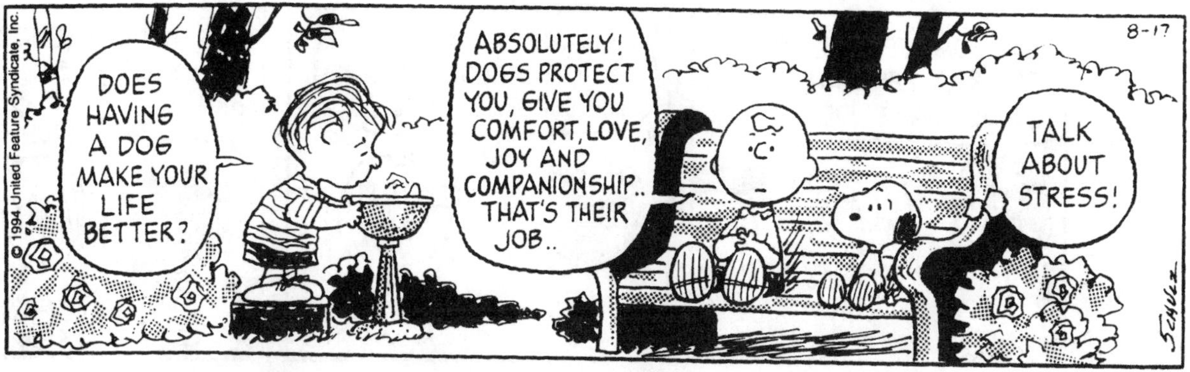

© 1994 United Feature Syndicate, Inc.
8-17
DOES HAVING A DOG MAKE YOUR LIFE BETTER?
ABSOLUTELY! DOGS PROTECT YOU, GIVE YOU COMFORT, LOVE, JOY AND COMPANIONSHIP.. THAT'S THEIR JOB..
TALK ABOUT STRESS!
SCHULZ

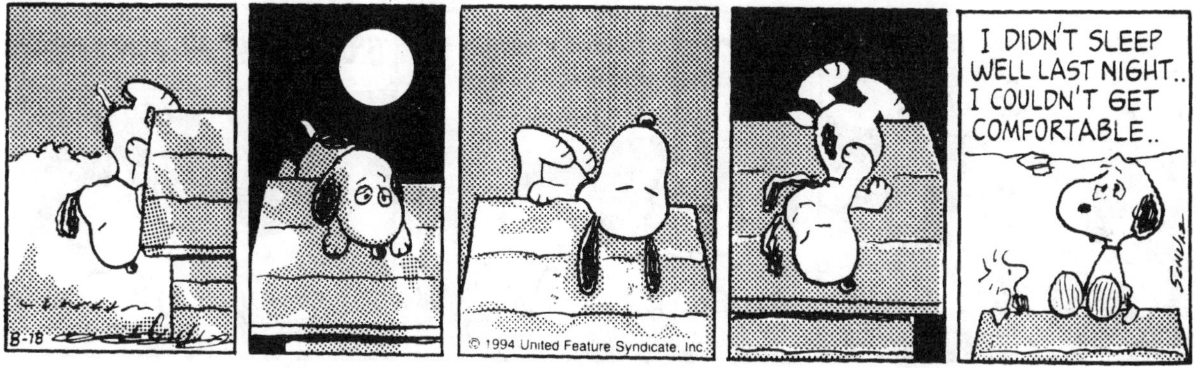

8-18
© 1994 United Feature Syndicate, Inc.
I DIDN'T SLEEP WELL LAST NIGHT.. I COULDN'T GET COMFORTABLE..
SCHULZ

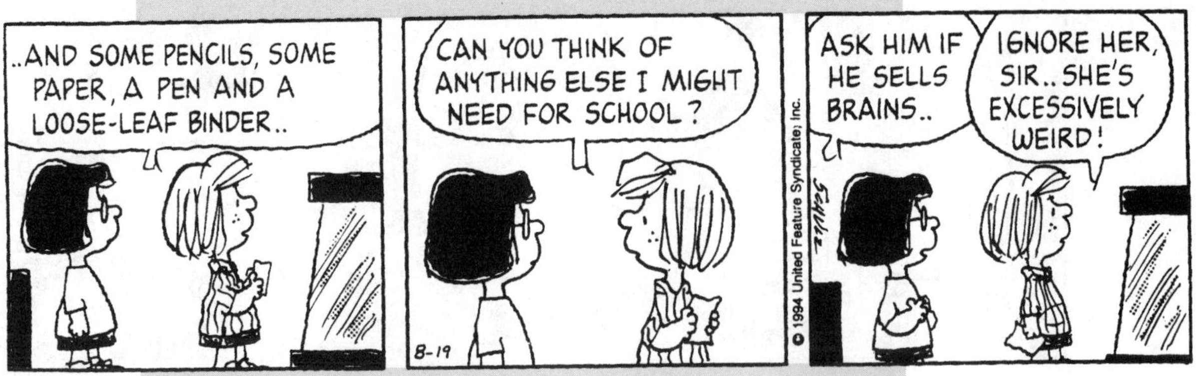
..AND SOME PENCILS, SOME PAPER, A PEN AND A LOOSE-LEAF BINDER..
CAN YOU THINK OF ANYTHING ELSE I MIGHT NEED FOR SCHOOL?
8-19
ASK HIM IF HE SELLS BRAINS..
IGNORE HER, SIR..SHE'S EXCESSIVELY WEIRD!
© 1994 United Feature Syndicate, Inc.
SCHULZ

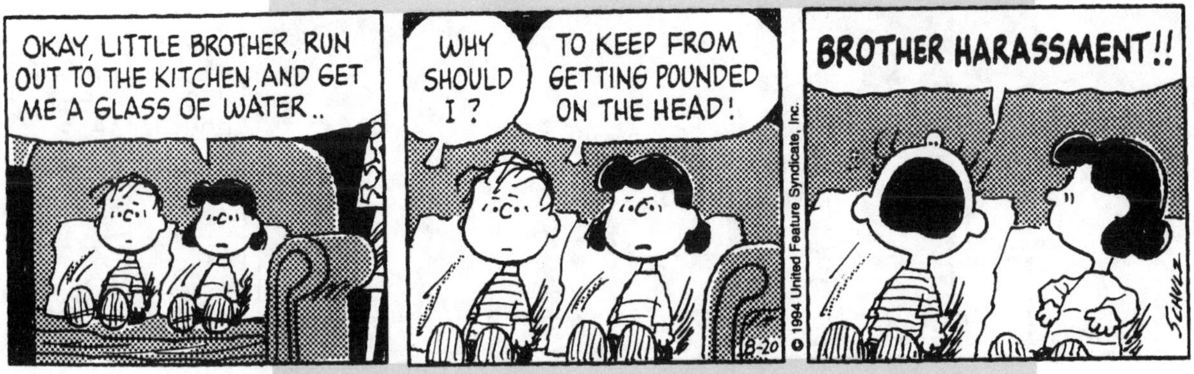
OKAY, LITTLE BROTHER, RUN OUT TO THE KITCHEN, AND GET ME A GLASS OF WATER..
WHY SHOULD I?
TO KEEP FROM GETTING POUNDED ON THE HEAD!
8-20
© 1994 United Feature Syndicate, Inc.
BROTHER HARASSMENT!!
SCHULZ

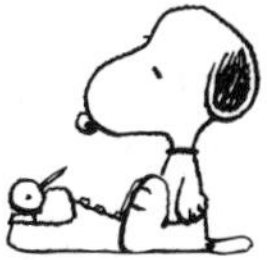

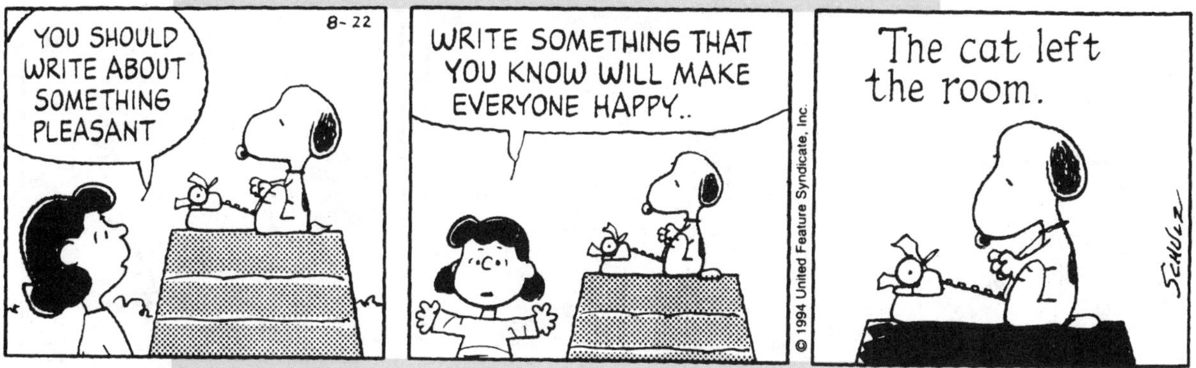
8-22
YOU SHOULD WRITE ABOUT SOMETHING PLEASANT
WRITE SOMETHING THAT YOU KNOW WILL MAKE EVERYONE HAPPY..
© 1994 United Feature Syndicate, Inc.
The cat left the room.
SCHULZ

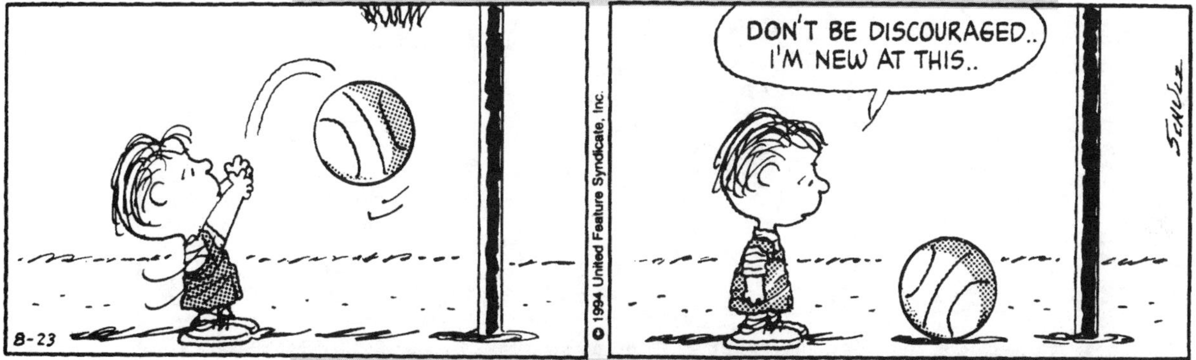
8-23
© 1994 United Feature Syndicate, Inc.
DON'T BE DISCOURAGED.. I'M NEW AT THIS..
SCHULZ

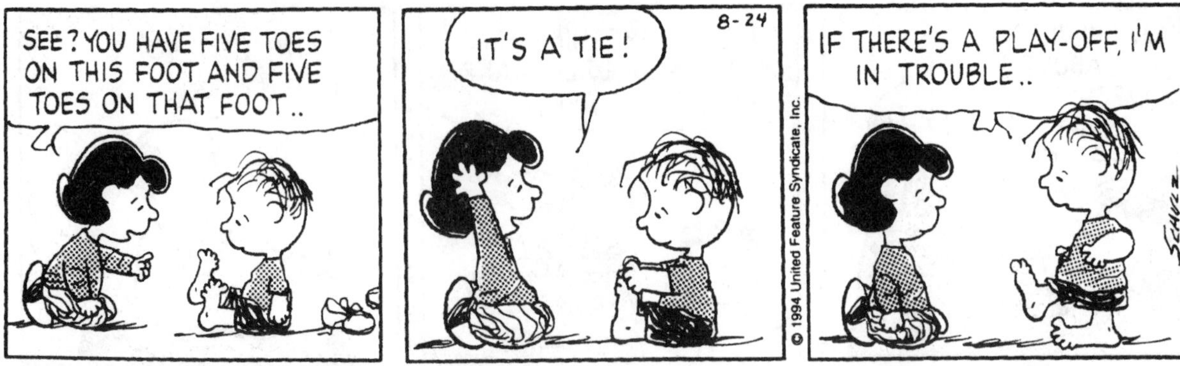
SEE? YOU HAVE FIVE TOES ON THIS FOOT AND FIVE TOES ON THAT FOOT..
8-24
IT'S A TIE!
© 1994 United Feature Syndicate, Inc.
IF THERE'S A PLAY-OFF, I'M IN TROUBLE..
SCHULZ

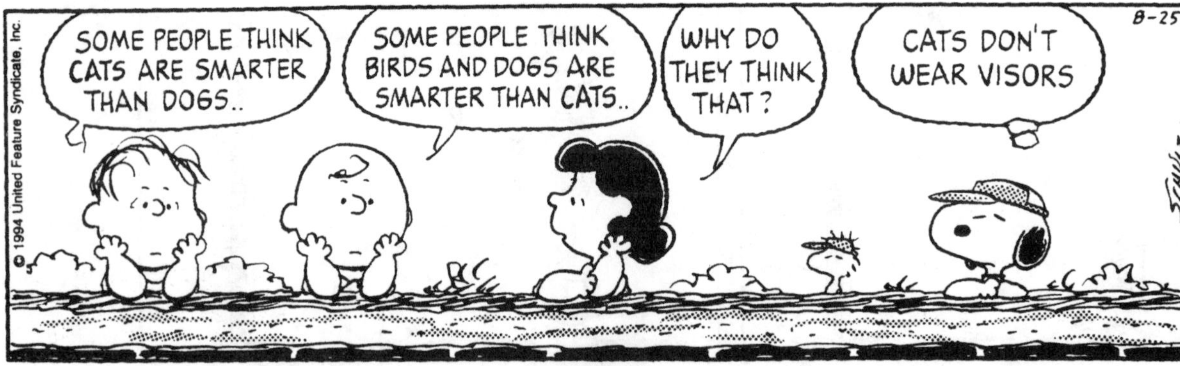
© 1994 United Feature Syndicate, Inc.
8-25
SOME PEOPLE THINK CATS ARE SMARTER THAN DOGS..
SOME PEOPLE THINK BIRDS AND DOGS ARE SMARTER THAN CATS..
WHY DO THEY THINK THAT?
CATS DON'T WEAR VISORS
SCHULZ

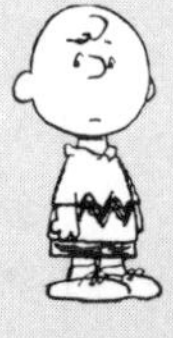

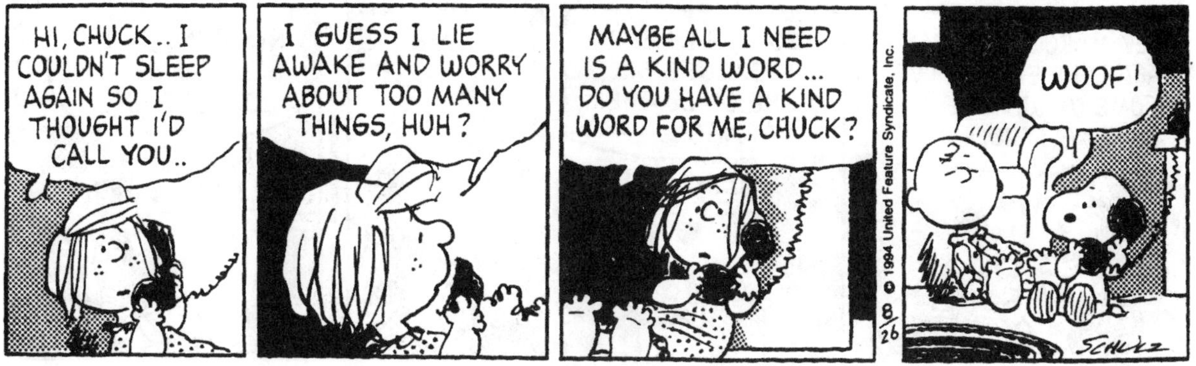
HI, CHUCK.. I COULDN'T SLEEP AGAIN SO I THOUGHT I'D CALL YOU..
I GUESS I LIE AWAKE AND WORRY ABOUT TOO MANY THINGS, HUH?
MAYBE ALL I NEED IS A KIND WORD... DO YOU HAVE A KIND WORD FOR ME, CHUCK?
© 1994 United Feature Syndicate, Inc.
8/26
WOOF!
SCHULZ

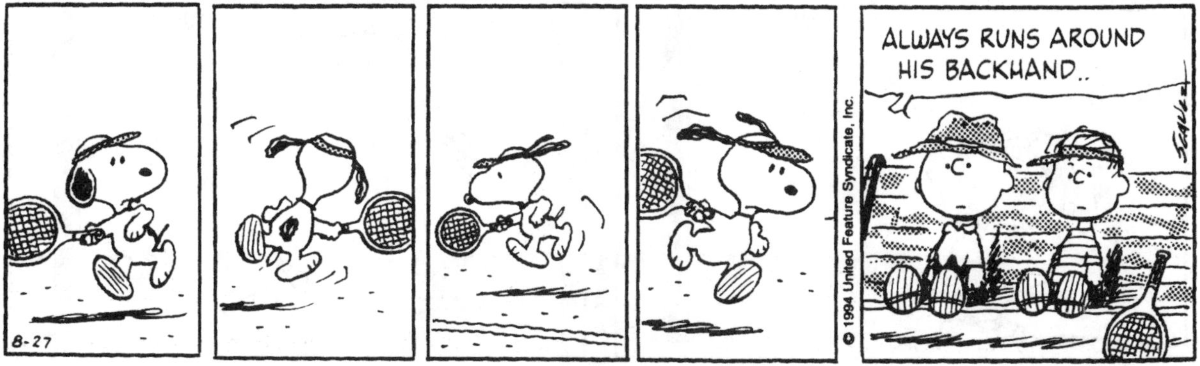
8-27
© 1994 United Feature Syndicate, Inc.
ALWAYS RUNS AROUND HIS BACKHAND..
SCHULZ

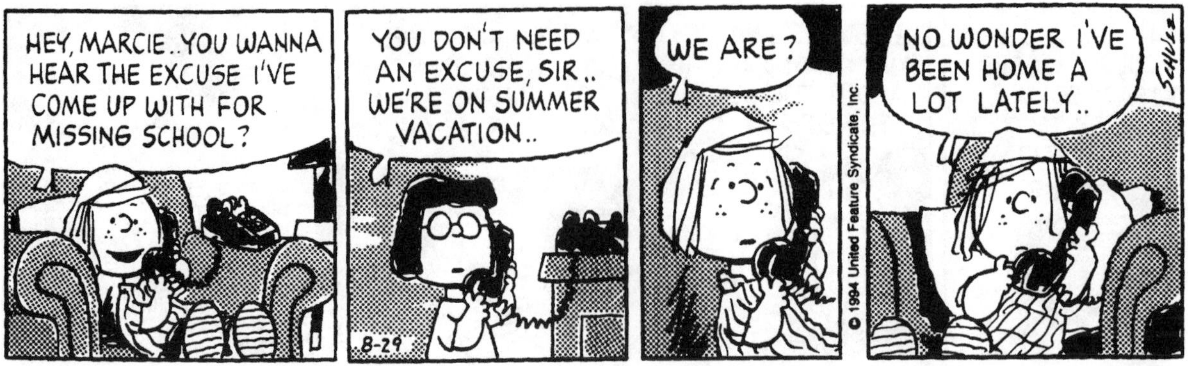
HEY, MARCIE..YOU WANNA HEAR THE EXCUSE I'VE COME UP WITH FOR MISSING SCHOOL?
YOU DON'T NEED AN EXCUSE, SIR.. WE'RE ON SUMMER VACATION..
WE ARE?
NO WONDER I'VE BEEN HOME A LOT LATELY..
8-29
© 1994 United Feature Syndicate, Inc.
SCHULZ

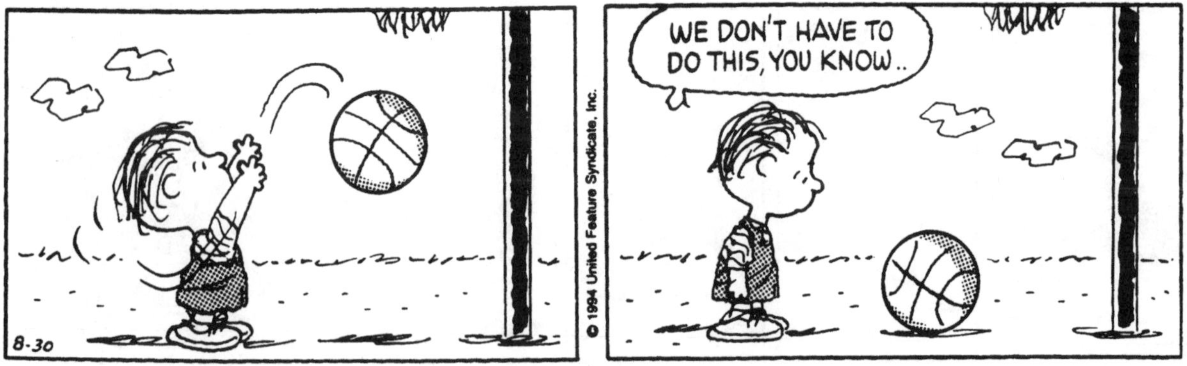
WE DON'T HAVE TO DO THIS, YOU KNOW..
8-30
© 1994 United Feature Syndicate, Inc.

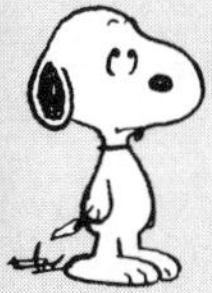

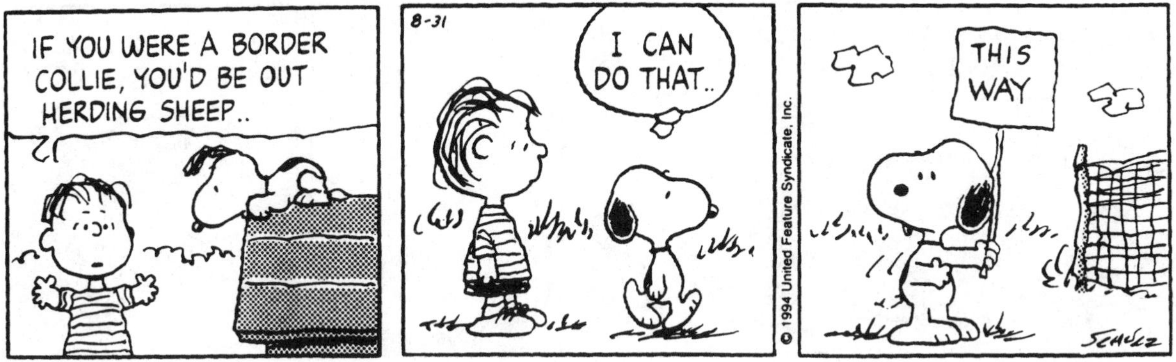
IF YOU WERE A BORDER COLLIE, YOU'D BE OUT HERDING SHEEP..
8-31
I CAN DO THAT..
© 1994 United Feature Syndicate, Inc.
THIS WAY
SCHULZ

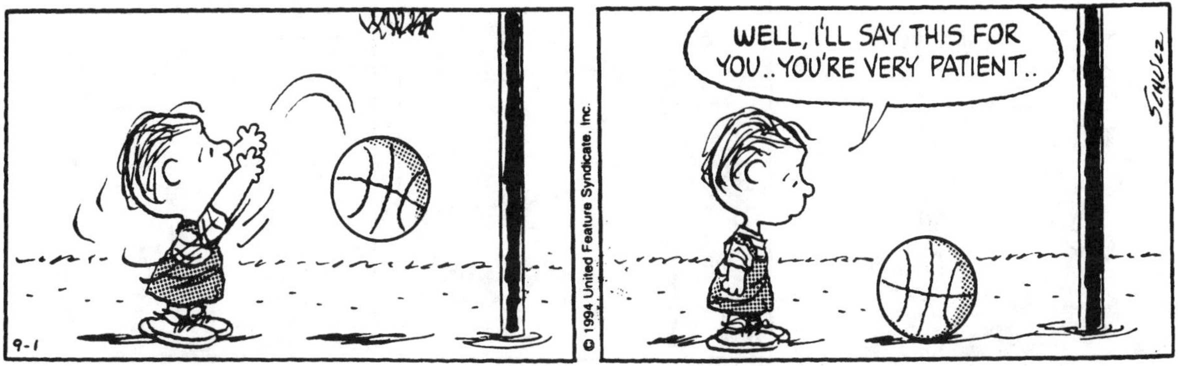
9-1
© 1994 United Feature Syndicate, Inc.
WELL, I'LL SAY THIS FOR YOU..YOU'RE VERY PATIENT..
SCHULZ

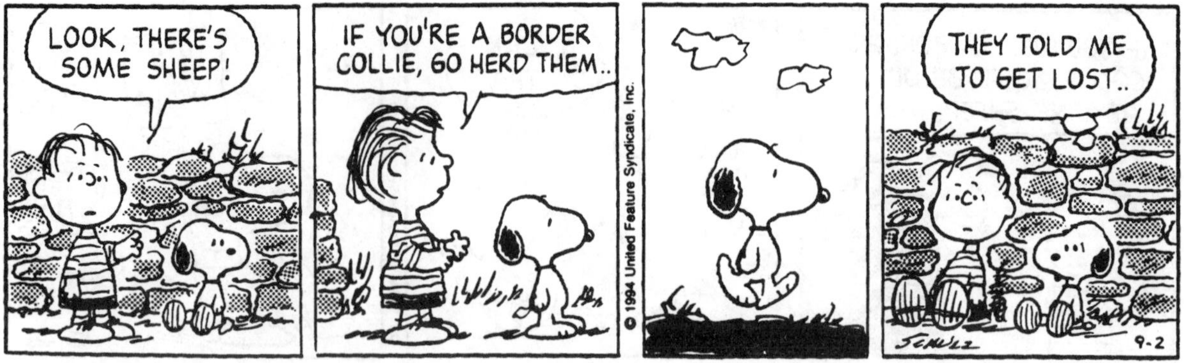
LOOK, THERE'S SOME SHEEP!
IF YOU'RE A BORDER COLLIE, GO HERD THEM..
© 1994 United Feature Syndicate, Inc.
THEY TOLD ME TO GET LOST..
SCHULZ
9-2

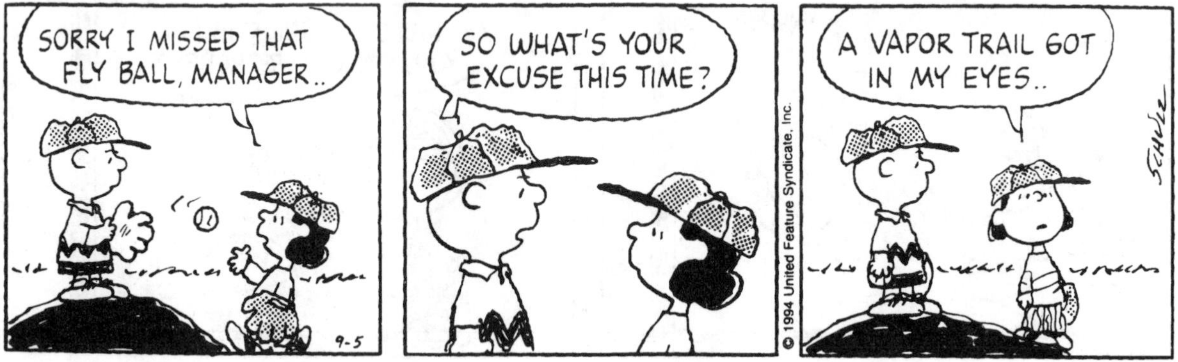
SORRY I MISSED THAT FLY BALL, MANAGER..
9-5
SO WHAT'S YOUR EXCUSE THIS TIME?
© 1994 United Feature Syndicate, Inc.
A VAPOR TRAIL GOT IN MY EYES..
SCHULZ

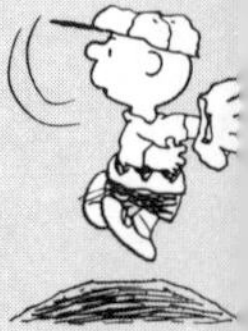

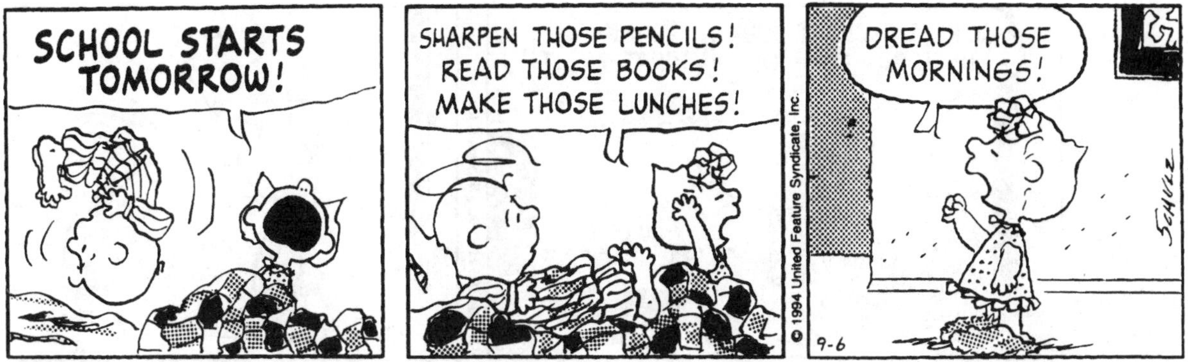
SCHOOL STARTS TOMORROW!
SHARPEN THOSE PENCILS! READ THOSE BOOKS! MAKE THOSE LUNCHES!
© 1994 United Feature Syndicate, Inc.
DREAD THOSE MORNINGS!
9-6

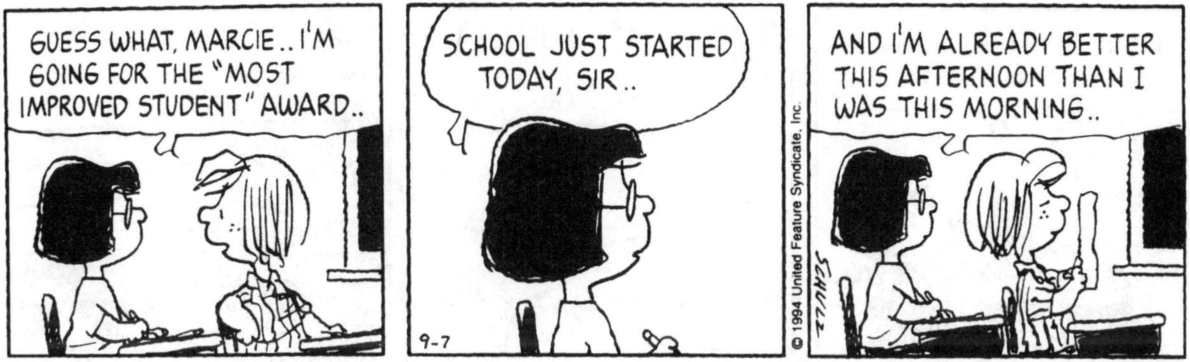
GUESS WHAT, MARCIE.. I'M GOING FOR THE "MOST IMPROVED STUDENT" AWARD..
SCHOOL JUST STARTED TODAY, SIR..
9-7
© 1994 United Feature Syndicate, Inc.
AND I'M ALREADY BETTER THIS AFTERNOON THAN I WAS THIS MORNING..

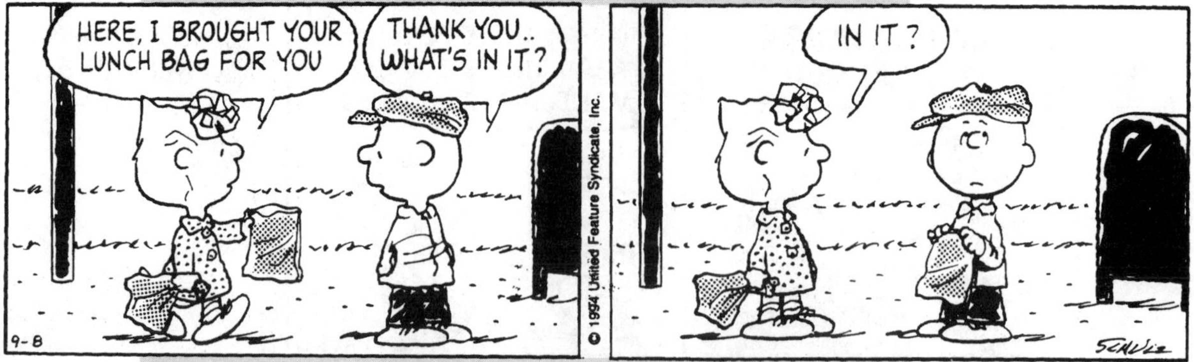
HERE, I BROUGHT YOUR LUNCH BAG FOR YOU
THANK YOU.. WHAT'S IN IT?
IN IT?
9-8
© 1994 United Feature Syndicate, Inc.
SCHULZ

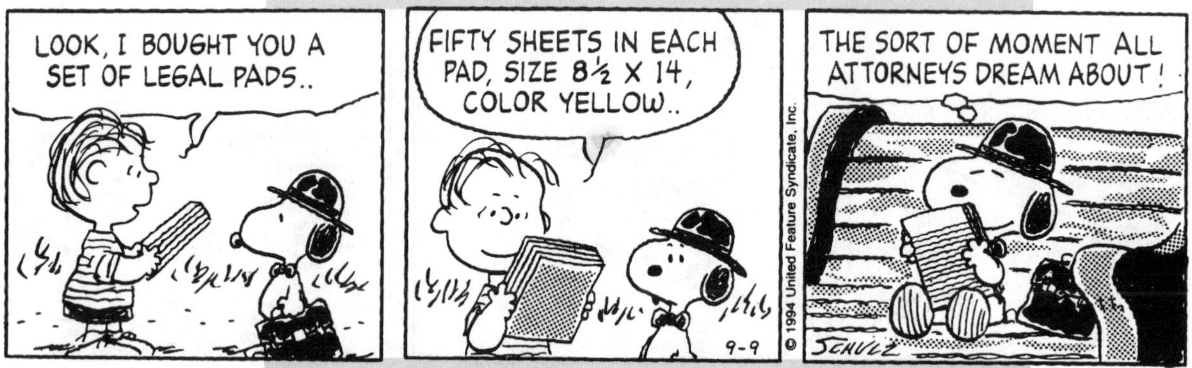
LOOK, I BOUGHT YOU A SET OF LEGAL PADS..
FIFTY SHEETS IN EACH PAD, SIZE 8½ X 14, COLOR YELLOW..
9-9
© 1994 United Feature Syndicate, Inc.
THE SORT OF MOMENT ALL ATTORNEYS DREAM ABOUT!
SCHULZ

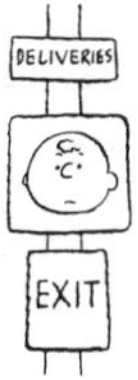
DELIVERIES
EXIT

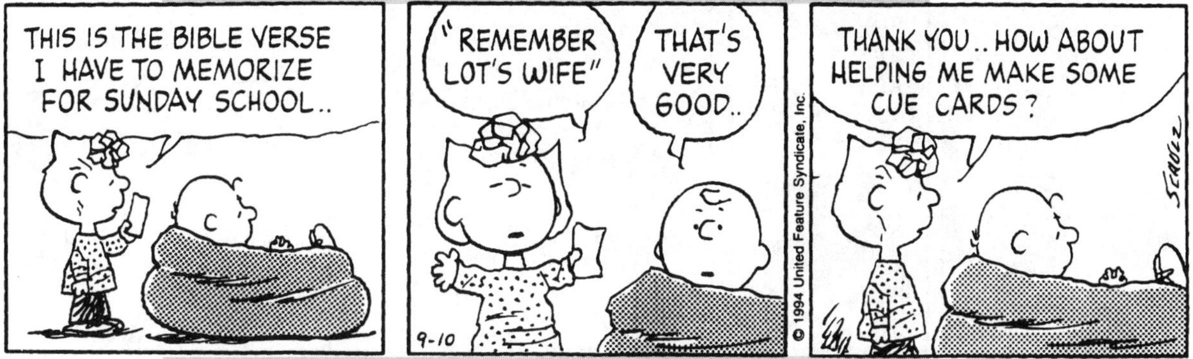
THIS IS THE BIBLE VERSE I HAVE TO MEMORIZE FOR SUNDAY SCHOOL..
"REMEMBER LOT'S WIFE"
THAT'S VERY GOOD..
9-10
© 1994 United Feature Syndicate, Inc.
THANK YOU.. HOW ABOUT HELPING ME MAKE SOME CUE CARDS?
SCHULZ

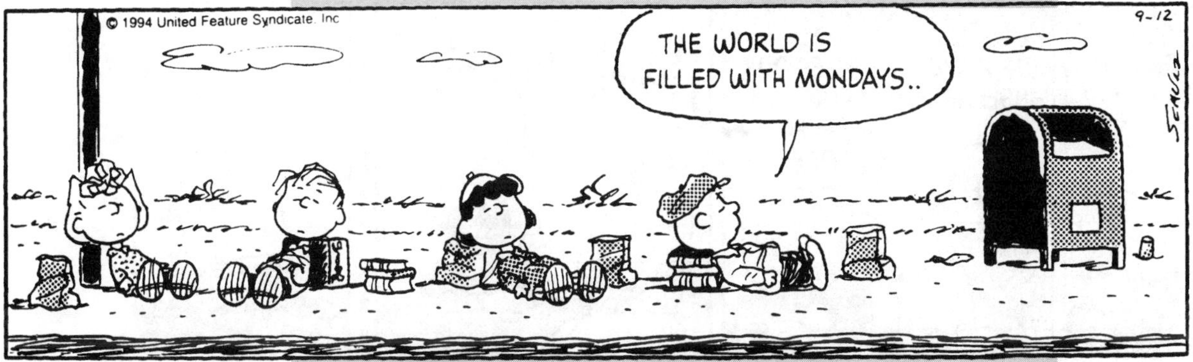
© 1994 United Feature Syndicate, Inc
9-12
THE WORLD IS FILLED WITH MONDAYS..
SCHULZ

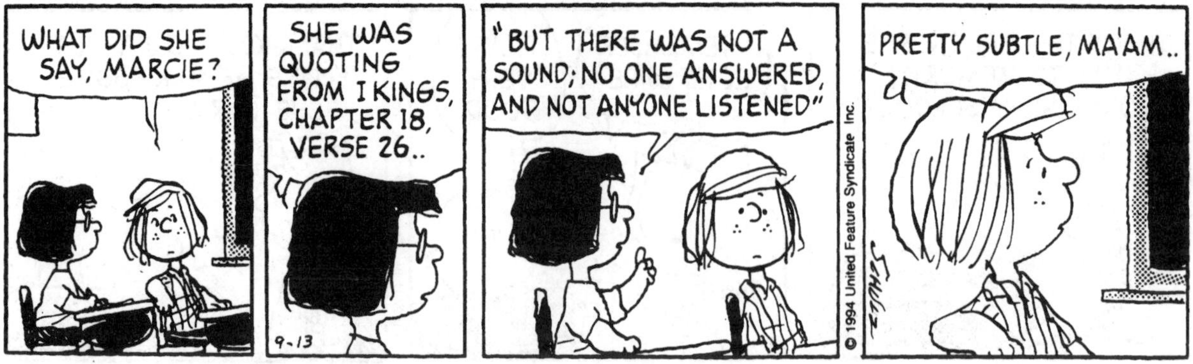
WHAT DID SHE SAY, MARCIE?
SHE WAS QUOTING FROM I KINGS, CHAPTER 18, VERSE 26..
9-13
"BUT THERE WAS NOT A SOUND; NO ONE ANSWERED, AND NOT ANYONE LISTENED"
© 1994 United Feature Syndicate Inc.
SCHULZ
PRETTY SUBTLE, MA'AM..

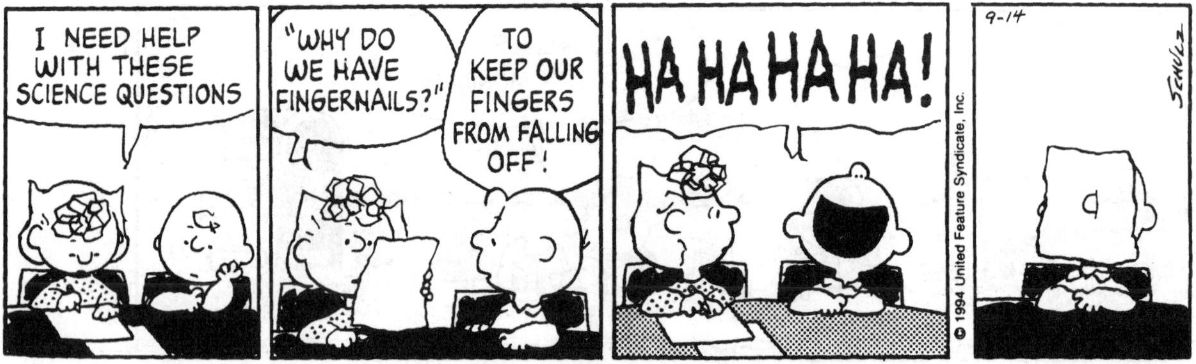
I NEED HELP WITH THESE SCIENCE QUESTIONS
"WHY DO WE HAVE FINGERNAILS?"
TO KEEP OUR FINGERS FROM FALLING OFF!
HA HA HA HA HA!
© 1994 United Feature Syndicate, Inc.
9-14
SCHULZ

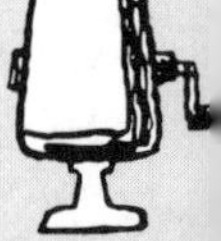

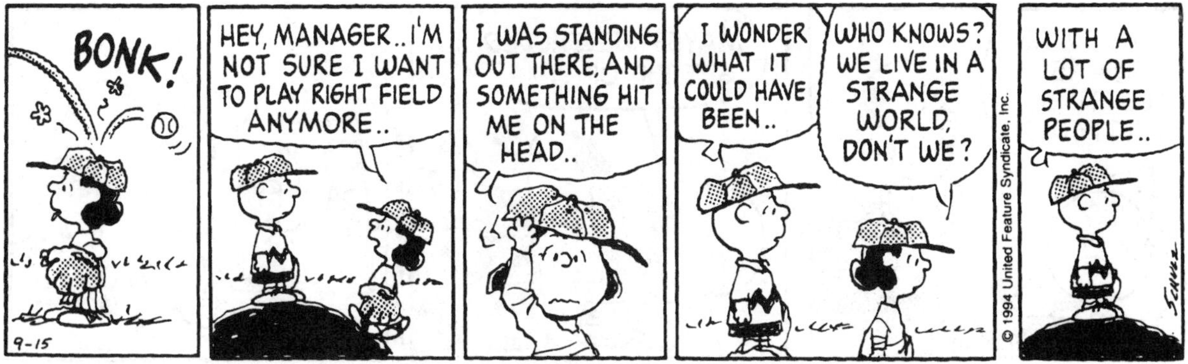
BONK!
9-15
HEY, MANAGER.. I'M NOT SURE I WANT TO PLAY RIGHT FIELD ANYMORE..
I WAS STANDING OUT THERE, AND SOMETHING HIT ME ON THE HEAD..
I WONDER WHAT IT COULD HAVE BEEN..
WHO KNOWS? WE LIVE IN A STRANGE WORLD, DON'T WE?
© 1994 United Feature Syndicate, Inc.
WITH A LOT OF STRANGE PEOPLE..
SCHULZ

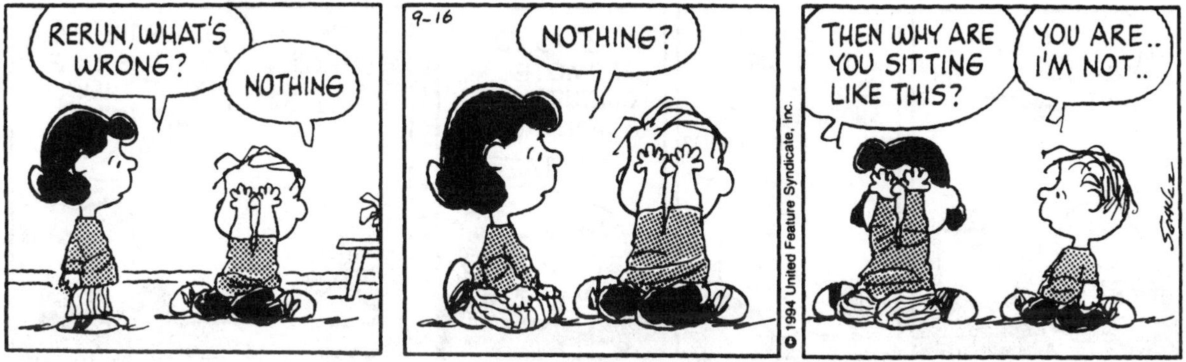
RERUN, WHAT'S WRONG?
NOTHING
9-16
NOTHING?
© 1994 United Feature Syndicate, Inc.
THEN WHY ARE YOU SITTING LIKE THIS?
YOU ARE.. I'M NOT..
SCHULZ

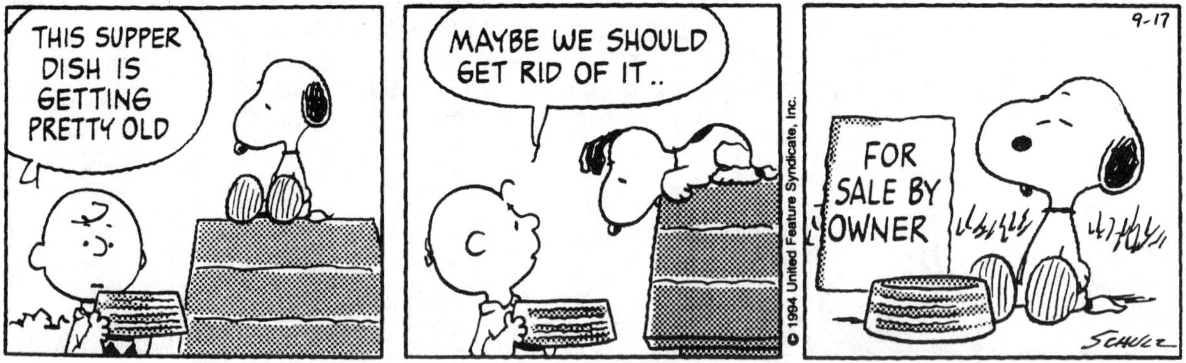
THIS SUPPER DISH IS GETTING PRETTY OLD
MAYBE WE SHOULD GET RID OF IT..
© 1994 United Feature Syndicate, Inc.
9-17
FOR SALE BY OWNER
SCHULZ

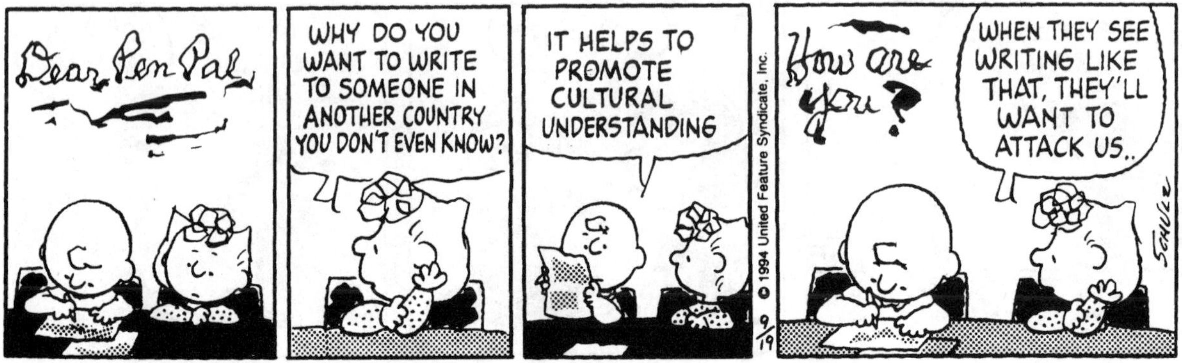
Dear Pen Pal
WHY DO YOU WANT TO WRITE TO SOMEONE IN ANOTHER COUNTRY YOU DON'T EVEN KNOW?
IT HELPS TO PROMOTE CULTURAL UNDERSTANDING
© 1994 United Feature Syndicate, Inc.
9/19
How are you?
WHEN THEY SEE WRITING LIKE THAT, THEY'LL WANT TO ATTACK US..
SCHULZ

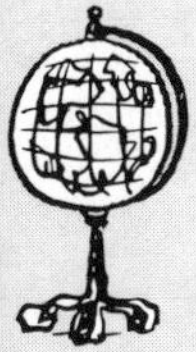

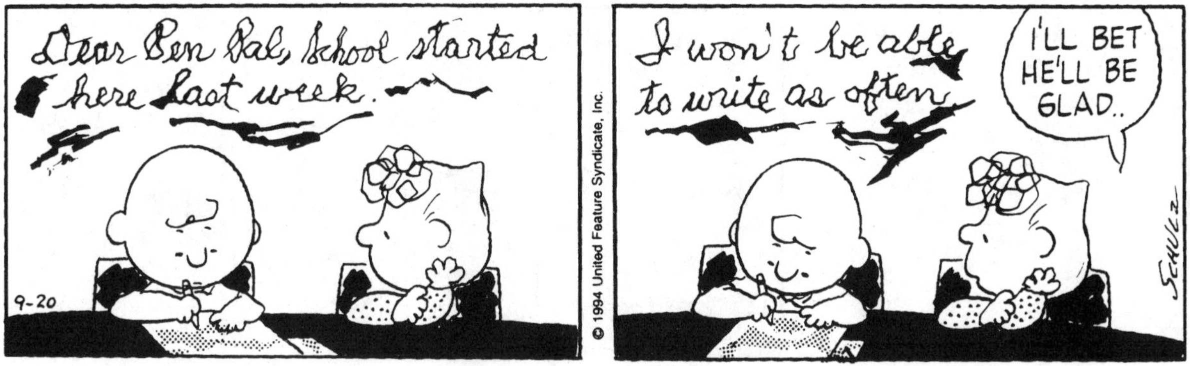
Dear Pen Pal, School started here last week.
9-20
© 1994 United Feature Syndicate, Inc.
I won't be able to write as often
I'LL BET HE'LL BE GLAD..
SCHULZ

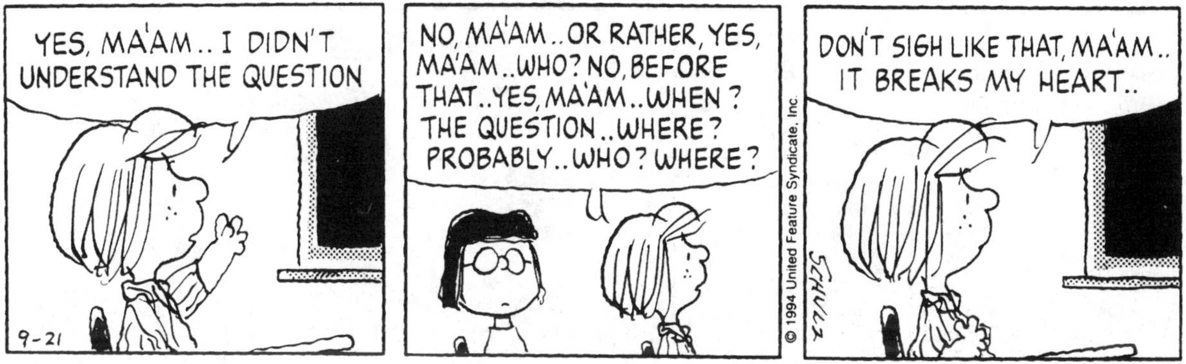
YES, MA'AM.. I DIDN'T UNDERSTAND THE QUESTION
9-21
NO, MA'AM..OR RATHER, YES, MA'AM..WHO? NO, BEFORE THAT..YES, MA'AM..WHEN? THE QUESTION..WHERE? PROBABLY..WHO? WHERE?
© 1994 United Feature Syndicate, Inc.
SCHULZ
DON'T SIGH LIKE THAT, MA'AM.. IT BREAKS MY HEART..

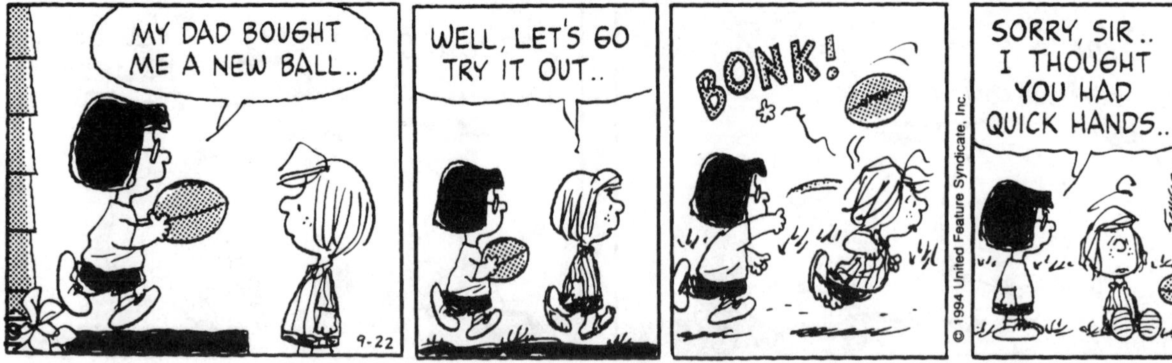
MY DAD BOUGHT ME A NEW BALL..
9-22
WELL, LET'S GO TRY IT OUT..
BONK!
© 1994 United Feature Syndicate, Inc.
SORRY, SIR.. I THOUGHT YOU HAD QUICK HANDS..
SCHULZ

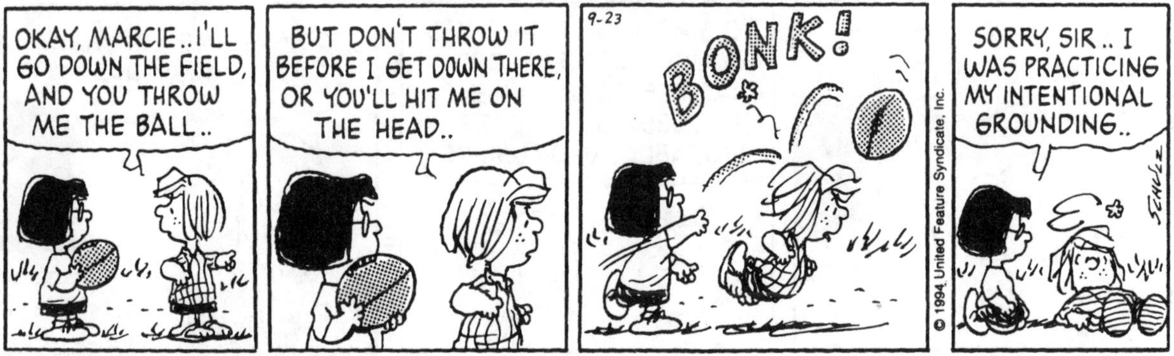
OKAY, MARCIE..I'LL GO DOWN THE FIELD, AND YOU THROW ME THE BALL..
BUT DON'T THROW IT BEFORE I GET DOWN THERE, OR YOU'LL HIT ME ON THE HEAD..
9-23
BONK!
© 1994 United Feature Syndicate, Inc.
SORRY, SIR.. I WAS PRACTICING MY INTENTIONAL GROUNDING..
SCHULZ

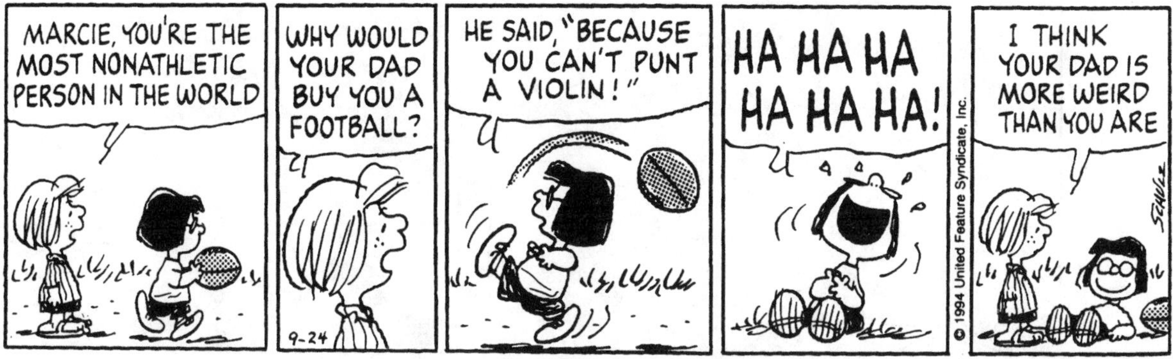

MARCIE, YOU'RE THE MOST NONATHLETIC PERSON IN THE WORLD
WHY WOULD YOUR DAD BUY YOU A FOOTBALL?
9-24
HE SAID, "BECAUSE YOU CAN'T PUNT A VIOLIN!"
HA HA HA HA HA HA!
© 1994 United Feature Syndicate, Inc.
I THINK YOUR DAD IS MORE WEIRD THAN YOU ARE
SCHULZ

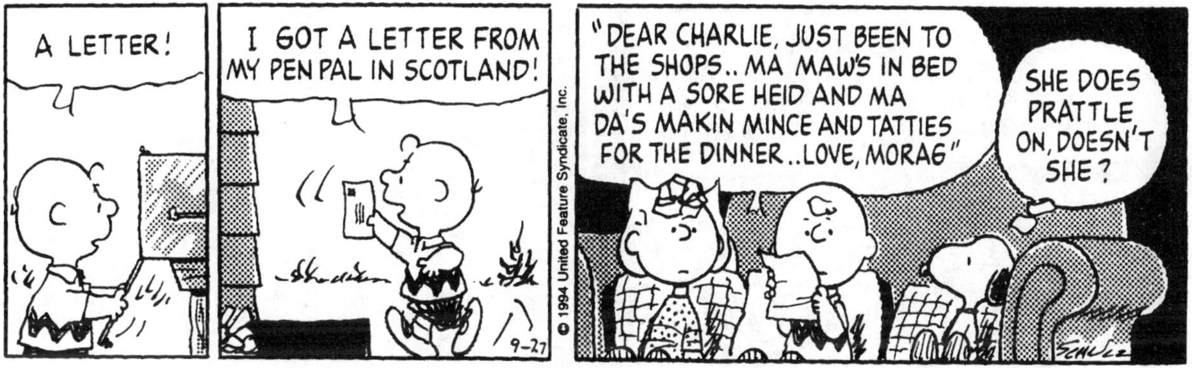

A LETTER!
I GOT A LETTER FROM MY PEN PAL IN SCOTLAND!
9-27
© 1994 United Feature Syndicate, Inc.
"DEAR CHARLIE, JUST BEEN TO THE SHOPS.. MA MAW'S IN BED WITH A SORE HEID AND MA DA'S MAKIN MINCE AND TATTIES FOR THE DINNER..LOVE, MORAG"
SHE DOES PRATTLE ON, DOESN'T SHE?
SCHULZ

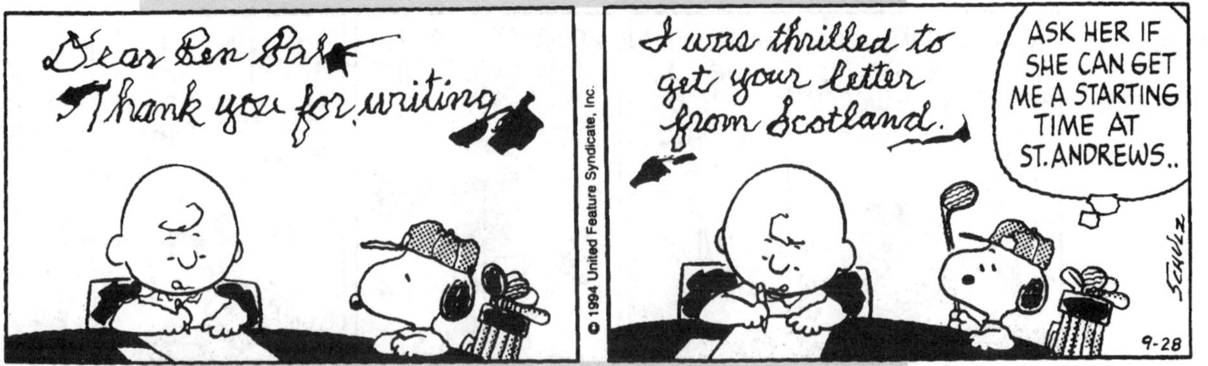
Dear Pen Pal
Thank you for writing
I was thrilled to get your letter from Scotland.
ASK HER IF SHE CAN GET ME A STARTING TIME AT ST. ANDREWS..
© 1994 United Feature Syndicate, Inc.
SCHULZ
9-28

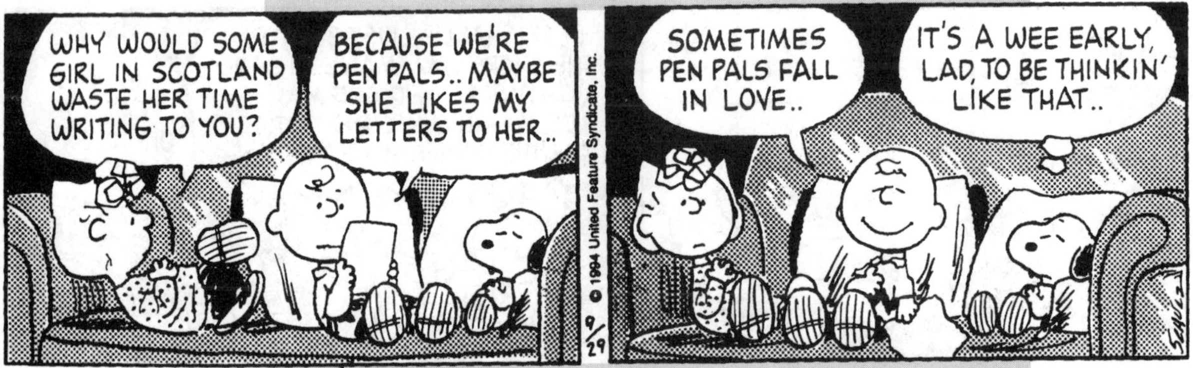
WHY WOULD SOME GIRL IN SCOTLAND WASTE HER TIME WRITING TO YOU?
BECAUSE WE'RE PEN PALS.. MAYBE SHE LIKES MY LETTERS TO HER..
© 1994 United Feature Syndicate, Inc.
9/29
SOMETIMES PEN PALS FALL IN LOVE..
IT'S A WEE EARLY, LAD, TO BE THINKIN' LIKE THAT..
SCHULZ

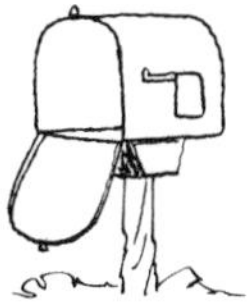

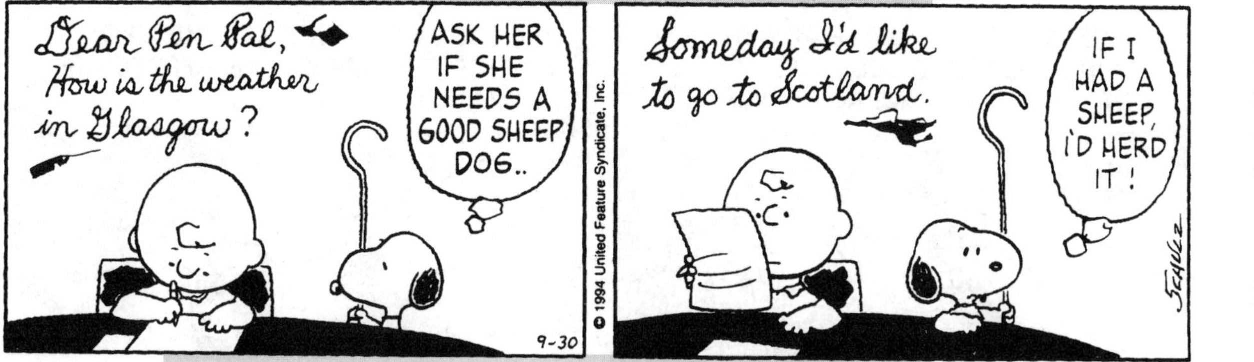
Dear Pen Pal,
How is the weather in Glasgow?
ASK HER IF SHE NEEDS A GOOD SHEEP DOG..
9-30
© 1994 United Feature Syndicate, Inc.
Someday I'd like to go to Scotland.
IF I HAD A SHEEP, I'D HERD IT!
SCHULZ

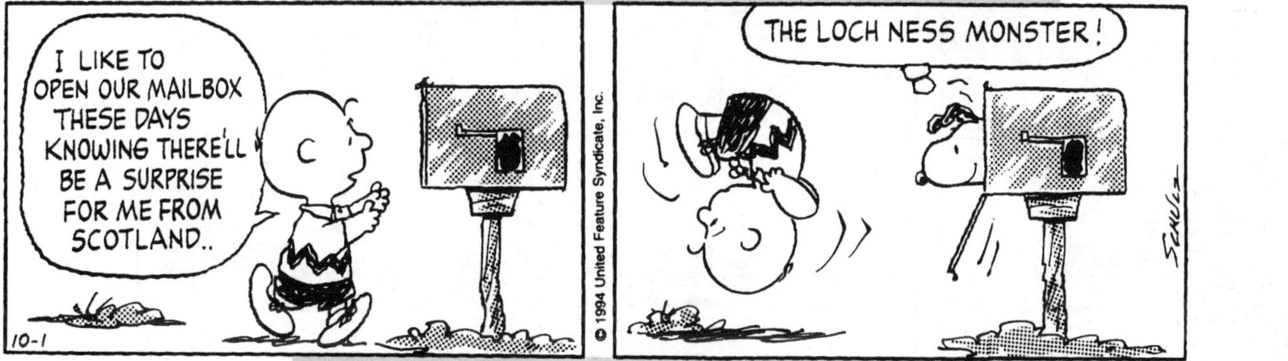
I LIKE TO OPEN OUR MAILBOX THESE DAYS KNOWING THERE'LL BE A SURPRISE FOR ME FROM SCOTLAND..
10-1
© 1994 United Feature Syndicate, Inc.
THE LOCH NESS MONSTER!
SCHULZ

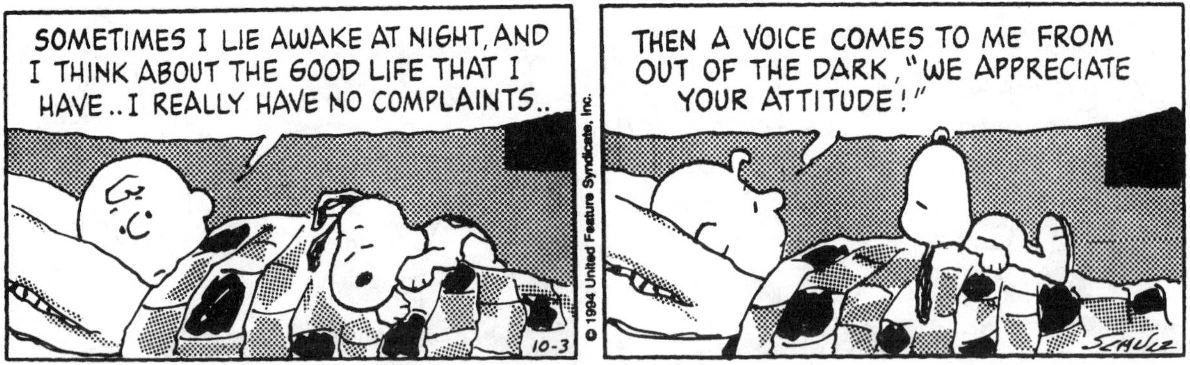
SOMETIMES I LIE AWAKE AT NIGHT, AND I THINK ABOUT THE GOOD LIFE THAT I HAVE..I REALLY HAVE NO COMPLAINTS..
THEN A VOICE COMES TO ME FROM OUT OF THE DARK, "WE APPRECIATE YOUR ATTITUDE!"
10-3
© 1994 United Feature Syndicate, Inc.
SCHULZ

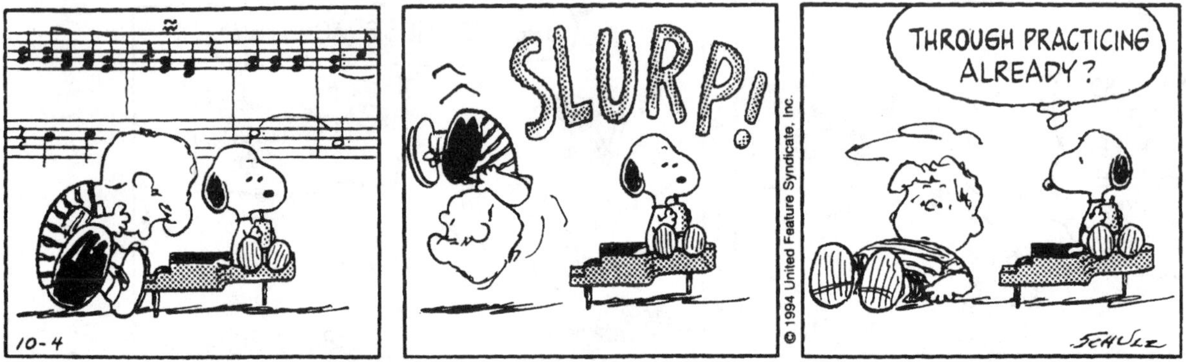
SLURP!
THROUGH PRACTICING ALREADY?
10-4
© 1994 United Feature Syndicate, Inc.
SCHULZ

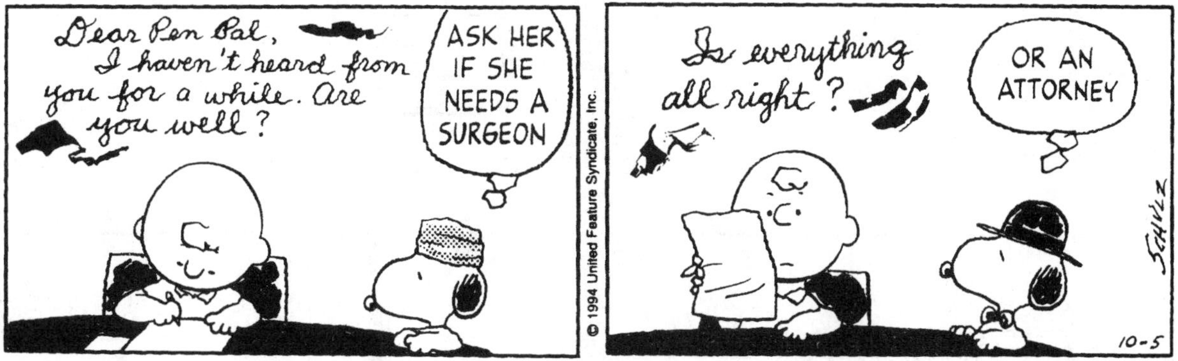
Dear Pen Pal,
I haven't heard from you for a while. Are you well?
ASK HER IF SHE NEEDS A SURGEON
© 1994 United Feature Syndicate, Inc.
Is everything all right?
OR AN ATTORNEY
SCHULZ
10-5

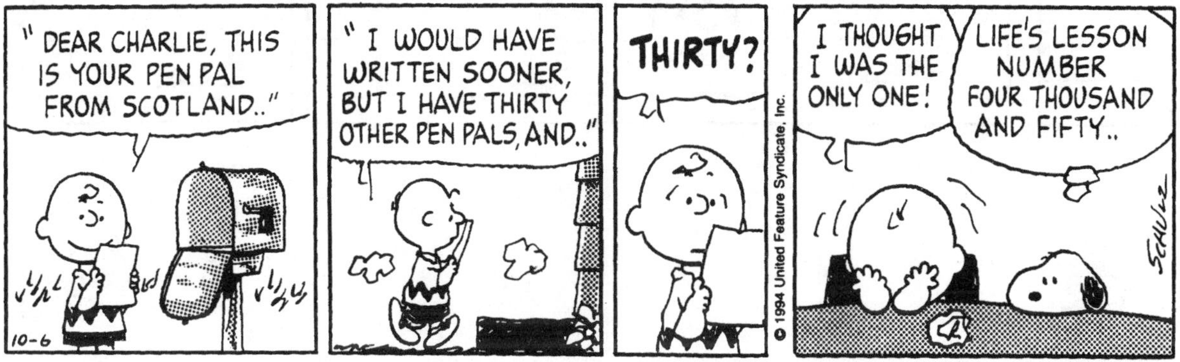
" DEAR CHARLIE, THIS IS YOUR PEN PAL FROM SCOTLAND.."
10-6
" I WOULD HAVE WRITTEN SOONER, BUT I HAVE THIRTY OTHER PEN PALS, AND.."
THIRTY?
© 1994 United Feature Syndicate, Inc.
I THOUGHT I WAS THE ONLY ONE!
LIFE'S LESSON NUMBER FOUR THOUSAND AND FIFTY..
SCHULZ

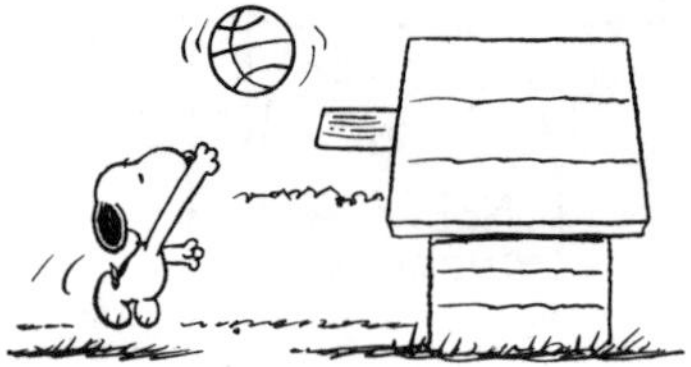

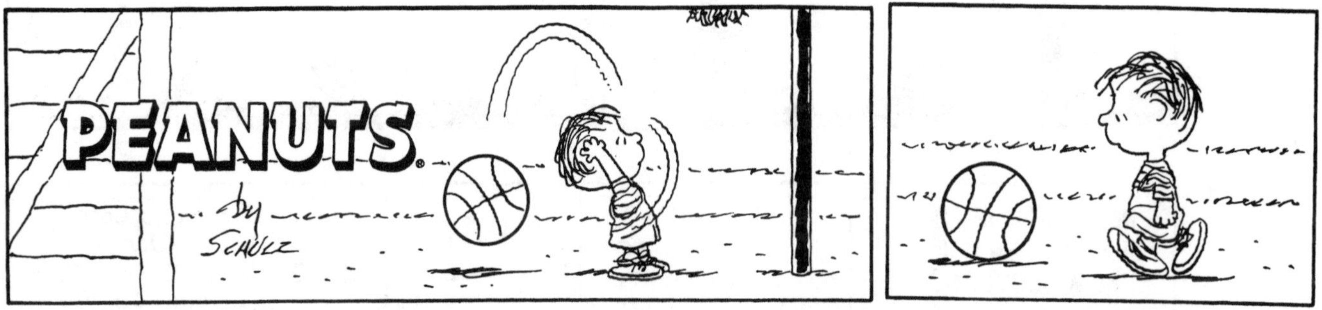
PEANUTS
by SCHULZ

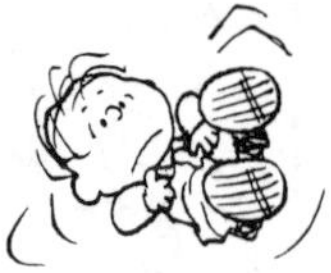

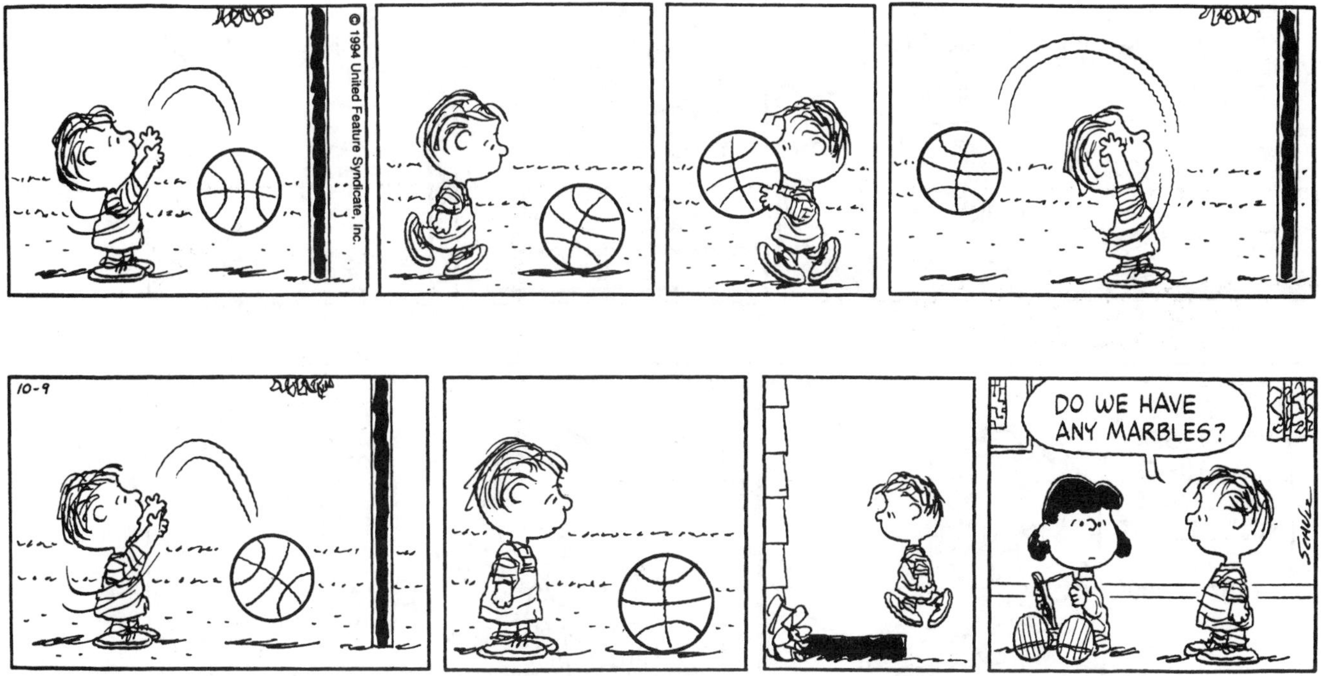
© 1994 United Feature Syndicate, Inc.
10-9
DO WE HAVE ANY MARBLES?
SCHULZ

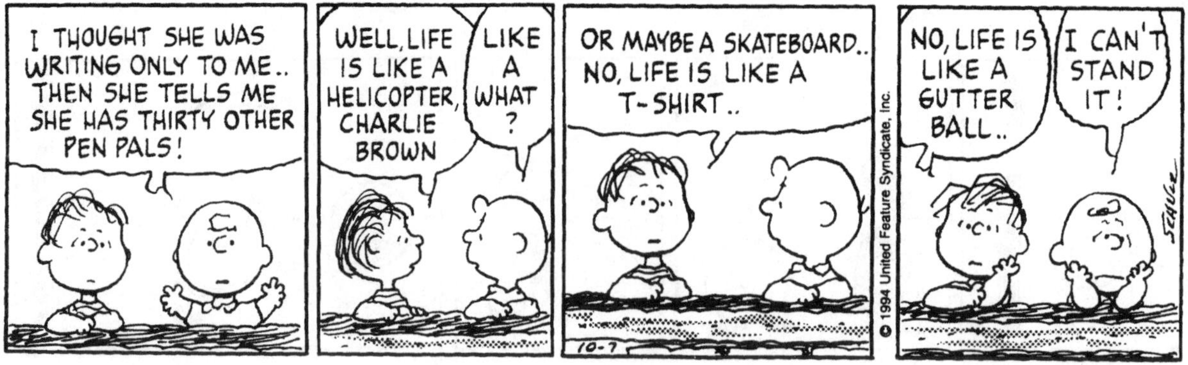
I THOUGHT SHE WAS WRITING ONLY TO ME.. THEN SHE TELLS ME SHE HAS THIRTY OTHER PEN PALS!
WELL, LIFE IS LIKE A HELICOPTER, CHARLIE BROWN
LIKE A WHAT ?
OR MAYBE A SKATEBOARD.. NO, LIFE IS LIKE A T-SHIRT..
10-7
© 1994 United Feature Syndicate, Inc.
NO, LIFE IS LIKE A GUTTER BALL..
I CAN'T STAND IT!
SCHULZ

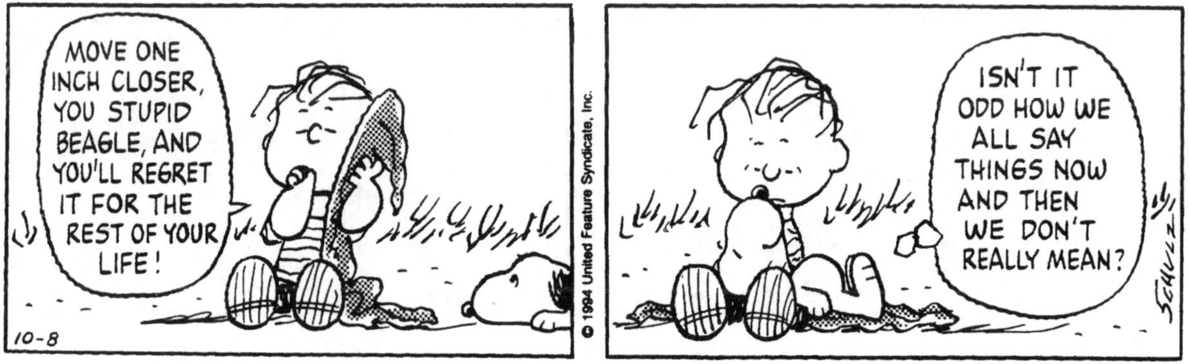
MOVE ONE INCH CLOSER, YOU STUPID BEAGLE, AND YOU'LL REGRET IT FOR THE REST OF YOUR LIFE!
10-8
© 1994 United Feature Syndicate, Inc.
ISN'T IT ODD HOW WE ALL SAY THINGS NOW AND THEN WE DON'T REALLY MEAN?
SCHULZ

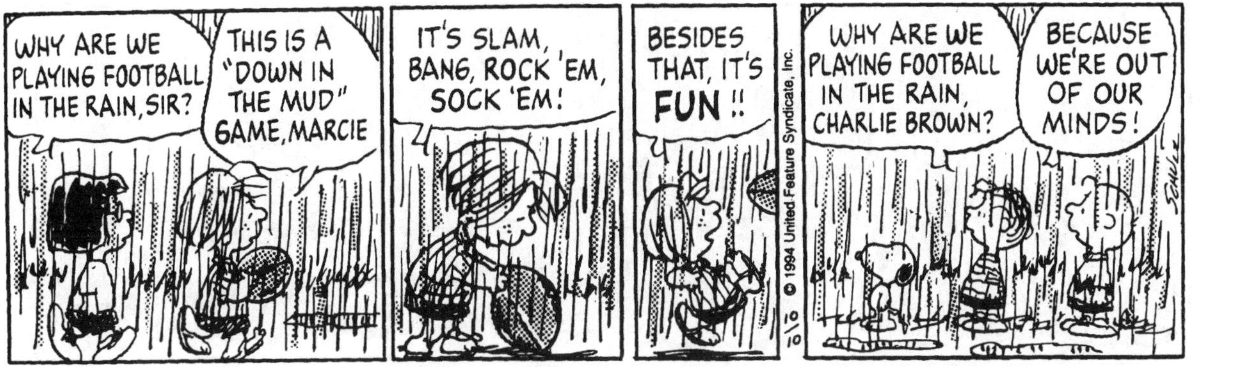
WHY ARE WE PLAYING FOOTBALL IN THE RAIN, SIR?
THIS IS A "DOWN IN THE MUD" GAME, MARCIE
IT'S SLAM, BANG, ROCK 'EM, SOCK 'EM!
BESIDES THAT, IT'S FUN !!
10/10
© 1994 United Feature Syndicate, Inc.
WHY ARE WE PLAYING FOOTBALL IN THE RAIN, CHARLIE BROWN?
BECAUSE WE'RE OUT OF OUR MINDS!

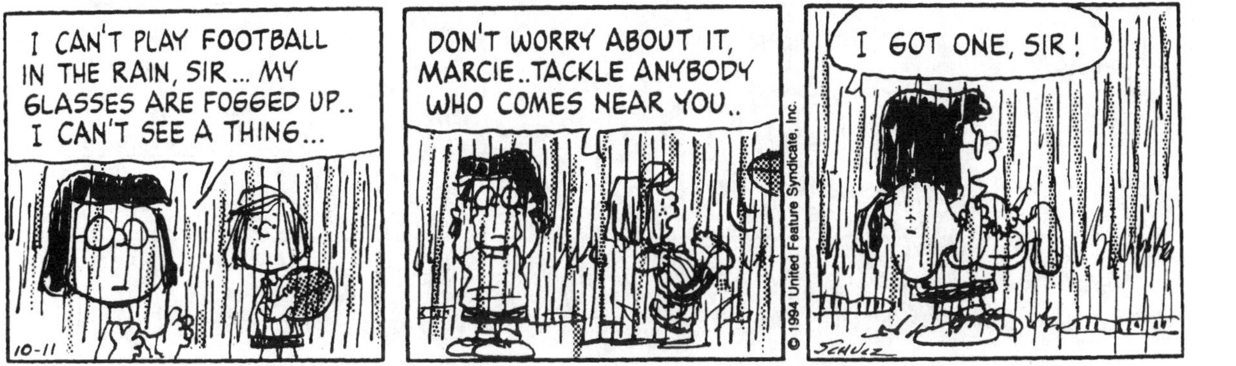
I CAN'T PLAY FOOTBALL IN THE RAIN, SIR... MY GLASSES ARE FOGGED UP.. I CAN'T SEE A THING...
10-11
DON'T WORRY ABOUT IT, MARCIE..TACKLE ANYBODY WHO COMES NEAR YOU..
© 1994 United Feature Syndicate, Inc.
I GOT ONE, SIR!

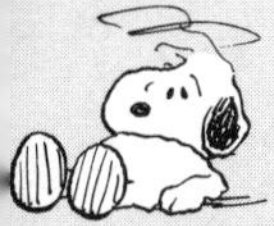

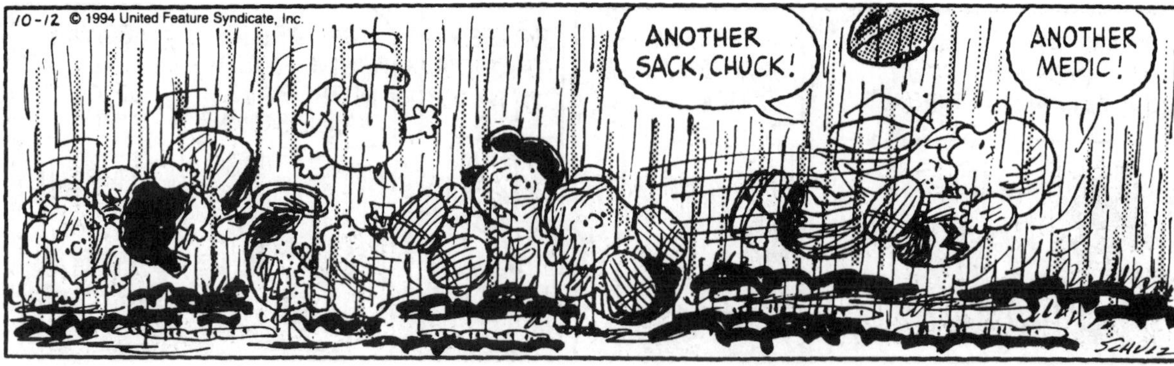
10-12 © 1994 United Feature Syndicate, Inc.
ANOTHER SACK, CHUCK!
ANOTHER MEDIC!
SCHULZ

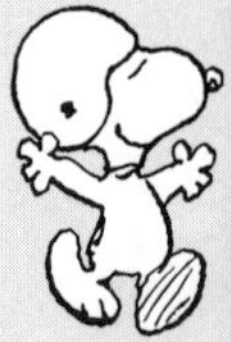

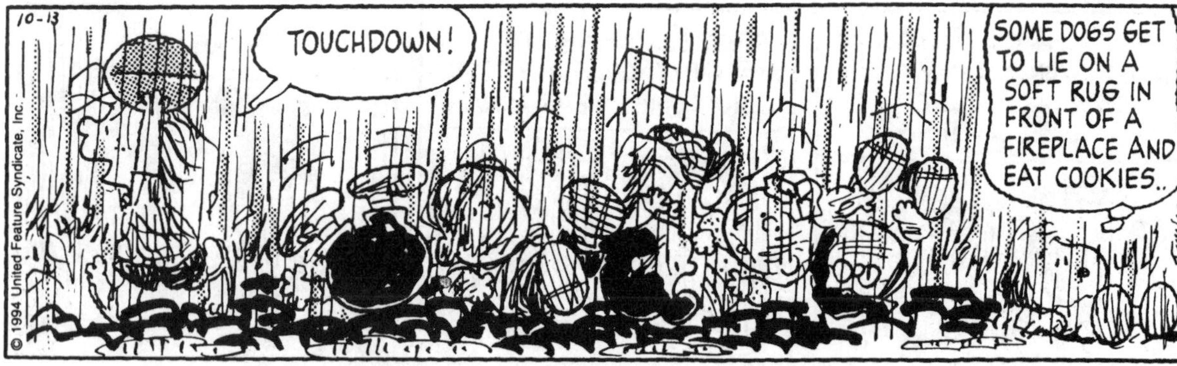
10-13
© 1994 United Feature Syndicate, Inc.
TOUCHDOWN!
SOME DOGS GET TO LIE ON A SOFT RUG IN FRONT OF A FIREPLACE AND EAT COOKIES..
SCHULZ

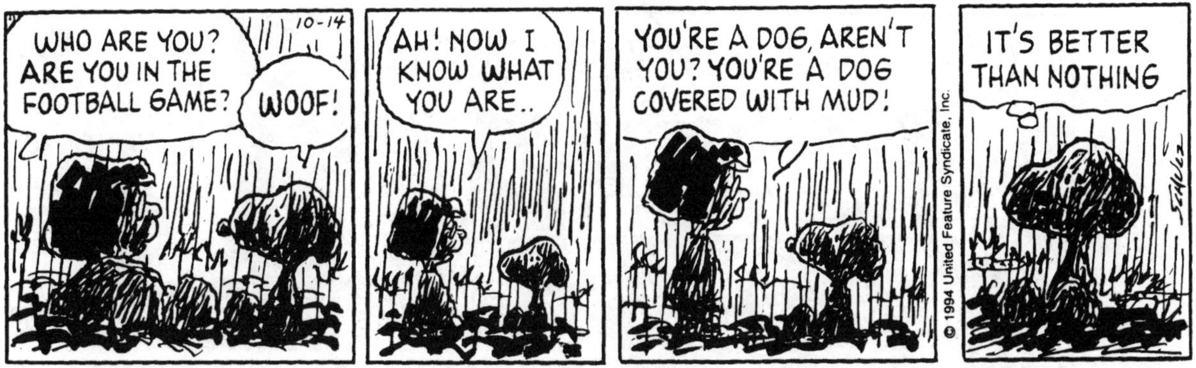
10-14
WHO ARE YOU? ARE YOU IN THE FOOTBALL GAME?
WOOF!
AH! NOW I KNOW WHAT YOU ARE..
YOU'RE A DOG, AREN'T YOU? YOU'RE A DOG COVERED WITH MUD!
© 1994 United Feature Syndicate, Inc.
IT'S BETTER THAN NOTHING

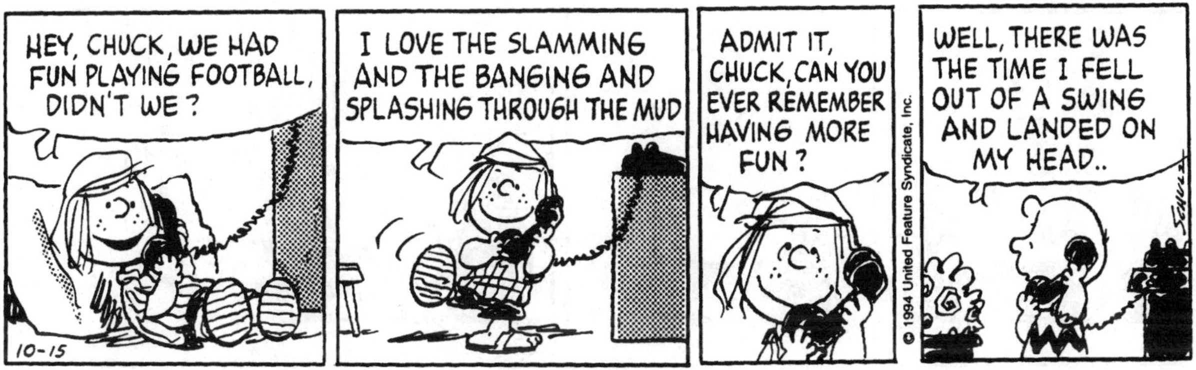
HEY, CHUCK, WE HAD FUN PLAYING FOOTBALL, DIDN'T WE?
10-15
I LOVE THE SLAMMING AND THE BANGING AND SPLASHING THROUGH THE MUD
ADMIT IT, CHUCK, CAN YOU EVER REMEMBER HAVING MORE FUN?
© 1994 United Feature Syndicate, Inc.
WELL, THERE WAS THE TIME I FELL OUT OF A SWING AND LANDED ON MY HEAD..

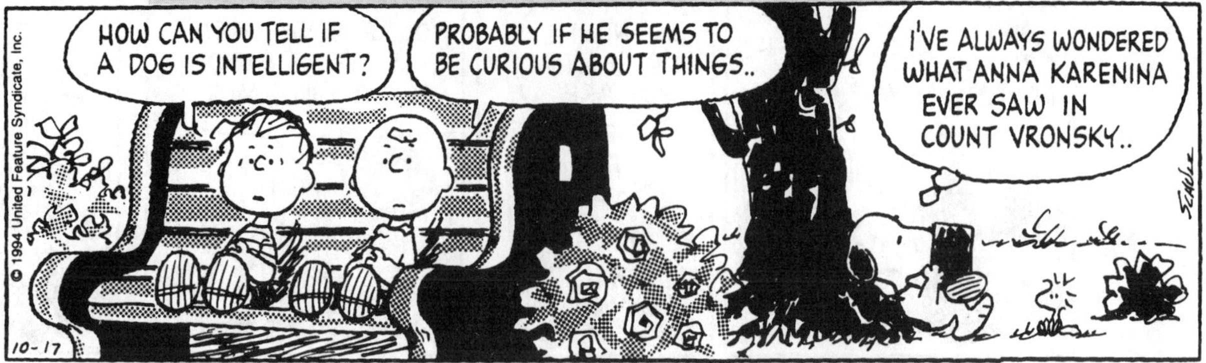
© 1994 United Feature Syndicate, Inc.
10-17
HOW CAN YOU TELL IF A DOG IS INTELLIGENT?
PROBABLY IF HE SEEMS TO BE CURIOUS ABOUT THINGS..
I'VE ALWAYS WONDERED WHAT ANNA KARENINA EVER SAW IN COUNT VRONSKY..
SCHULZ

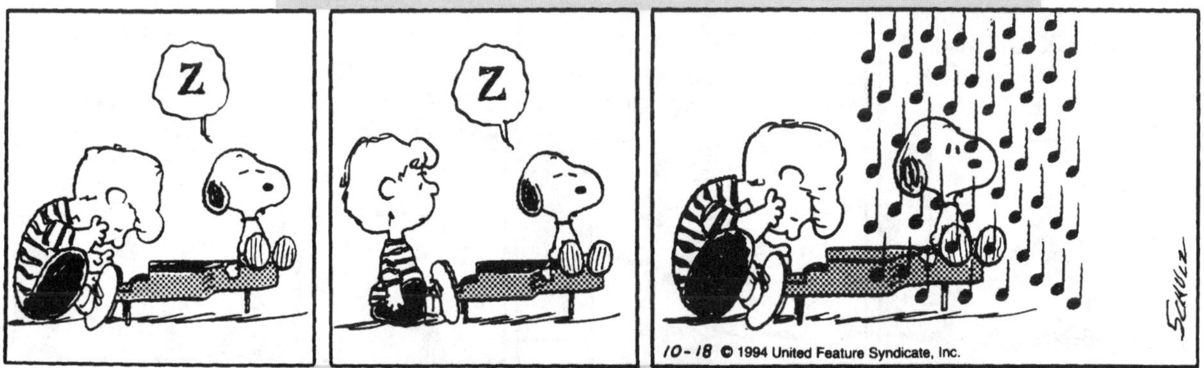
Z
Z
SCHULZ
10-18 © 1994 United Feature Syndicate, Inc.

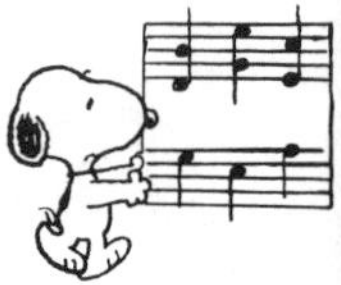

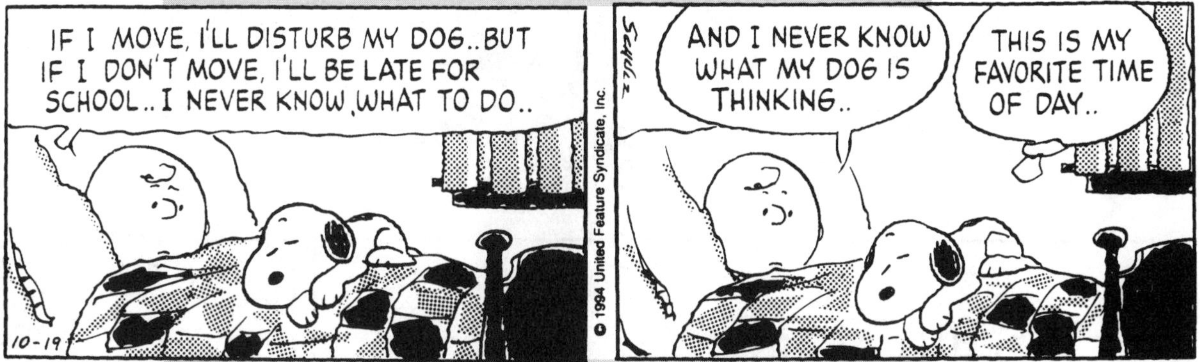
IF I MOVE, I'LL DISTURB MY DOG.. BUT IF I DON'T MOVE, I'LL BE LATE FOR SCHOOL.. I NEVER KNOW WHAT TO DO..
AND I NEVER KNOW WHAT MY DOG IS THINKING..
THIS IS MY FAVORITE TIME OF DAY..
10-19
© 1994 United Feature Syndicate, Inc.
SCHULZ

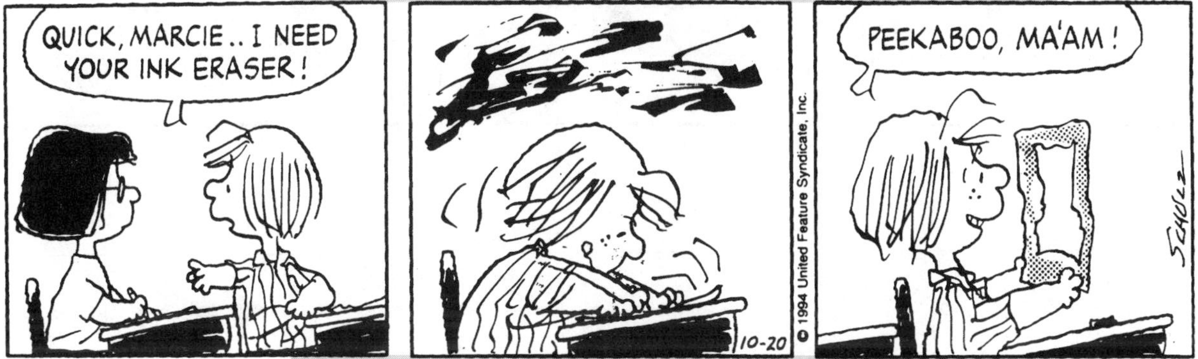
QUICK, MARCIE.. I NEED YOUR INK ERASER!
PEEKABOO, MA'AM!
10-20
© 1994 United Feature Syndicate, Inc.
SCHULZ

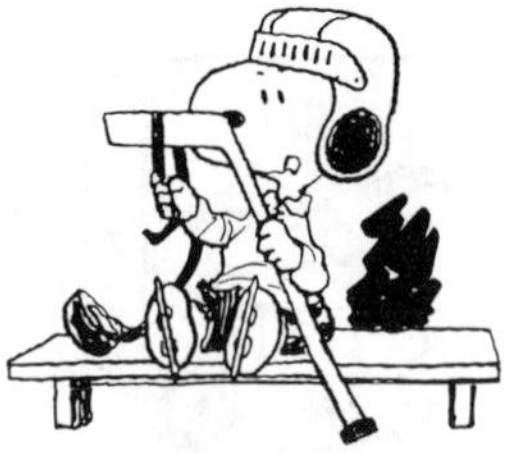

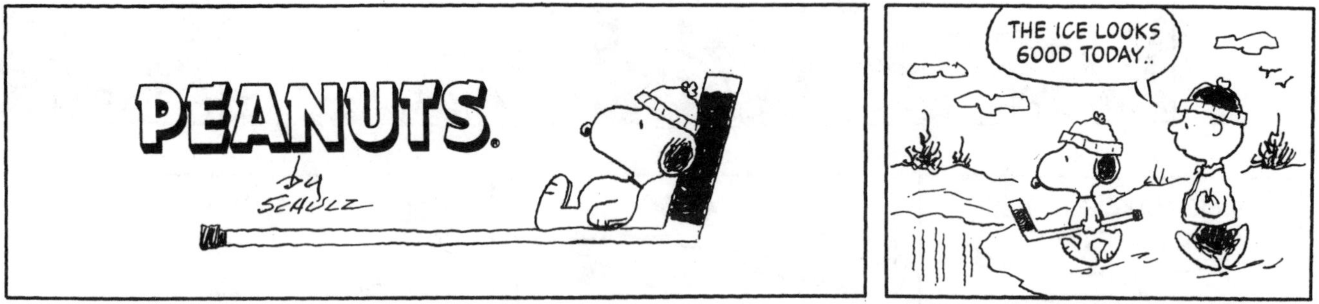
PEANUTS.
by SCHULZ
THE ICE LOOKS GOOD TODAY..

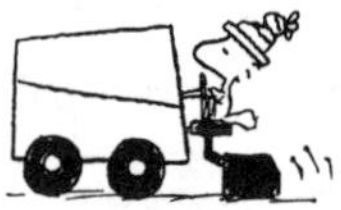

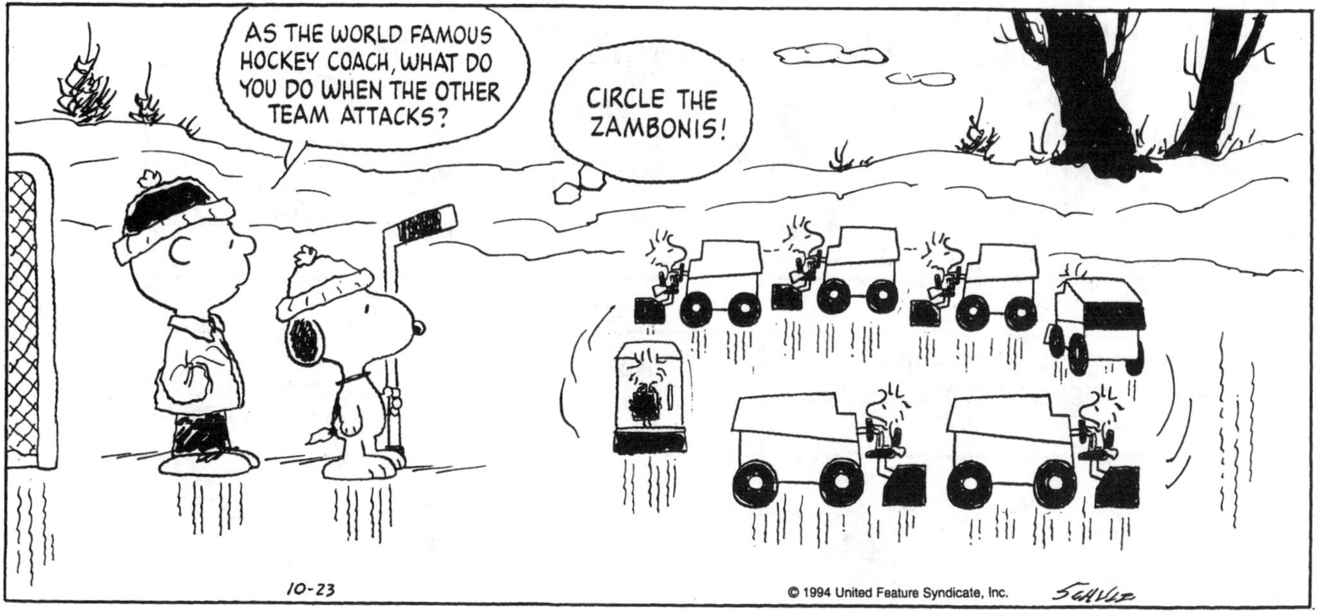
AS THE WORLD FAMOUS HOCKEY COACH, WHAT DO YOU DO WHEN THE OTHER TEAM ATTACKS?
CIRCLE THE ZAMBONIS!
10-23
© 1994 United Feature Syndicate, Inc.
SCHULZ

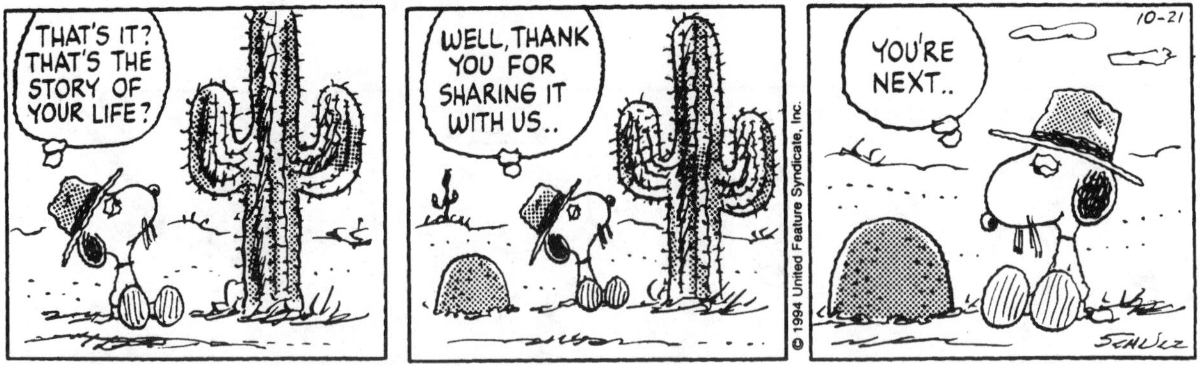
THAT'S IT? THAT'S THE STORY OF YOUR LIFE?
WELL, THANK YOU FOR SHARING IT WITH US..
YOU'RE NEXT..
10-21
© 1994 United Feature Syndicate, Inc.

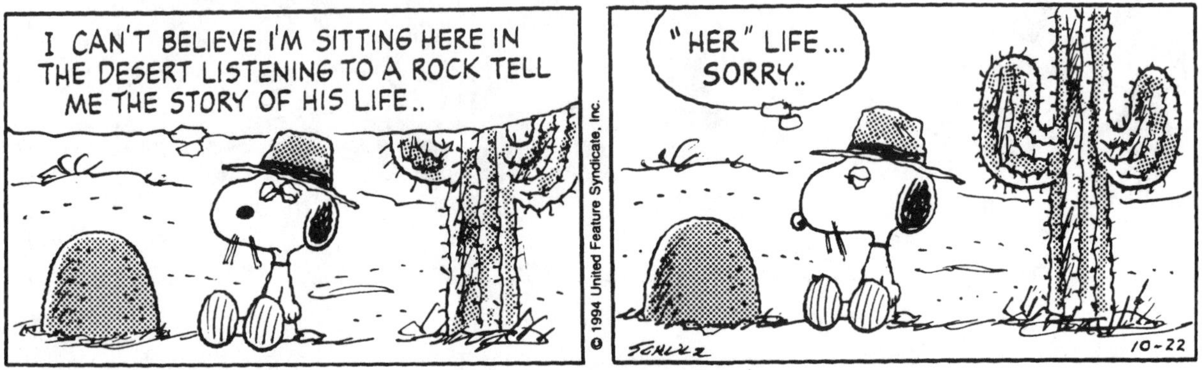
I CAN'T BELIEVE I'M SITTING HERE IN THE DESERT LISTENING TO A ROCK TELL ME THE STORY OF HIS LIFE..
"HER" LIFE... SORRY..
10-22
© 1994 United Feature Syndicate, Inc.

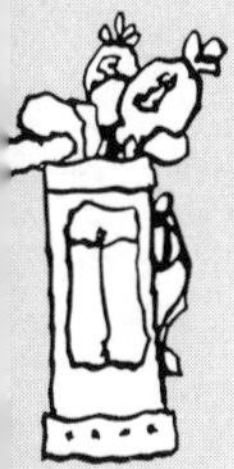

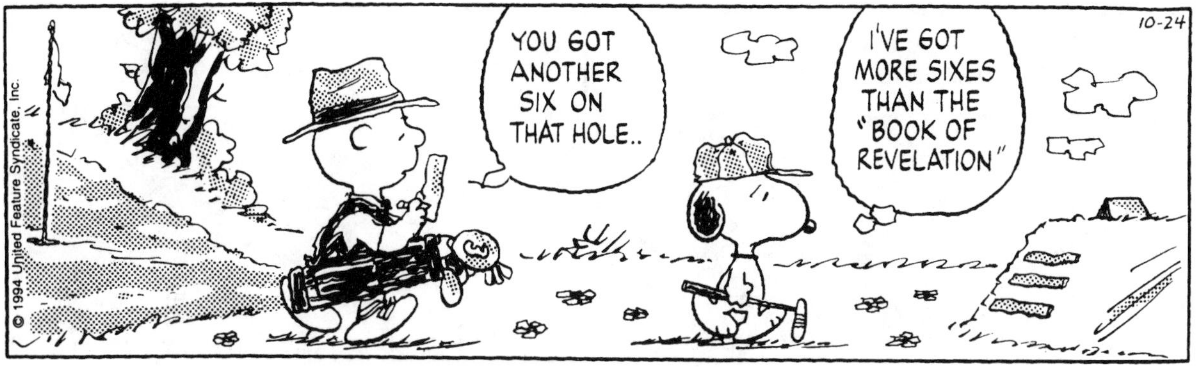
© 1994 United Feature Syndicate, Inc.
10-24
YOU GOT ANOTHER SIX ON THAT HOLE..
I'VE GOT MORE SIXES THAN THE "BOOK OF REVELATION"

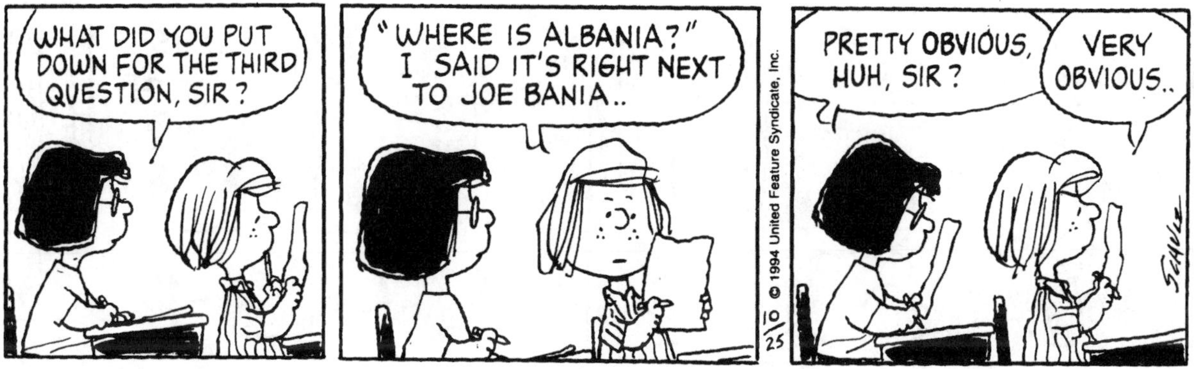
WHAT DID YOU PUT DOWN FOR THE THIRD QUESTION, SIR?
"WHERE IS ALBANIA?" I SAID IT'S RIGHT NEXT TO JOE BANIA..
© 1994 United Feature Syndicate, Inc.
10/25
PRETTY OBVIOUS, HUH, SIR?
VERY OBVIOUS..
SCHULZ

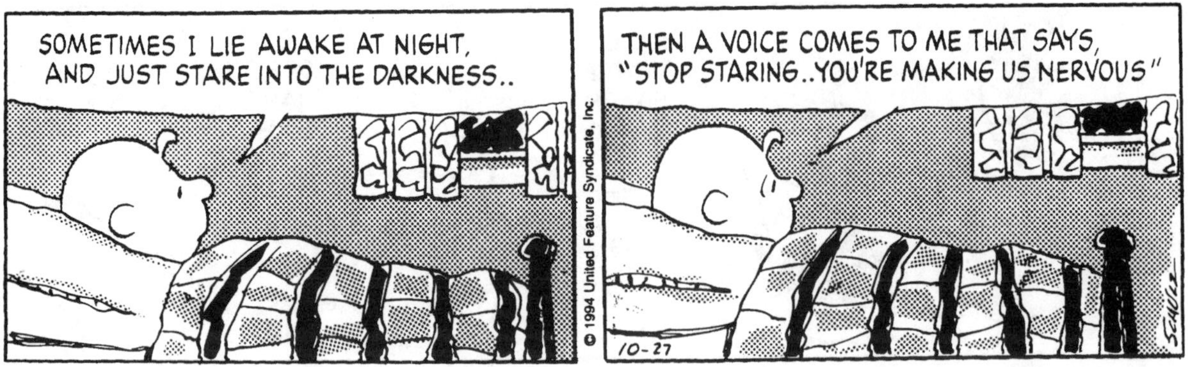
SOMETIMES I LIE AWAKE AT NIGHT, AND JUST STARE INTO THE DARKNESS..
THEN A VOICE COMES TO ME THAT SAYS, "STOP STARING..YOU'RE MAKING US NERVOUS"
© 1994 United Feature Syndicate, Inc.
10-27
SCHULZ

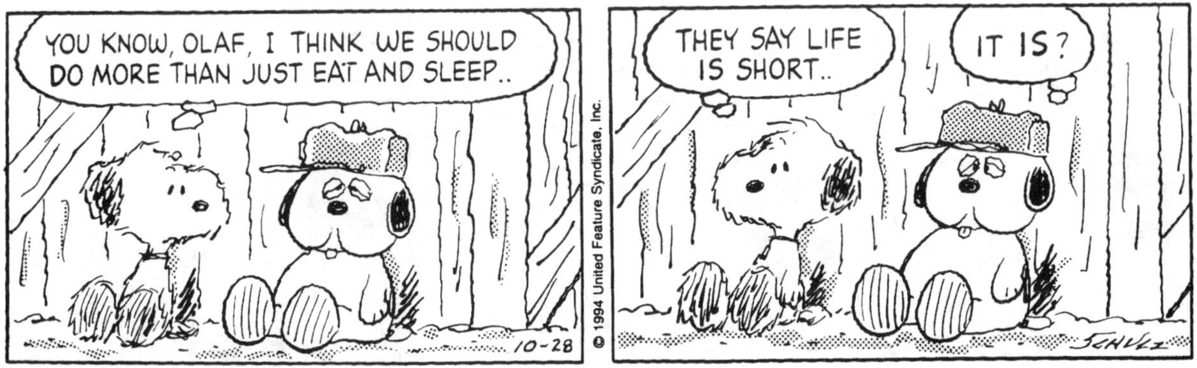
YOU KNOW, OLAF, I THINK WE SHOULD DO MORE THAN JUST EAT AND SLEEP..
10-28
THEY SAY LIFE IS SHORT..
IT IS?
© 1994 United Feature Syndicate, Inc.
SCHULZ

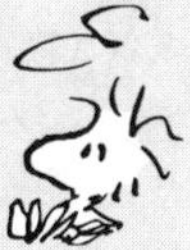

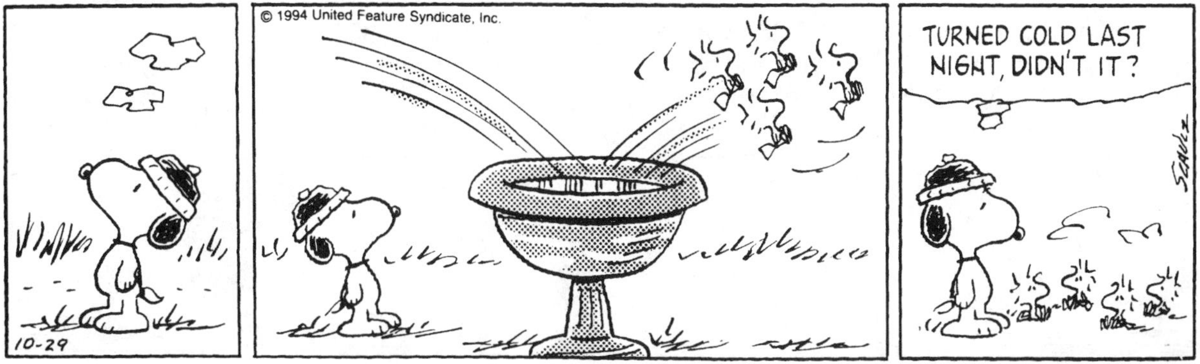
© 1994 United Feature Syndicate, Inc.
TURNED COLD LAST NIGHT, DIDN'T IT?
10-29
SCHULZ

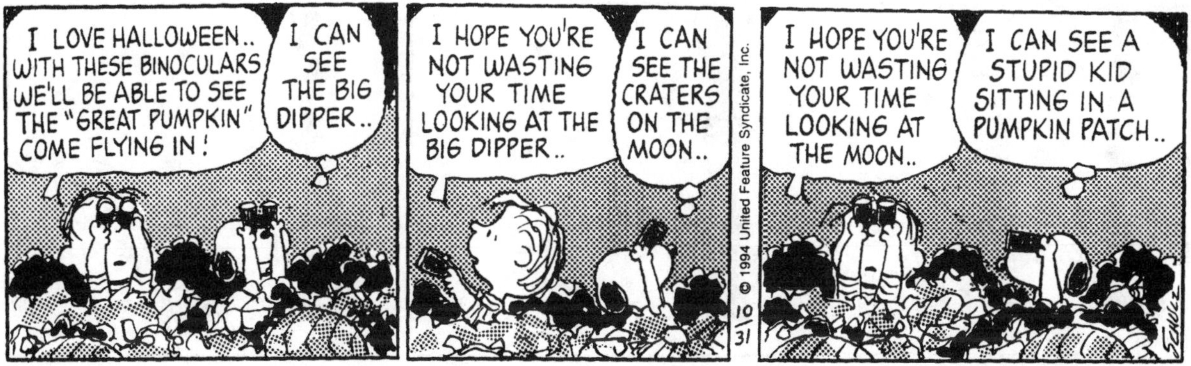
I LOVE HALLOWEEN.. WITH THESE BINOCULARS WE'LL BE ABLE TO SEE THE "GREAT PUMPKIN" COME FLYING IN!
I CAN SEE THE BIG DIPPER..
I HOPE YOU'RE NOT WASTING YOUR TIME LOOKING AT THE BIG DIPPER..
I CAN SEE THE CRATERS ON THE MOON..
© 1994 United Feature Syndicate, Inc.
10/31
I HOPE YOU'RE NOT WASTING YOUR TIME LOOKING AT THE MOON..
I CAN SEE A STUPID KID SITTING IN A PUMPKIN PATCH..
SCHULZ

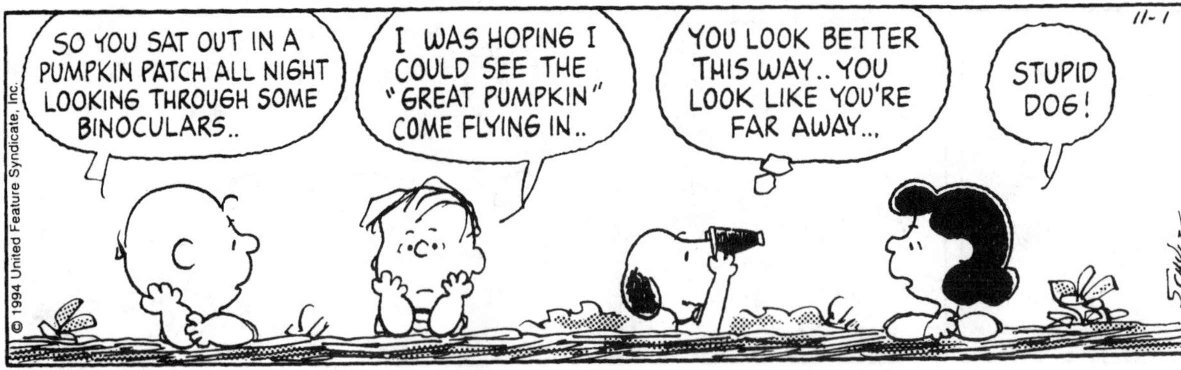
11-1
SO YOU SAT OUT IN A PUMPKIN PATCH ALL NIGHT LOOKING THROUGH SOME BINOCULARS..
I WAS HOPING I COULD SEE THE "GREAT PUMPKIN" COME FLYING IN..
YOU LOOK BETTER THIS WAY.. YOU LOOK LIKE YOU'RE FAR AWAY...
STUPID DOG!
SCHULZ
© 1994 United Feature Syndicate, Inc.

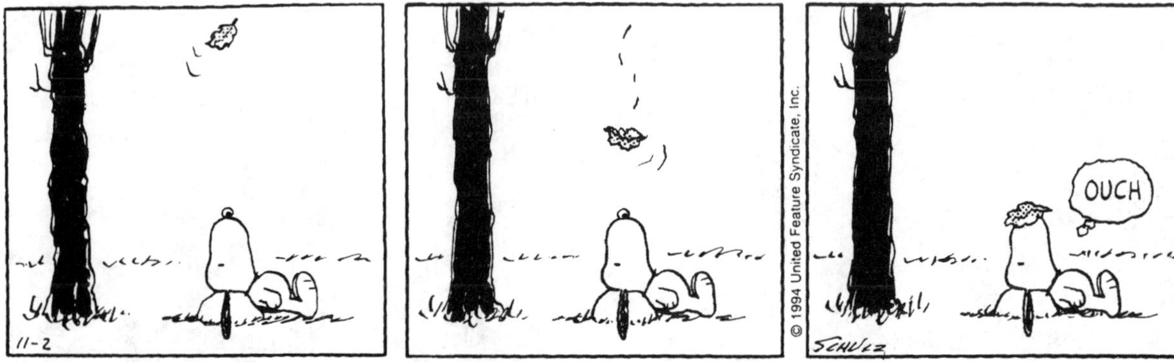
11-2
OUCH
© 1994 United Feature Syndicate, Inc.
SCHULZ

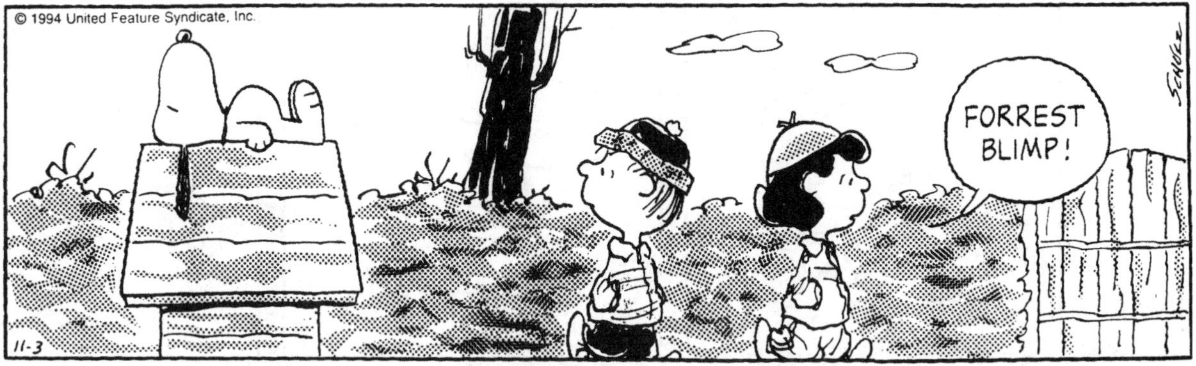

© 1994 United Feature Syndicate, Inc.
FORREST BLIMP!

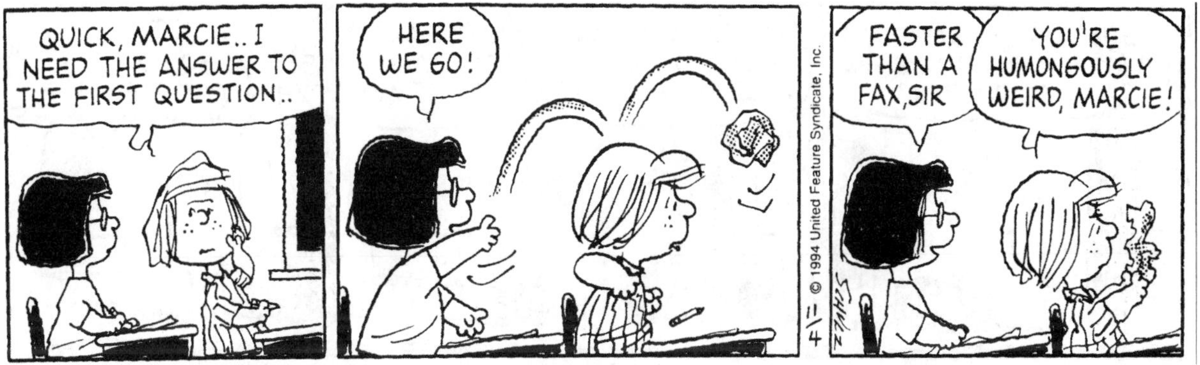

QUICK, MARCIE.. I NEED THE ANSWER TO THE FIRST QUESTION..
HERE WE GO!
© 1994 United Feature Syndicate, Inc.
FASTER THAN A FAX, SIR
YOU'RE HUMONGOUSLY WEIRD, MARCIE!

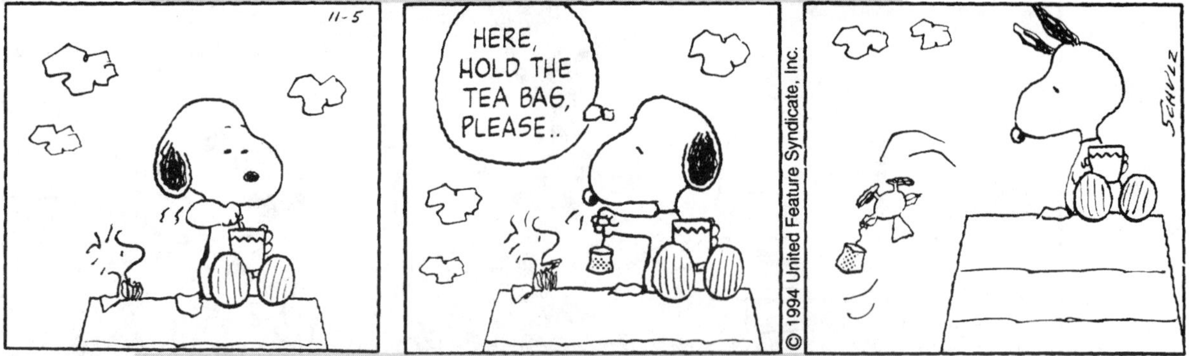
11-5
HERE, HOLD THE TEA BAG, PLEASE..
© 1994 United Feature Syndicate, Inc.
SCHULZ

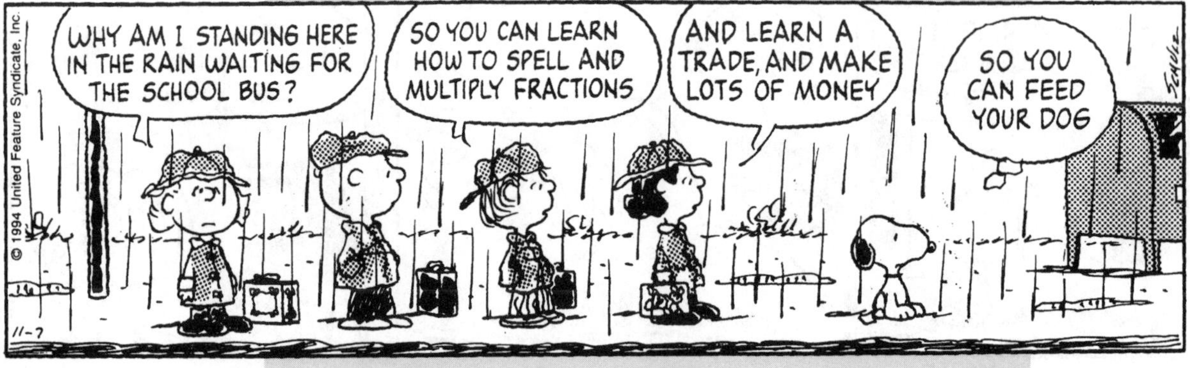
© 1994 United Feature Syndicate, Inc.
WHY AM I STANDING HERE IN THE RAIN WAITING FOR THE SCHOOL BUS?
SO YOU CAN LEARN HOW TO SPELL AND MULTIPLY FRACTIONS
AND LEARN A TRADE, AND MAKE LOTS OF MONEY
SO YOU CAN FEED YOUR DOG
SCHULZ
11-7

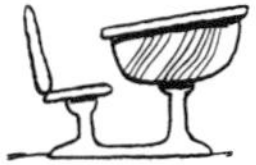

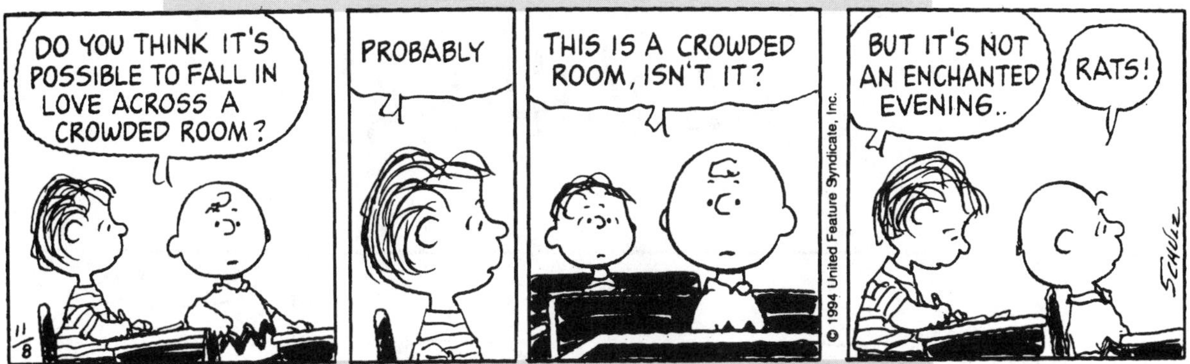
DO YOU THINK IT'S POSSIBLE TO FALL IN LOVE ACROSS A CROWDED ROOM?
PROBABLY
THIS IS A CROWDED ROOM, ISN'T IT?
BUT IT'S NOT AN ENCHANTED EVENING..
RATS!
11/8
© 1994 United Feature Syndicate, Inc.
SCHULZ

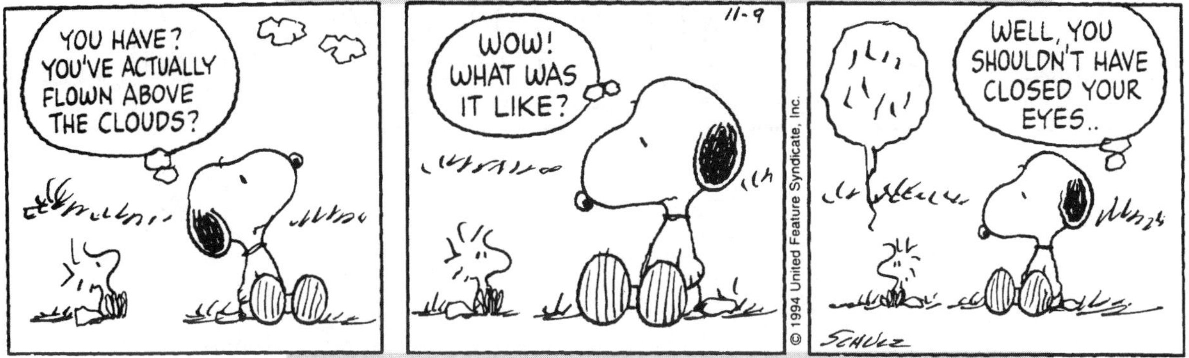
YOU HAVE? YOU'VE ACTUALLY FLOWN ABOVE THE CLOUDS?
11-9
WOW! WHAT WAS IT LIKE?
WELL, YOU SHOULDN'T HAVE CLOSED YOUR EYES..
© 1994 United Feature Syndicate, Inc.
SCHULZ

HAHAHAHA!

PEANUTS
by SCHULZ
LAST MONDAY..

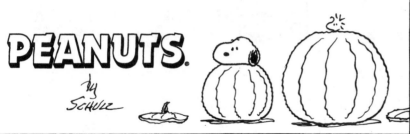

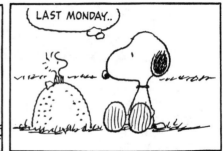

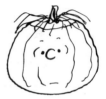

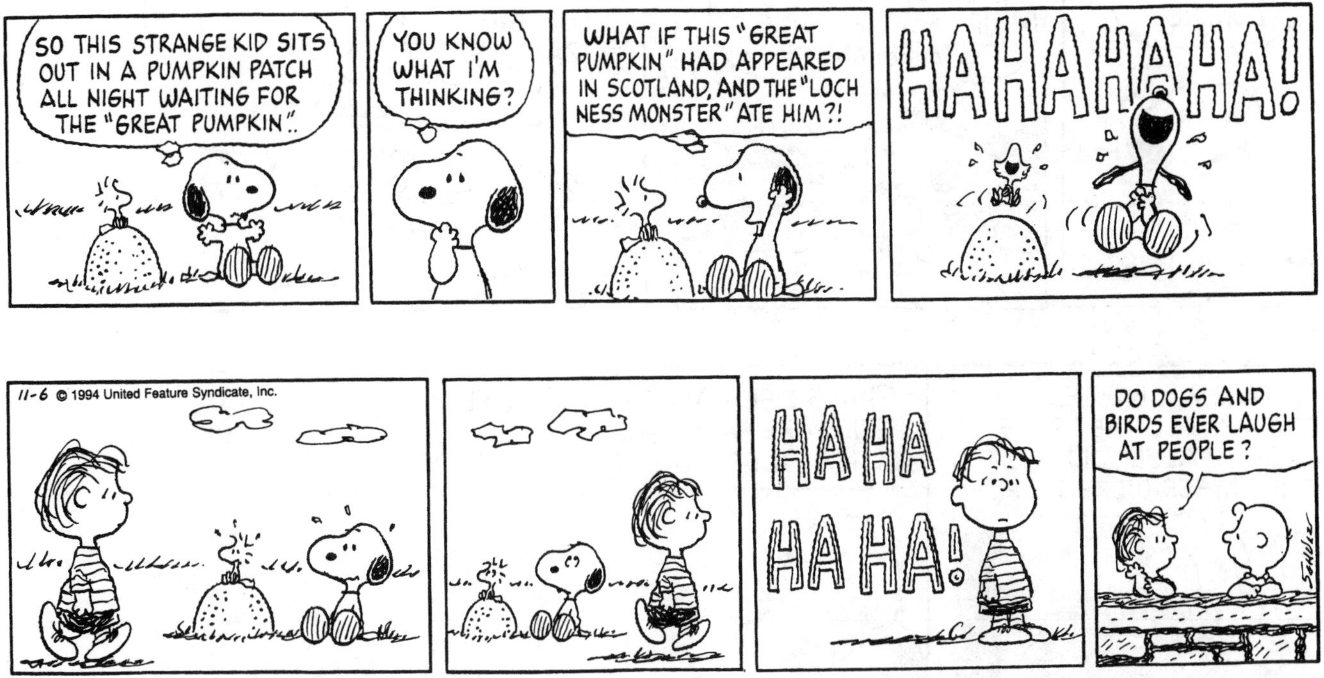
SO THIS STRANGE KID SITS OUT IN A PUMPKIN PATCH ALL NIGHT WAITING FOR THE "GREAT PUMPKIN"..
YOU KNOW WHAT I'M THINKING?
WHAT IF THIS "GREAT PUMPKIN" HAD APPEARED IN SCOTLAND, AND THE "LOCH NESS MONSTER" ATE HIM?!
HAHAHAHAHA!
11-6 © 1994 United Feature Syndicate, Inc.
HAHA HAHA!
DO DOGS AND BIRDS EVER LAUGH AT PEOPLE?
SCHULZ

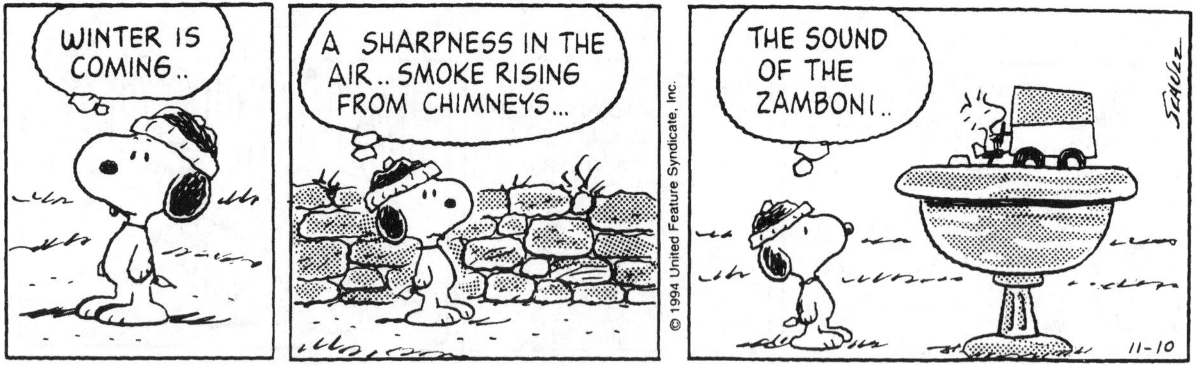
WINTER IS COMING..
A SHARPNESS IN THE AIR.. SMOKE RISING FROM CHIMNEYS...
© 1994 United Feature Syndicate, Inc.
THE SOUND OF THE ZAMBONI..
SCHULZ
11-10

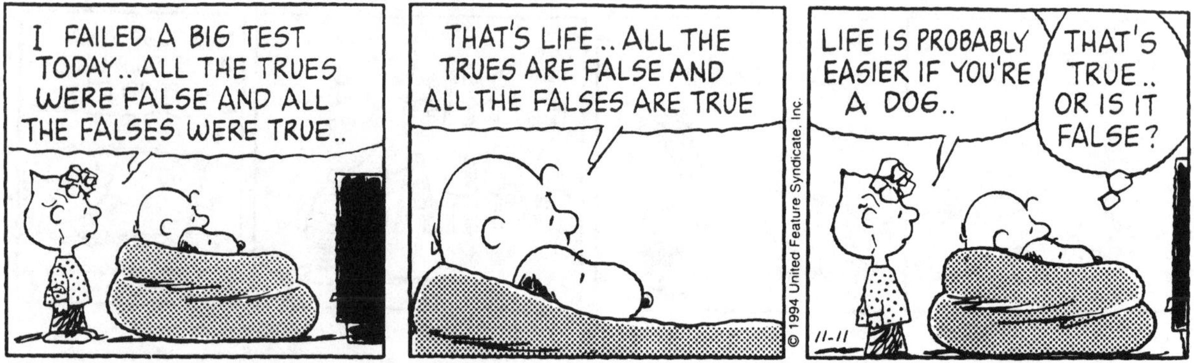
I FAILED A BIG TEST TODAY.. ALL THE TRUES WERE FALSE AND ALL THE FALSES WERE TRUE..
THAT'S LIFE.. ALL THE TRUES ARE FALSE AND ALL THE FALSES ARE TRUE
© 1994 United Feature Syndicate, Inc.
LIFE IS PROBABLY EASIER IF YOU'RE A DOG..
THAT'S TRUE.. OR IS IT FALSE?
11-11

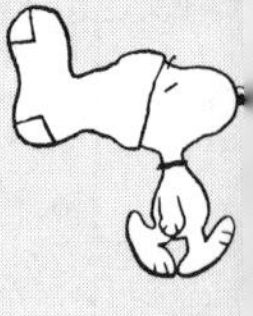

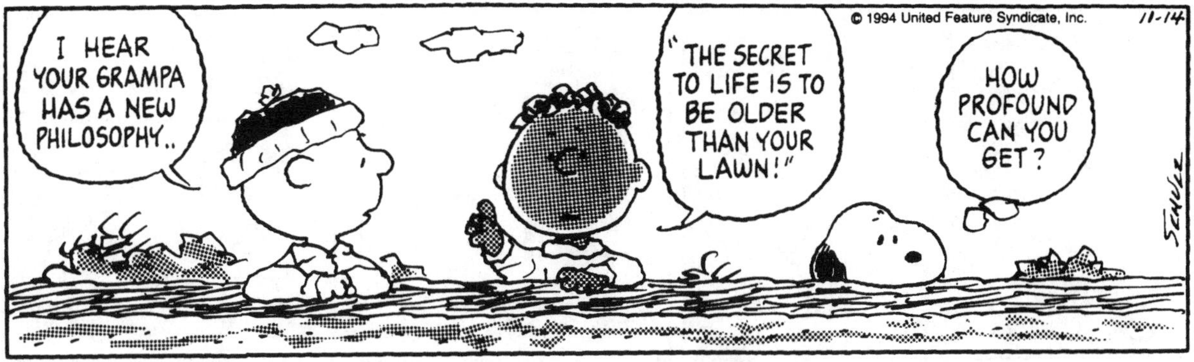
© 1994 United Feature Syndicate, Inc.
11-14
I HEAR YOUR GRAMPA HAS A NEW PHILOSOPHY..
"THE SECRET TO LIFE IS TO BE OLDER THAN YOUR LAWN!"
HOW PROFOUND CAN YOU GET?
SCHULZ

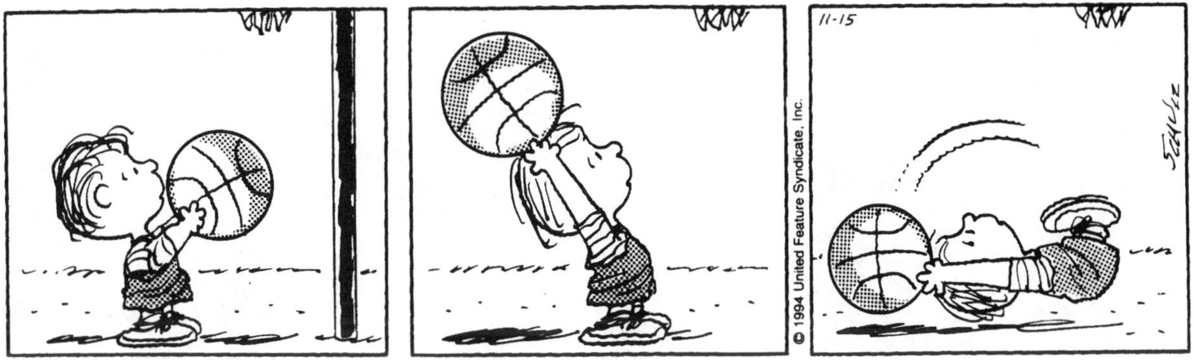
© 1994 United Feature Syndicate, Inc.
11-15
SCHULZ

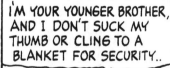

I'M YOUR YOUNGER BROTHER, AND I DON'T SUCK MY THUMB OR CLING TO A BLANKET FOR SECURITY..

HOORAY FOR YOU

AS THE YEARS GO BY, YOU'LL PROBABLY DEVELOP A REAL RESENTMENT TOWARD ME..

11-16

AND FIND DIFFERENT WAYS TO GET EVEN..

© 1994 United Feature Syndicate, Inc.

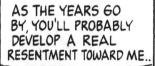

HI, MY NAME IS RERUN.. CAN YOUR DOG COME OUT TO PLAY?

WELL, I DON'T KNOW.. I'LL HAVE TO SEE..

11-17

WHO ARE YOU, HIS AGENT?

© 1994 United Feature Syndicate, Inc.

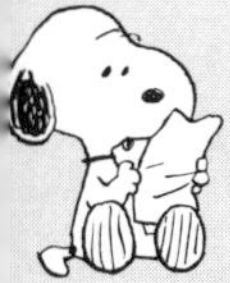

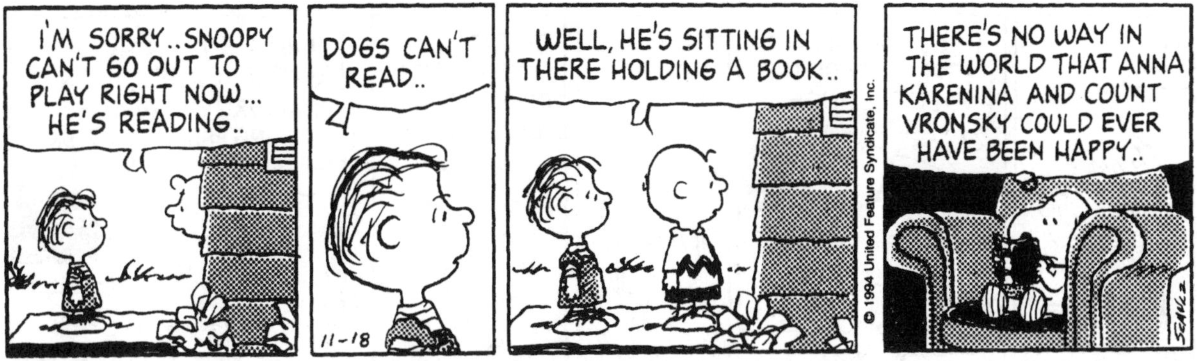
I'M SORRY.. SNOOPY CAN'T GO OUT TO PLAY RIGHT NOW... HE'S READING..
DOGS CAN'T READ..
11-18
WELL, HE'S SITTING IN THERE HOLDING A BOOK..
© 1994 United Feature Syndicate, Inc.
THERE'S NO WAY IN THE WORLD THAT ANNA KARENINA AND COUNT VRONSKY COULD EVER HAVE BEEN HAPPY..
SCHULZ

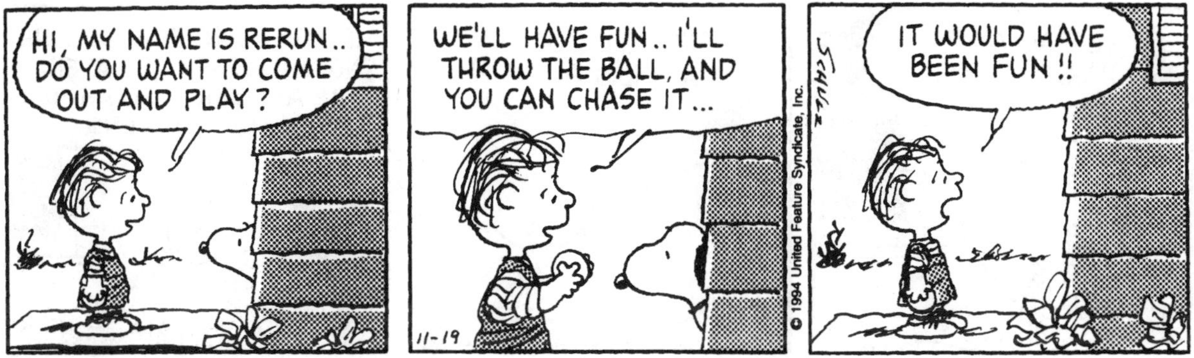
HI, MY NAME IS RERUN.. DO YOU WANT TO COME OUT AND PLAY?
WE'LL HAVE FUN.. I'LL THROW THE BALL, AND YOU CAN CHASE IT...
11-19
© 1994 United Feature Syndicate, Inc.
SCHULZ
IT WOULD HAVE BEEN FUN!!

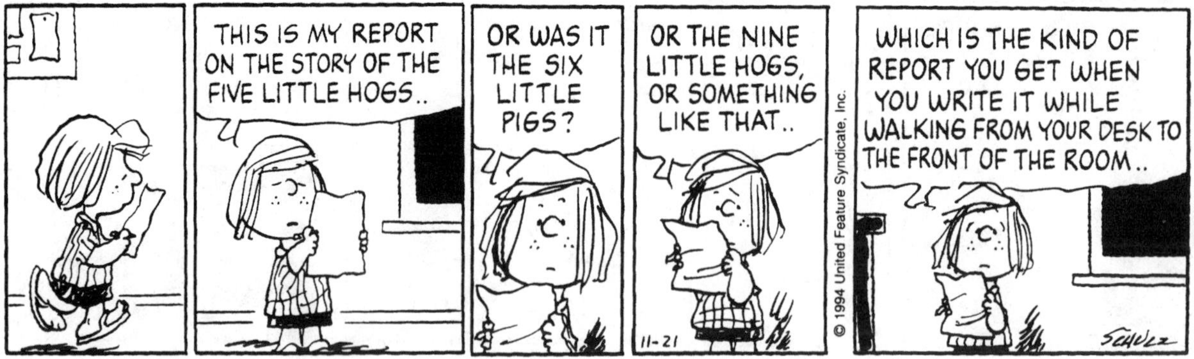
THIS IS MY REPORT ON THE STORY OF THE FIVE LITTLE HOGS..
OR WAS IT THE SIX LITTLE PIGS?
OR THE NINE LITTLE HOGS, OR SOMETHING LIKE THAT..
11-21
© 1994 United Feature Syndicate, Inc.
WHICH IS THE KIND OF REPORT YOU GET WHEN YOU WRITE IT WHILE WALKING FROM YOUR DESK TO THE FRONT OF THE ROOM..
SCHULZ

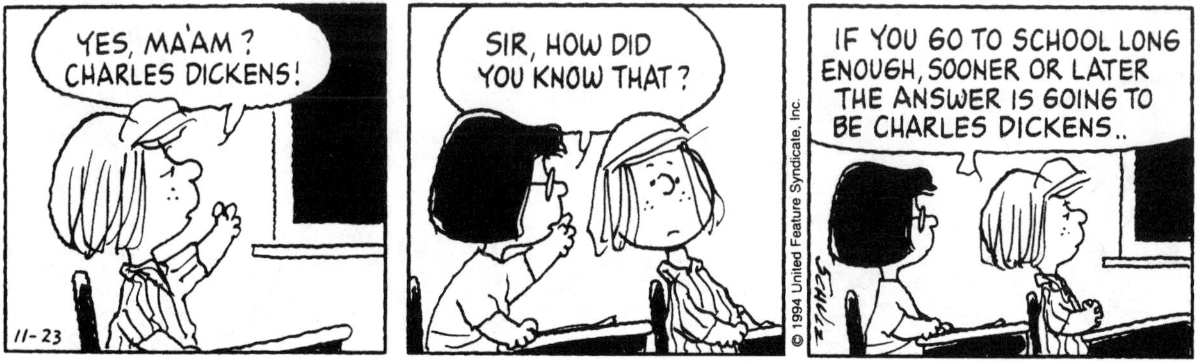
YES, MA'AM? CHARLES DICKENS!
11-23
SIR, HOW DID YOU KNOW THAT?
© 1994 United Feature Syndicate, Inc.
SCHULZ
IF YOU GO TO SCHOOL LONG ENOUGH, SOONER OR LATER THE ANSWER IS GOING TO BE CHARLES DICKENS..

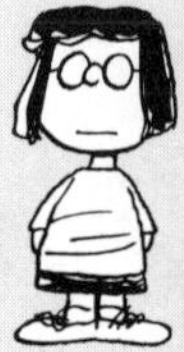

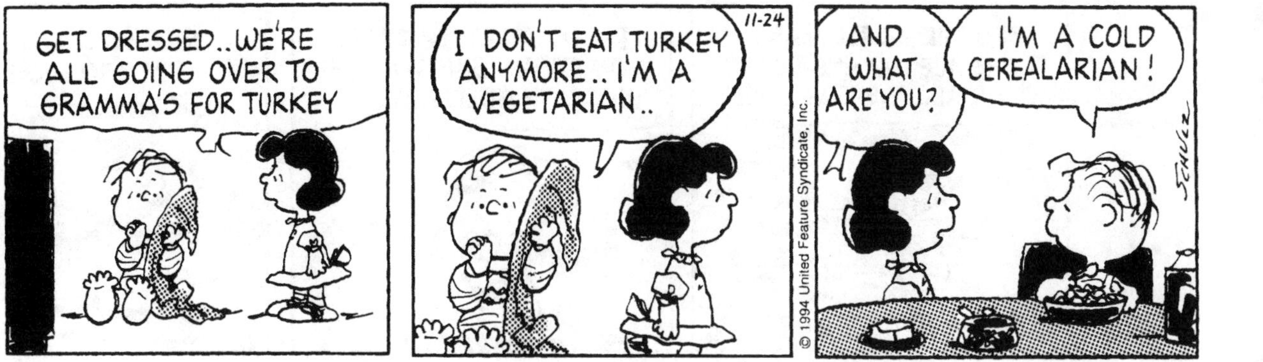
GET DRESSED..WE'RE ALL GOING OVER TO GRAMMA'S FOR TURKEY
11-24
I DON'T EAT TURKEY ANYMORE.. I'M A VEGETARIAN..
AND WHAT ARE YOU?
I'M A COLD CEREALARIAN!
SCHULZ
© 1994 United Feature Syndicate, Inc.

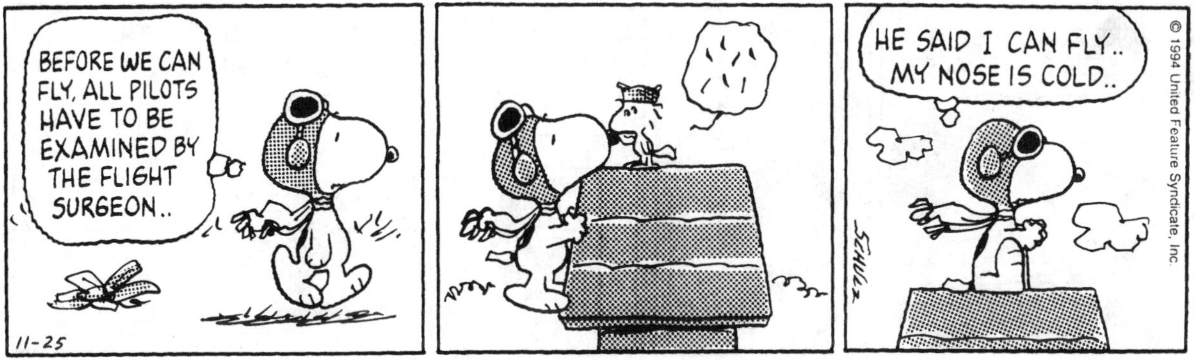
BEFORE WE CAN FLY, ALL PILOTS HAVE TO BE EXAMINED BY THE FLIGHT SURGEON..
11-25
HE SAID I CAN FLY.. MY NOSE IS COLD..
SCHULZ
© 1994 United Feature Syndicate, Inc.

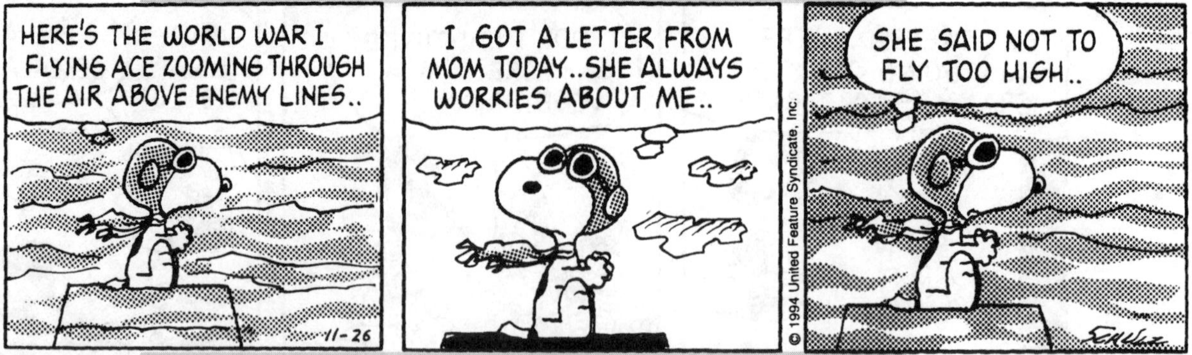
HERE'S THE WORLD WAR I FLYING ACE ZOOMING THROUGH THE AIR ABOVE ENEMY LINES..
11-26
I GOT A LETTER FROM MOM TODAY..SHE ALWAYS WORRIES ABOUT ME..
© 1994 United Feature Syndicate, Inc.
SHE SAID NOT TO FLY TOO HIGH..
SCHULZ

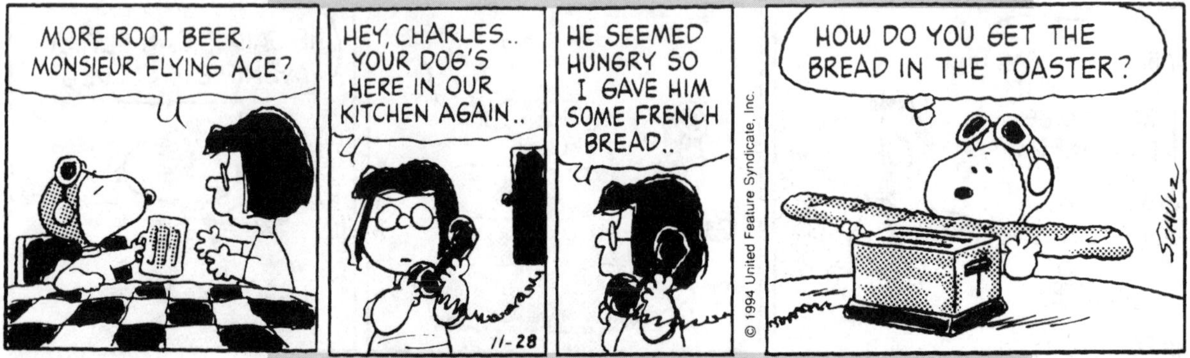
MORE ROOT BEER, MONSIEUR FLYING ACE?
HEY, CHARLES.. YOUR DOG'S HERE IN OUR KITCHEN AGAIN..
11-28
HE SEEMED HUNGRY SO I GAVE HIM SOME FRENCH BREAD..
© 1994 United Feature Syndicate, Inc.
HOW DO YOU GET THE BREAD IN THE TOASTER?
SCHULZ

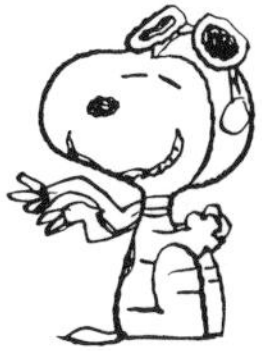

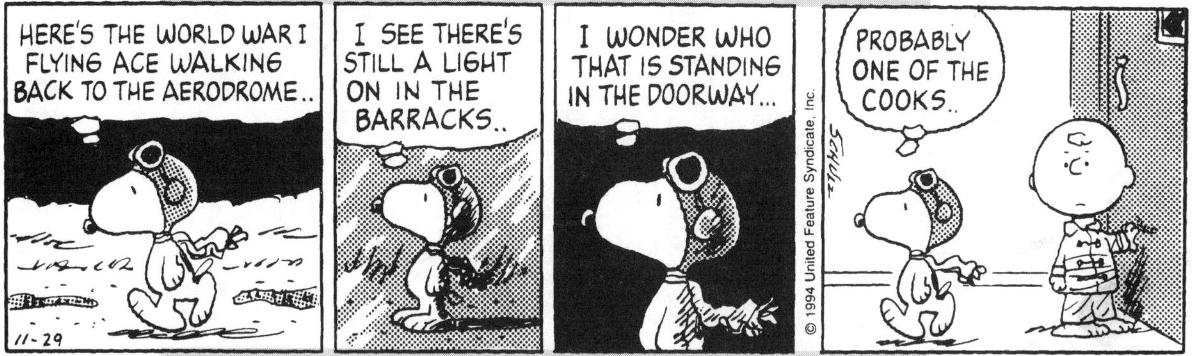
HERE'S THE WORLD WAR I FLYING ACE WALKING BACK TO THE AERODROME..
11-29
I SEE THERE'S STILL A LIGHT ON IN THE BARRACKS..
I WONDER WHO THAT IS STANDING IN THE DOORWAY...
© 1994 United Feature Syndicate, Inc.
SCHULZ
PROBABLY ONE OF THE COOKS..

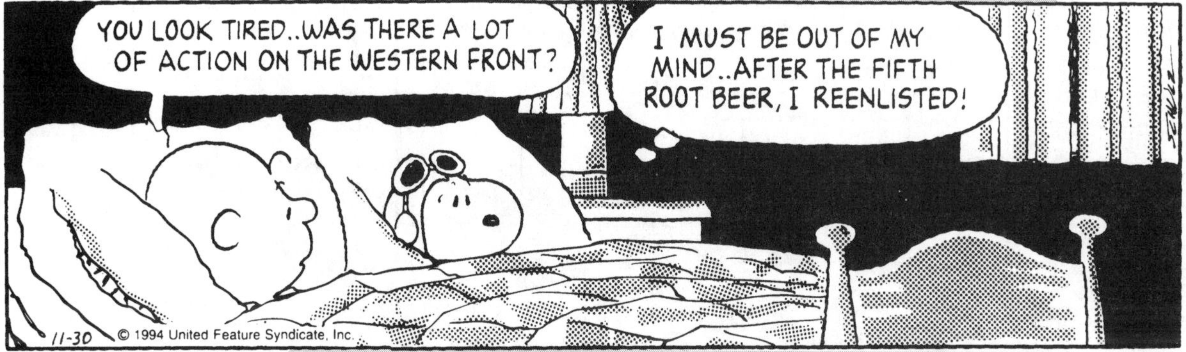
YOU LOOK TIRED..WAS THERE A LOT OF ACTION ON THE WESTERN FRONT?
I MUST BE OUT OF MY MIND..AFTER THE FIFTH ROOT BEER, I REENLISTED!
SCHULZ
11-30
© 1994 United Feature Syndicate, Inc.

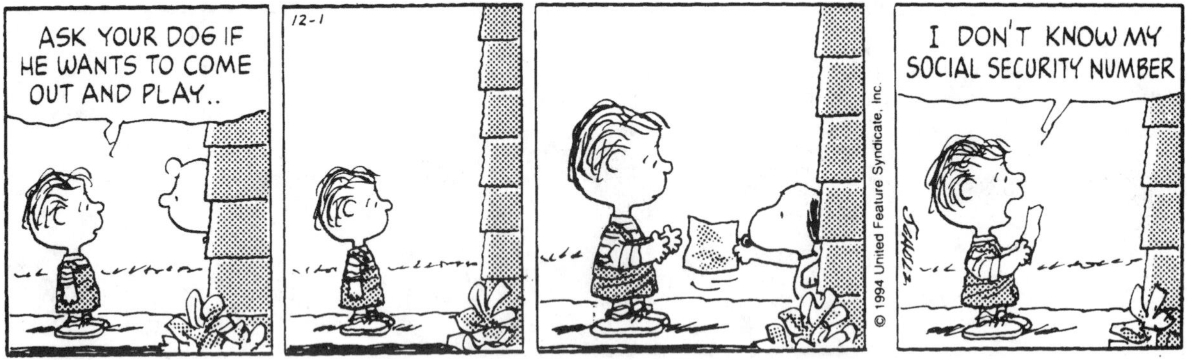
ASK YOUR DOG IF HE WANTS TO COME OUT AND PLAY..
12-1
© 1994 United Feature Syndicate, Inc.
I DON'T KNOW MY SOCIAL SECURITY NUMBER

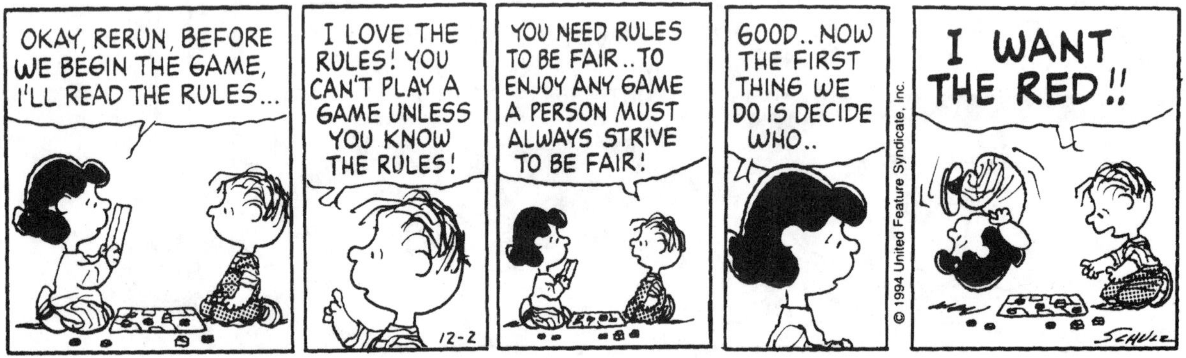
OKAY, RERUN, BEFORE WE BEGIN THE GAME, I'LL READ THE RULES...
I LOVE THE RULES! YOU CAN'T PLAY A GAME UNLESS YOU KNOW THE RULES!
12-2
YOU NEED RULES TO BE FAIR..TO ENJOY ANY GAME A PERSON MUST ALWAYS STRIVE TO BE FAIR!
GOOD.. NOW THE FIRST THING WE DO IS DECIDE WHO..
© 1994 United Feature Syndicate, Inc.
I WANT THE RED!!

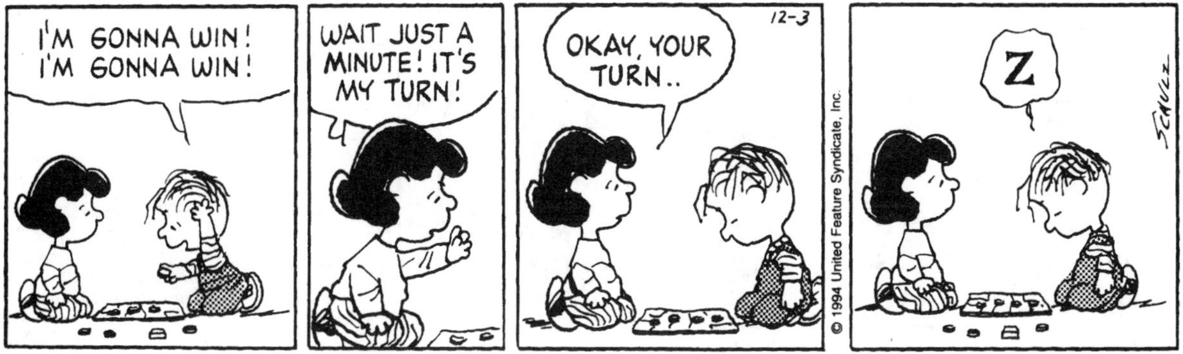

I'M GONNA WIN! I'M GONNA WIN!
WAIT JUST A MINUTE! IT'S MY TURN!
12-3
OKAY, YOUR TURN..
© 1994 United Feature Syndicate, Inc.
Z
SCHULZ

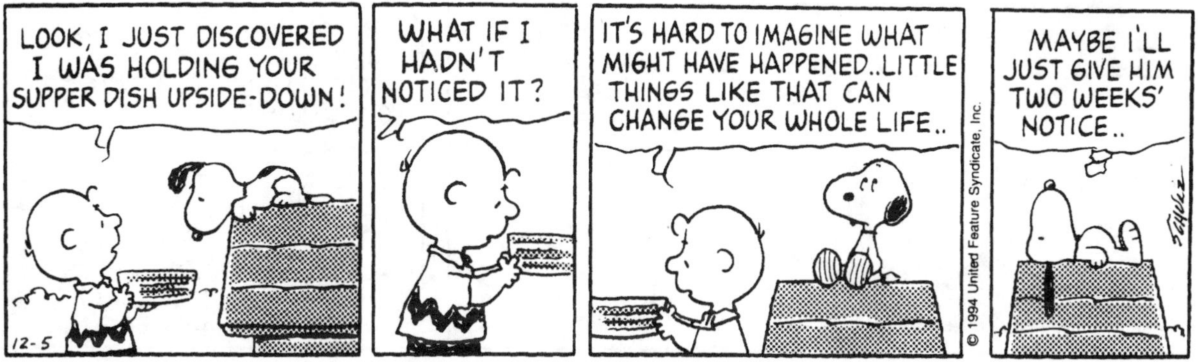

LOOK, I JUST DISCOVERED I WAS HOLDING YOUR SUPPER DISH UPSIDE-DOWN!
12-5
WHAT IF I HADN'T NOTICED IT?
IT'S HARD TO IMAGINE WHAT MIGHT HAVE HAPPENED..LITTLE THINGS LIKE THAT CAN CHANGE YOUR WHOLE LIFE..
© 1994 United Feature Syndicate, Inc.
MAYBE I'LL JUST GIVE HIM TWO WEEKS' NOTICE..
SCHULZ

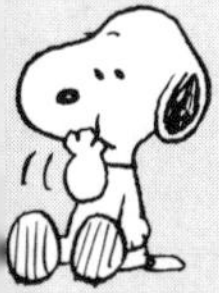

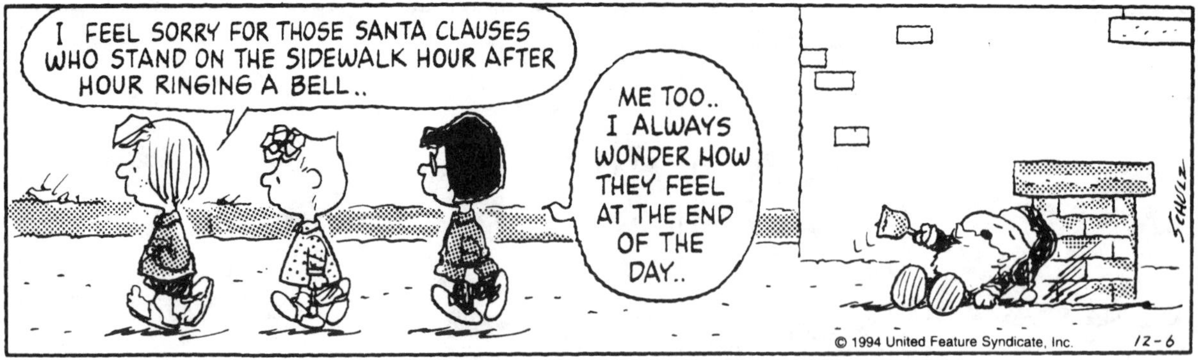
I FEEL SORRY FOR THOSE SANTA CLAUSES WHO STAND ON THE SIDEWALK HOUR AFTER HOUR RINGING A BELL..
ME TOO.. I ALWAYS WONDER HOW THEY FEEL AT THE END OF THE DAY..
SCHULZ
© 1994 United Feature Syndicate, Inc.
12-6

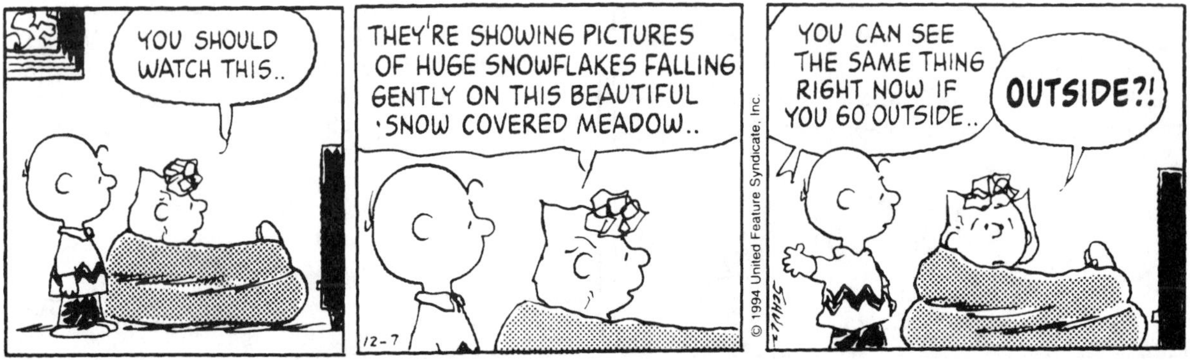
YOU SHOULD WATCH THIS..
THEY'RE SHOWING PICTURES OF HUGE SNOWFLAKES FALLING GENTLY ON THIS BEAUTIFUL SNOW COVERED MEADOW..
12-7
© 1994 United Feature Syndicate, Inc.
SCHULZ
YOU CAN SEE THE SAME THING RIGHT NOW IF YOU GO OUTSIDE..
OUTSIDE?!

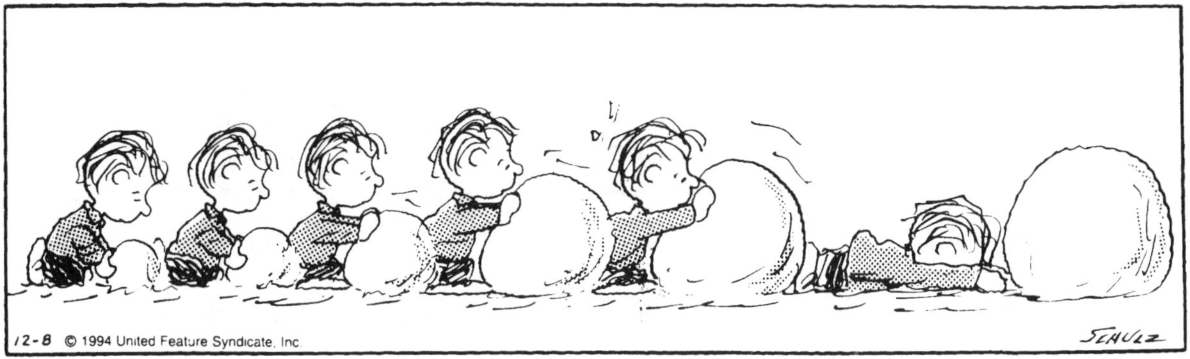
12-8 © 1994 United Feature Syndicate, Inc.
SCHULZ

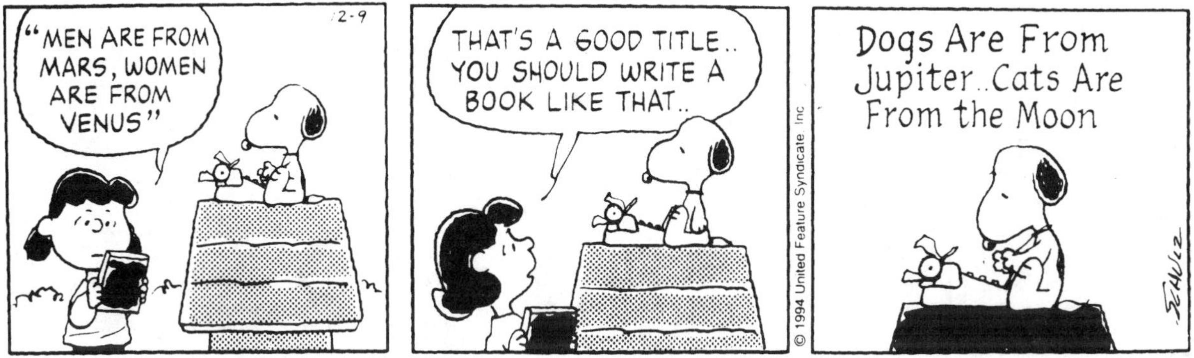
12-9
"MEN ARE FROM MARS, WOMEN ARE FROM VENUS"
THAT'S A GOOD TITLE.. YOU SHOULD WRITE A BOOK LIKE THAT..
© 1994 United Feature Syndicate, Inc.
Dogs Are From Jupiter..Cats Are From the Moon
SCHULZ

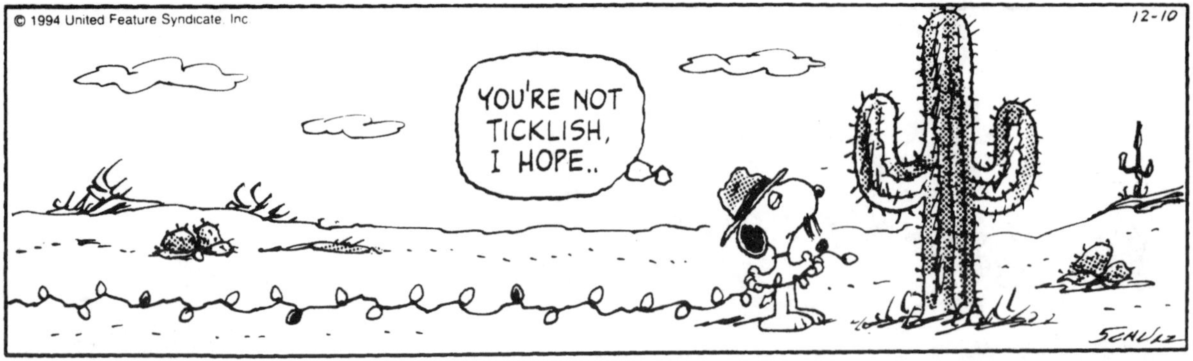
© 1994 United Feature Syndicate, Inc.
12-10
YOU'RE NOT TICKLISH, I HOPE..
SCHULZ

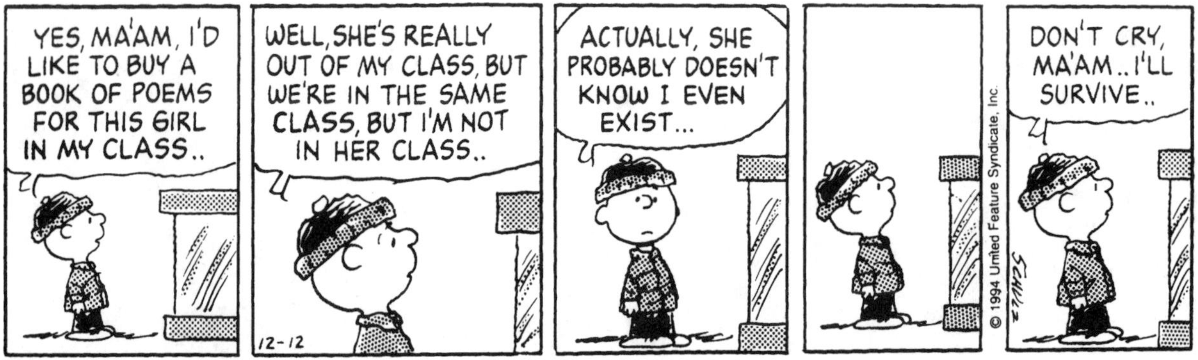
YES, MA'AM, I'D LIKE TO BUY A BOOK OF POEMS FOR THIS GIRL IN MY CLASS..
WELL, SHE'S REALLY OUT OF MY CLASS, BUT WE'RE IN THE SAME CLASS, BUT I'M NOT IN HER CLASS..
12-12
ACTUALLY, SHE PROBABLY DOESN'T KNOW I EVEN EXIST...
© 1994 United Feature Syndicate, Inc.
SCHULZ
DON'T CRY, MA'AM.. I'LL SURVIVE..

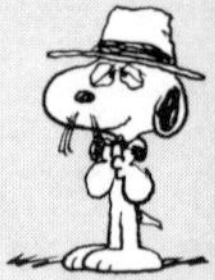

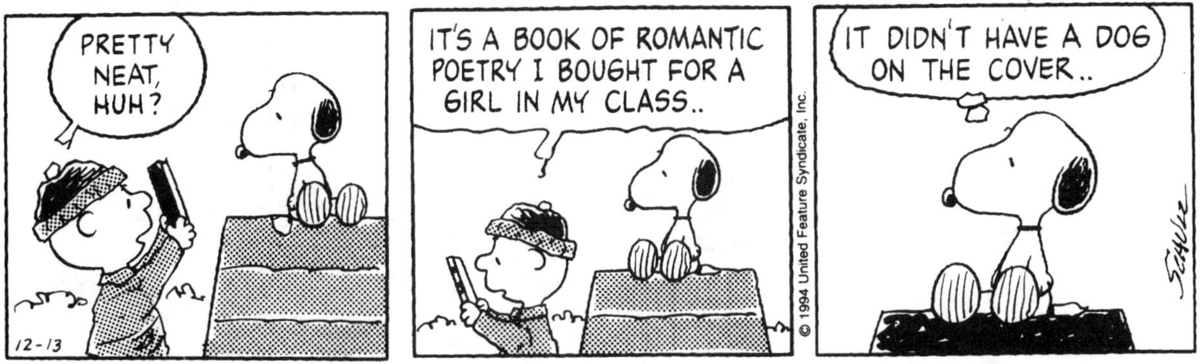
PRETTY NEAT, HUH?
12-13
IT'S A BOOK OF ROMANTIC POETRY I BOUGHT FOR A GIRL IN MY CLASS..
© 1994 United Feature Syndicate, Inc.
IT DIDN'T HAVE A DOG ON THE COVER..

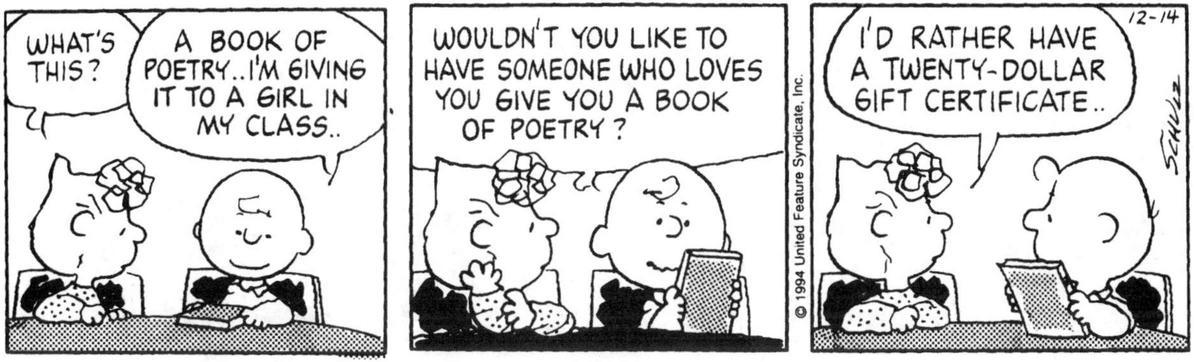
WHAT'S THIS?
A BOOK OF POETRY..I'M GIVING IT TO A GIRL IN MY CLASS..
WOULDN'T YOU LIKE TO HAVE SOMEONE WHO LOVES YOU GIVE YOU A BOOK OF POETRY?
© 1994 United Feature Syndicate, Inc.
12-14
I'D RATHER HAVE A TWENTY-DOLLAR GIFT CERTIFICATE..

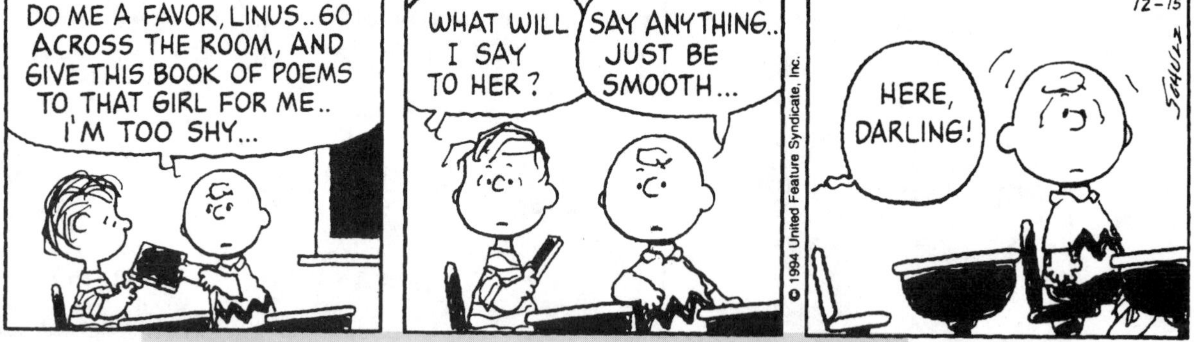
DO ME A FAVOR, LINUS..GO ACROSS THE ROOM, AND GIVE THIS BOOK OF POEMS TO THAT GIRL FOR ME.. I'M TOO SHY...
WHAT WILL I SAY TO HER?
SAY ANYTHING.. JUST BE SMOOTH...
© 1994 United Feature Syndicate, Inc.
12-15
SCHULZ
HERE, DARLING!

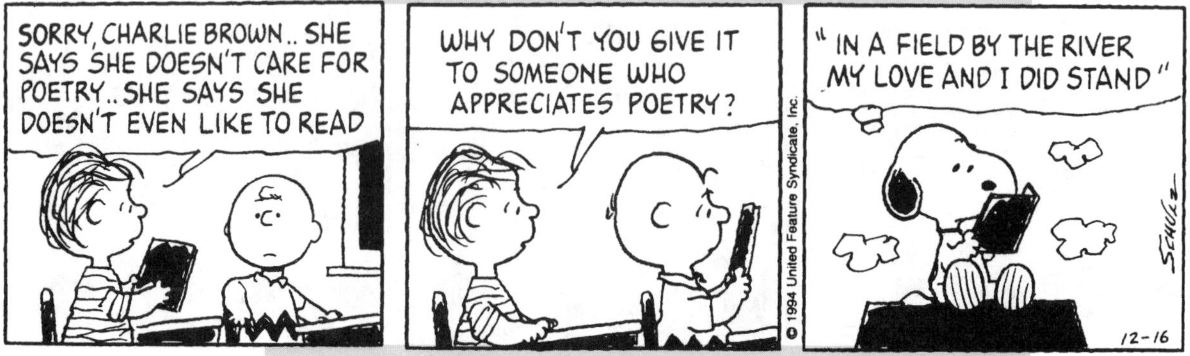
SORRY, CHARLIE BROWN.. SHE SAYS SHE DOESN'T CARE FOR POETRY.. SHE SAYS SHE DOESN'T EVEN LIKE TO READ
WHY DON'T YOU GIVE IT TO SOMEONE WHO APPRECIATES POETRY?
© 1994 United Feature Syndicate, Inc.
"IN A FIELD BY THE RIVER MY LOVE AND I DID STAND"
SCHULZ
12-16

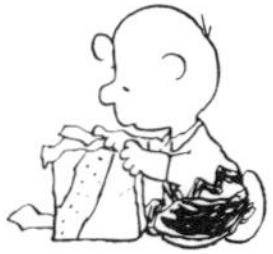

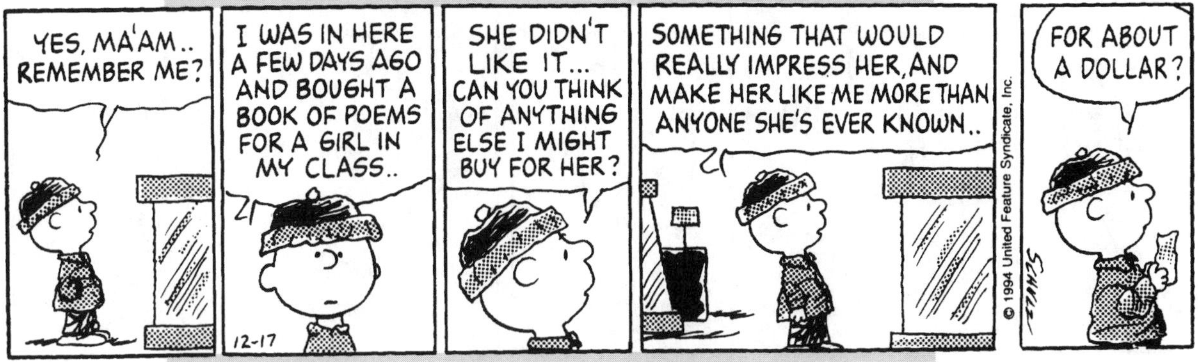
YES, MA'AM.. REMEMBER ME?
I WAS IN HERE A FEW DAYS AGO AND BOUGHT A BOOK OF POEMS FOR A GIRL IN MY CLASS..
12-17
SHE DIDN'T LIKE IT... CAN YOU THINK OF ANYTHING ELSE I MIGHT BUY FOR HER?
SOMETHING THAT WOULD REALLY IMPRESS HER, AND MAKE HER LIKE ME MORE THAN ANYONE SHE'S EVER KNOWN..
© 1994 United Feature Syndicate, Inc.
FOR ABOUT A DOLLAR?

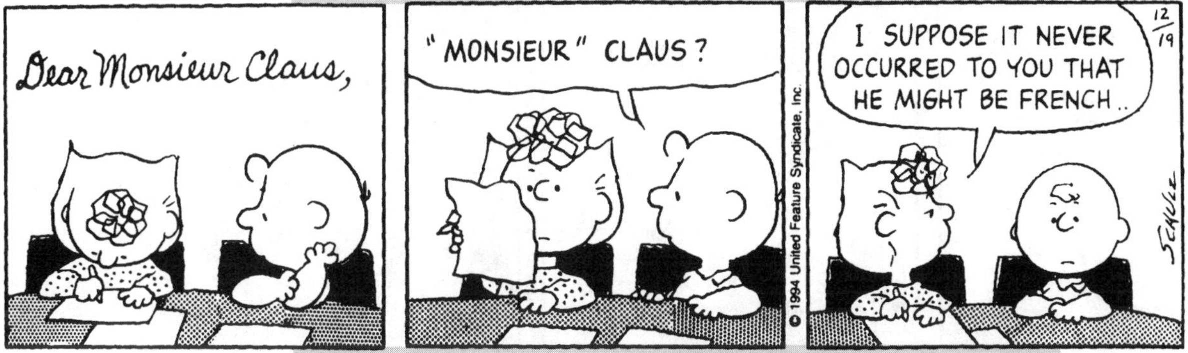
Dear Monsieur Claus,
"MONSIEUR" CLAUS?
© 1994 United Feature Syndicate, Inc.
12/19
I SUPPOSE IT NEVER OCCURRED TO YOU THAT HE MIGHT BE FRENCH..

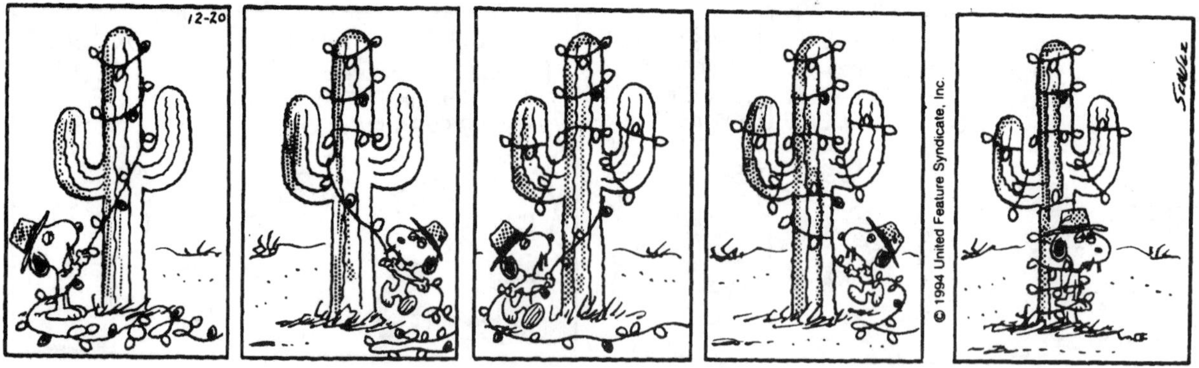
12-20
© 1994 United Feature Syndicate, Inc.

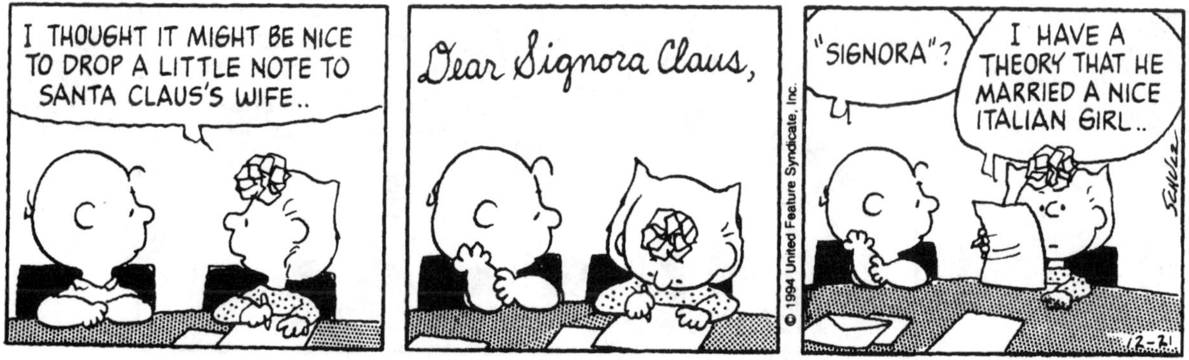
I THOUGHT IT MIGHT BE NICE TO DROP A LITTLE NOTE TO SANTA CLAUS'S WIFE..
Dear Signora Claus,
© 1994 United Feature Syndicate, Inc.
"SIGNORA"?
I HAVE A THEORY THAT HE MARRIED A NICE ITALIAN GIRL..
12-21

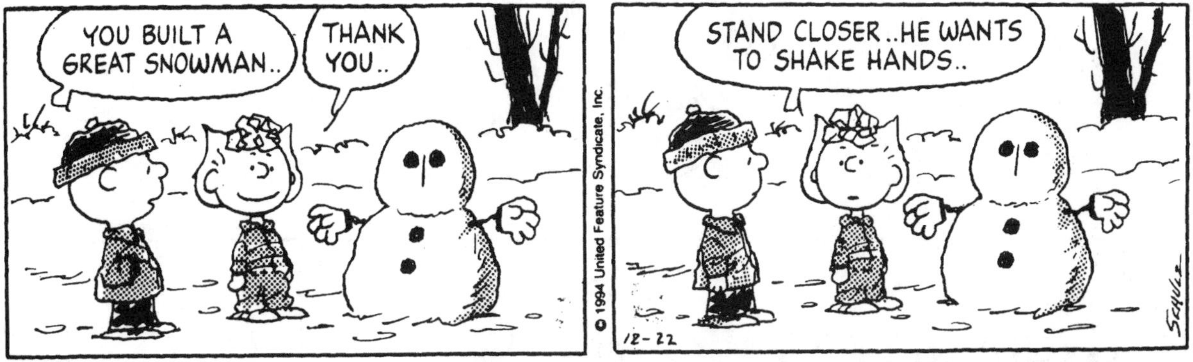
YOU BUILT A GREAT SNOWMAN..
THANK YOU..
STAND CLOSER..HE WANTS TO SHAKE HANDS..
© 1994 United Feature Syndicate, Inc.
12-22
SCHULZ

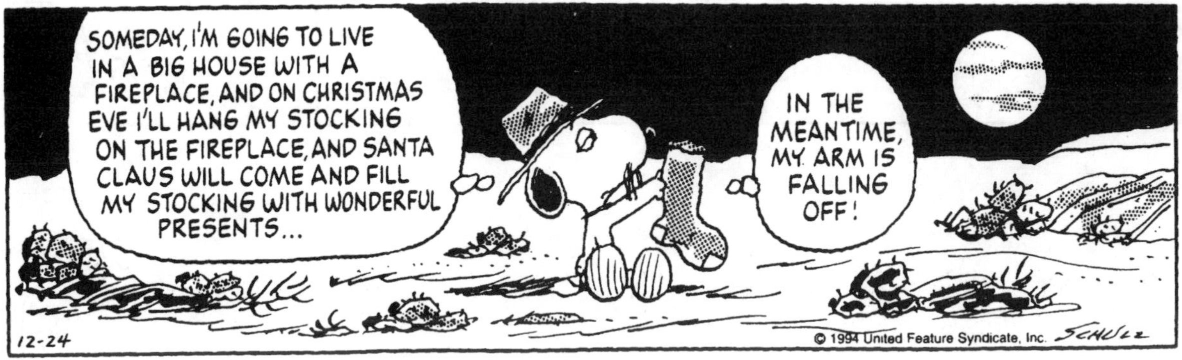
SOMEDAY, I'M GOING TO LIVE IN A BIG HOUSE WITH A FIREPLACE, AND ON CHRISTMAS EVE I'LL HANG MY STOCKING ON THE FIREPLACE, AND SANTA CLAUS WILL COME AND FILL MY STOCKING WITH WONDERFUL PRESENTS...
IN THE MEANTIME, MY ARM IS FALLING OFF!
12-24
© 1994 United Feature Syndicate, Inc.
SCHULZ

PEANUTS
by SCHULZ
HERE, I GUESS THIS IS FOR YOU..

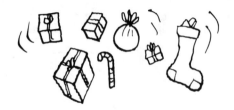

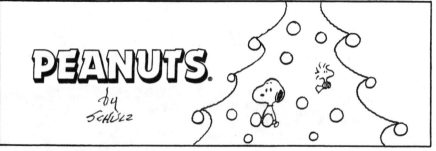

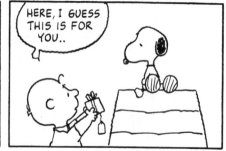

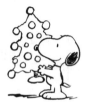

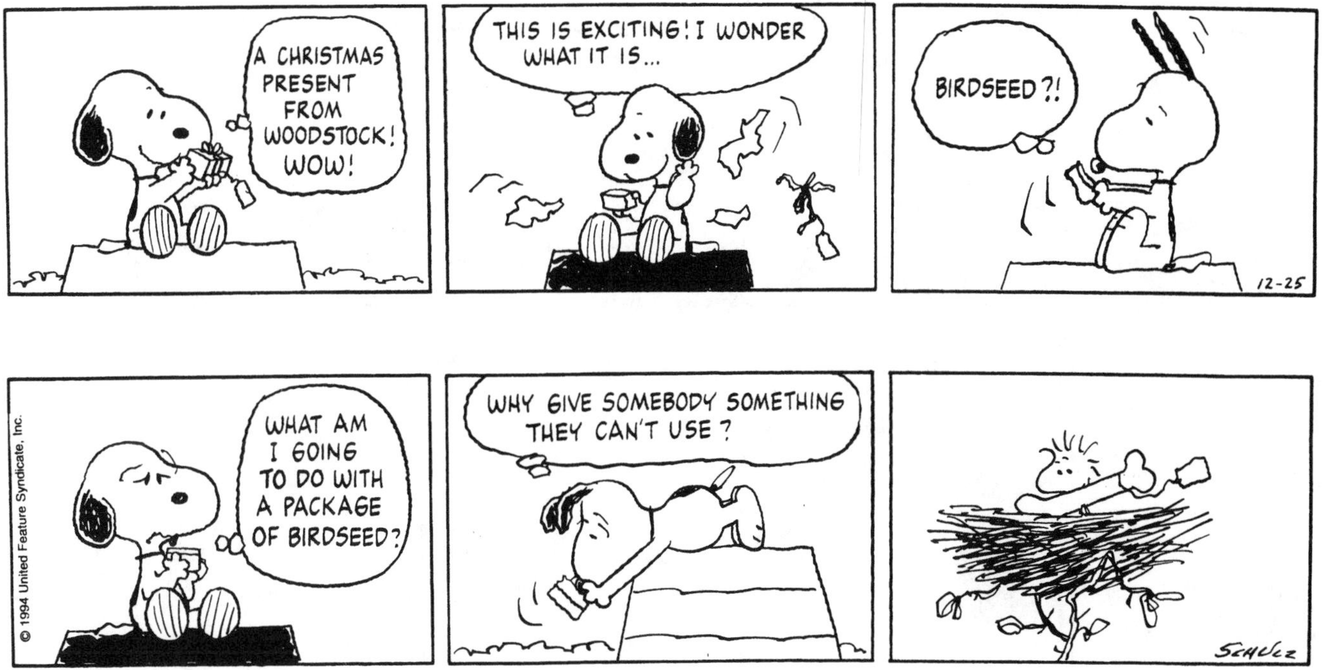
A CHRISTMAS PRESENT FROM WOODSTOCK! WOW!
THIS IS EXCITING! I WONDER WHAT IT IS...
BIRDSEED?!
12-25
WHAT AM I GOING TO DO WITH A PACKAGE OF BIRDSEED?
WHY GIVE SOMEBODY SOMETHING THEY CAN'T USE?
SCHULZ

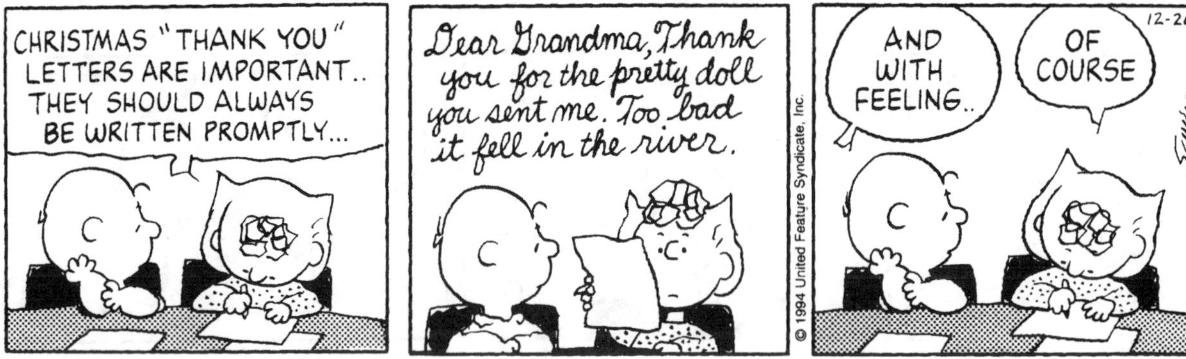
CHRISTMAS "THANK YOU" LETTERS ARE IMPORTANT.. THEY SHOULD ALWAYS BE WRITTEN PROMPTLY...
Dear Grandma, Thank you for the pretty doll you sent me. Too bad it fell in the river.
© 1994 United Feature Syndicate, Inc.
12-26
AND WITH FEELING..
OF COURSE
SCHULZ

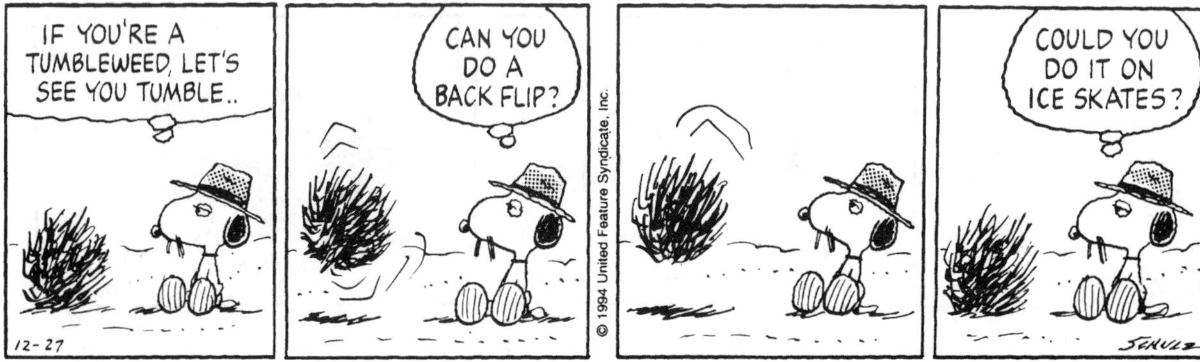
IF YOU'RE A TUMBLEWEED, LET'S SEE YOU TUMBLE..
12-27
CAN YOU DO A BACK FLIP?
© 1994 United Feature Syndicate, Inc.
COULD YOU DO IT ON ICE SKATES?
SCHULZ

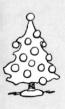

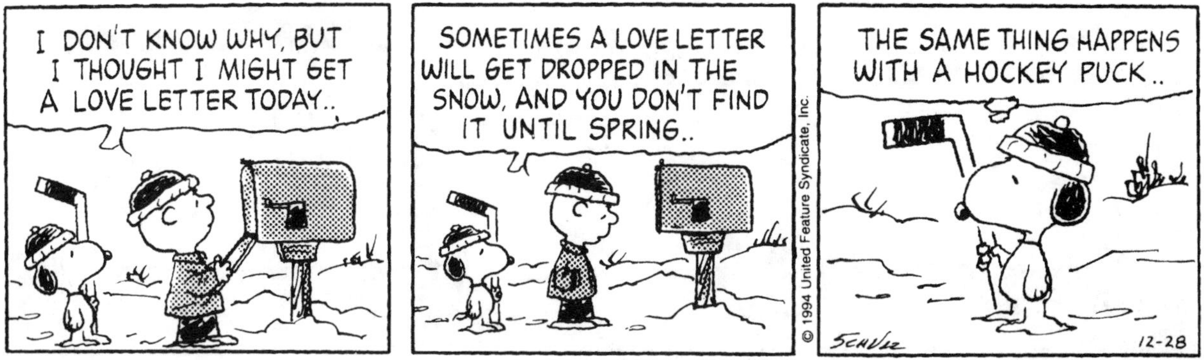
I DON'T KNOW WHY, BUT I THOUGHT I MIGHT GET A LOVE LETTER TODAY..
SOMETIMES A LOVE LETTER WILL GET DROPPED IN THE SNOW, AND YOU DON'T FIND IT UNTIL SPRING..
THE SAME THING HAPPENS WITH A HOCKEY PUCK..
© 1994 United Feature Syndicate, Inc.
SCHULZ
12-28

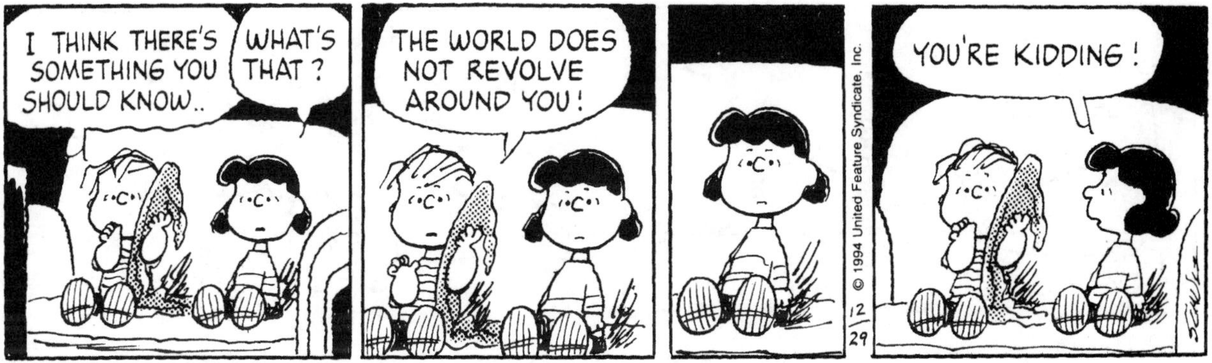
I THINK THERE'S SOMETHING YOU SHOULD KNOW..
WHAT'S THAT ?
THE WORLD DOES NOT REVOLVE AROUND YOU !
© 1994 United Feature Syndicate, Inc.
12/29
YOU'RE KIDDING !
SCHULZ

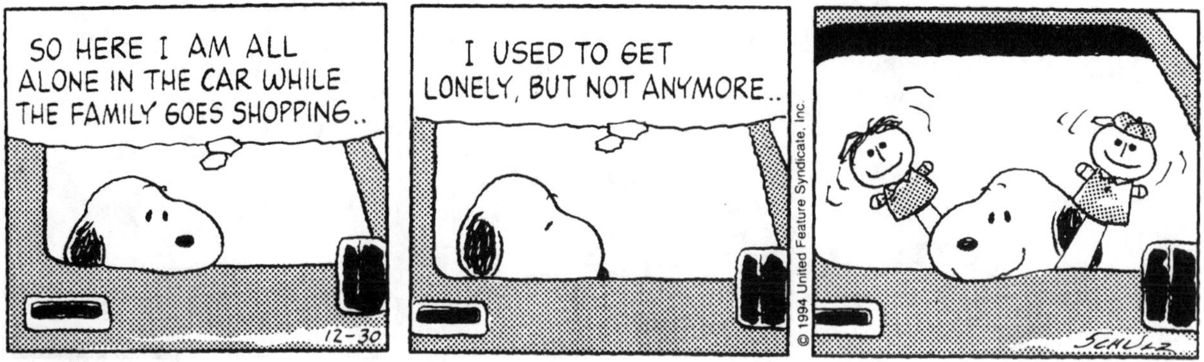
SO HERE I AM ALL ALONE IN THE CAR WHILE THE FAMILY GOES SHOPPING..
12-30
I USED TO GET LONELY, BUT NOT ANYMORE..
© 1994 United Feature Syndicate, Inc.
SCHULZ

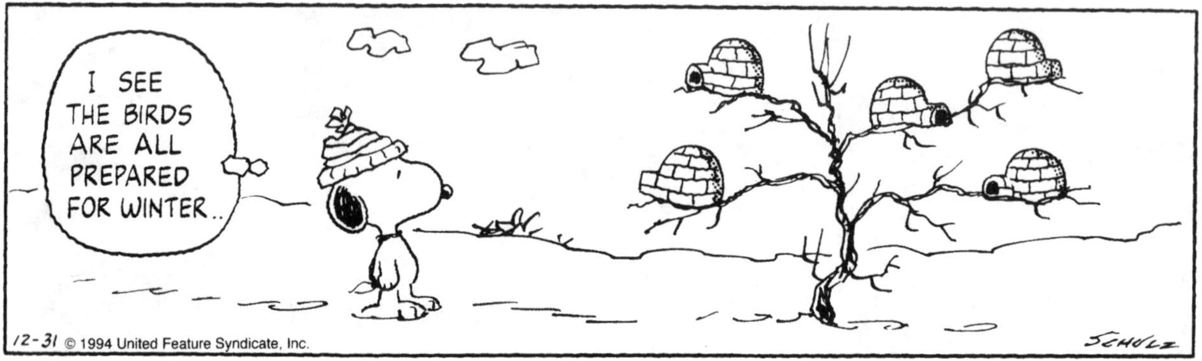
I SEE THE BIRDS ARE ALL PREPARED FOR WINTER..
12-31 © 1994 United Feature Syndicate, Inc.
SCHULZ

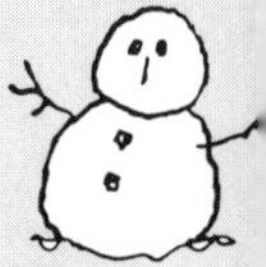